Monks and Wine

The Author

Desmond Seward was born in Paris of an Anglo-Irish family who have been wine merchants at Bordeaux since the 1860s. He was educated at Ampleforth and St Catharine's College, Cambridge, where he was an Exhibitioner in History. A Knight of Malta, he is the archivist of his order's British association. He has published six other historical books – including *The Monks of War,* the only modern general history of the military religious orders, besides contributing to historical and theological journals. He has also written for the *New York International Review of Food and Wine.*

Monks and Wine

Desmond Seward

With a Foreword by Hugh Johnson

Crown Publishers, Inc.
New York

Editor: Carolyn Ryden
Designer: Chris Bower
Picture Research: Paddy Poynder
Illustrator: Rodney Shackell
Cartographer: Patrick Leeson
Production: Julian Deeming

Monks and Wine
edited and designed
by Mitchell Beazley Publishers Ltd
87–89 Shaftesbury Avenue, London W1V 7AD

First published in the United States of America in 1979
by Crown Publishers, Inc., 1 Park Avenue, New York 10016

© Mitchell Beazley Publishers Ltd 1979
Text © Desmond Seward 1979

Library of Congress Catalog Card Number 79 2469
ISBN 0 517 539144

Printed and bound by Morrison and Gibb Ltd, Edinburgh
Photoset by Keyfilm (Trendbourne) Ltd), London
Origination by Culver Graphics Litho Ltd, Bucks

Publisher's Acknowledgements
Photographers and Archives: Bayerisches Nationalmuseum, Munich 104; Bildarchiv Foto Marburg/Photo: Lala Aufsberg 75; Mary Evans Picture Library 67; Fromm & Sichel/ Christian Brothers, San Francisco 108; Susan Griggs/Photo: Adam Woolfitt 106–7; Sonia Halliday 106 bottom; Pierre Mackiewicz 101, 102 top; Colin Maher 105; Lenz Moser 170 bottom; Prestel Verlag, Munich (from *Wein-leserbuch* by Karl Christoffel) 13, 27; Radio Times Hulton Picture Library 165; Scala 102–3; Verwaltung der Staatsweingüter, Eltville, Germany 102 bottom. *The publishers also gratefully acknowledge the assistance of the following*: Ampliaciones y Reproducciones Mas, Barcelona; Australian Wine Centre, London; Austrian Wine Institute, Vienna; Rev. Richard Rotter, Buckfast Abbey; Deutsche Wein-Information, Mainz; Dr P. Hallgarten, House of Hallgarten; Mission Vineyards, New Zealand; Moët & Chandon; N. F. Petch; Schneidersche Weingüter Verwaltung, Zell-Mosel; Sevenhill Cellar, South Australia; Standford J. Wolf & Associates Inc., Sunnyvale, California; Wine and Spirit Education Trust; Yapp Brothers, Wiltshire; and all those companies whose wine labels we are glad to be able to feature.

4

Contents

A Glossary of Wine-making Terms

Aguardiente (Sp.)—brandy

Cépage (Fr.)—the variety or varieties of grape from which a particular wine is made

Clos (Fr.)—vineyard

Cuvée (Fr.)—vintage

Cuverie (Fr.)—fermenting room

Estaminet (Fr.)—tavern

Fine (Eng.)—to clarify

Flor (Sp.)—a particular form of yeast carried in the air in the Jerez sherry-producing region of Spain. Unlike other bacteria it is not harmful to the wine—its presence is beneficial as it covers the liquid with a protective thick white film and imparts a fresh, yeasty flavor

Maderise (Eng.)—to brown with age

Marc (Fr.)—the residue (skins, pips and stalks) left after the grapes have been pressed

Marl (Eng.)—a limy clay often used as manure in viticulture

Must (Eng.)—unfermented or partially fermented grape-juice

Négociant (Fr.)—wine-broker

Oeil de perdrix (Fr.)—"partridge-eye"— a term used to describe the light red color of certain wines

Pourriture noble (Fr.)—"noble rot"—the popular name given to the mould *Botrytis cinerea*. It reduces the water content of the grape still on the vine, thus increasing the flavor and sugar content of the grapes with the result that they produce an especially intensely flavored wine

Solera system (Sp.)—method of progressively blending long-lived wines (e.g. sherry) by which the quality of the oldest stock is maintained throughout (*solera* translates as "inherited character"). Barrels of wine are stacked in tiers according to age, youngest at the top and oldest at the bottom. The wine moves downward to replace the oldest stock as it is drawn off

Tonneau (Fr.)—barrel

Vendange (Fr.)—grape-harvest

Vignoble (Fr.)—vineyard

Vin jaune (Fr.)—"yellow wine"—a dark white wine produced in the Jura

Vino rancio (Sp.)—old, mellow wine

Acknowledgements

It was the encouragement of Mr Hugh Johnson—the magisterial author of *The World Atlas of Wine*—after reading a synopsis, which finally decided me to write this book. Later, he read part of the typescript and kindly wrote the Foreword. I am sincerely grateful to him.

I owe much, too, to Mr Reresby Sitwell who also read the typescript and who made many constructive suggestions. It was he who first told me about English wine-growing and its history. (His own vineyard at Renishaw is the most northerly in Europe.)

I must acknowledge a special debt to the following for information about their own orders and wines:

Benedictines—Dom Alberic Stacpoole of Ampleforth; Dom Marcel Pierrot of Ligugé; and the community of Muri-Gries (Bolzano).

Carthusians—two fathers, who according to the custom of their order, must remain anonymous.

Knights of Malta—Fra Friedrich Kinsky von Wchinitz und Tettau, Prince Grand Prior of Austria; Major-General Viscount Monckton of Brenchley; Herr Ludolf von Kotze; Dr K. E. Eibenschutz; and Peter Drummond-Murray of Mastrick.

Jesuits—Fr. Philip Caraman; Fr. Thomas D. Terry of Novitiate Wines, Los Gatos, California; Fr. Richard Chisholm of the Jesuit novitiate in Rome; and Bro. John May of Sevenhill, South Australia.

Christian Brothers—Bro. Timothy of Napa Valley, California.

In addition I would like to thank Elisabeth, Viscountess Pollington; Sir John Pilcher; Professor Jonathan Riley-Smith; Colonel Peter Earle; Mr Julian Cotterell; Mr Harry Waugh; Mme François Lecointe; Mr Christopher Manning; and Mr Geoffrey Godbert. All gave me valuable information or advice or lent me otherwise unobtainable books.

As always I am indebted to the British Library and to the London Library. I am also obliged to the Wine and Food Society, who let me see their library in London.

Foreword

The glory of wine as a literary subject—and I feel no need to expand here on its other glories—is that it has so many dimensions. If I may be so vainglorious as to quote myself, from the first chapter I wrote on wine, "To me its fascination is that so many other subjects lie within its boundaries. Without geography and topography it is incomprehensible; without history it is colourless; without travel it remains unreal. It embraces botany, chemistry, agriculture, carpentry, economics—and any number of sciences whose names I do not even know. It leads you up paths of knowledge and byways of expertise you would never glimpse without it. Best of all, it brings you into friendly contact with some of the most skilful and devoted craftsmen, the most generous and entertaining hosts you will find anywhere."

Among whom, from every point of view, monks must be accounted the pioneers. When we think what we owe to them it is strange that no book that I know has ever before told the story. When Desmond Seward told me that he was collecting material I was immediately interested. I heard him talk with authority on topics that were totally new to me and yet had played a vital part in the history of wine. He asked me what monastic cellars I had visited. I began to realize that here was one of the central issues of a subject I profess to study, begging to be chronicled.

To me perhaps the most interesting part of the whole story is his lucid explanation of the monastic orders; how they came about and how they developed; their attitudes to property and land; their common need for wine and their ways of meeting it. The figures in the story range from self-mortifying ascetics—the monk you picture with nose and fingers blue with cold pacing the draughty cloister, to his colleague with nose of a different hue, like the ninth-century abbot of Angers, who, in the lovely language of Helen Waddell,

> " . . . would have his wine all times and seasons.
> Never did a day or night go by
> But it found him wine-soaked and wavering
> Even as a tree which the high winds sway."

Desmond Seward seems to me very fair on the temptations as well as the toil and triumphs along the way, and even devotes a chapter to the bibulous brethren who included, in a phrase I specially like, "the great boozers of European literature"—the heroes of Rabelais.

The great monastic triumph—aside, that is, from ensuring the survival of wine at all—was the creation of champagne. Dom Pérignon, the blind Benedictine cellarer of Hautvillers, was perhaps the greatest innovator in the history of wine—certainly before the technological revolution of the present century. This excellent man—all accounts show him a true Christian—was not only apparently the first to use a cork as part of the wine-making and maturing process but the first to make white wine with black grapes, to match grape variety with soil and situation, to harvest methodically as the grapes ripened and to master the art of blending.

All these are achievements whose repercussions spread far beyond champagne, affecting the way fine wine is made and matured everywhere, in the New World as well as the Old. California owes the origins of its wine industry to its missionary monks. Desmond Seward paints a remarkable picture of grey-headed Spaniards teaching California's under-sized Indians the fandango as part of what we would no doubt call their cultural exchange programme. Unfortunately for California the monasteries were suppressed: not that their original Mission wine was good, but the influence of monasteries on wine-making has everywhere been intelligent and progressive.

Indeed, the doyen of California's wine-makers once again today is a Christian Brother, a member of a lay teaching order with more than a touch of Pérignon in his patient, devoted research—curiously enough, like Pérignon, a man who believes in the importance of blending, against the trend of the day; who knows that the fine tuning of the human senses can improve on nature's individual productions.

There are important regions of the vine—Bordeaux by far the greatest —where the church has never been a major influence. Bordeaux wine-making has been commercial from the very first. In others—Germany in particular—the domination of the church has dwindled to memories and relics. Yet what a relic is the city of Trier and its religious and charitable wine-making institutions: one of the greatest concentrations of first-class vineyards on earth. In Austria the monasteries still combine tradition with progressive techniques to make some of the country's best wine.

Desmond Seward suggests in an appendix where you can go to see the great tradition still at work. Prompted by him I have made some monastic wine-pilgrimages myself. I have never been disappointed.

H. J.

Boire du vin, c'est honorer Dieu.

FÉNÉLON

To happy Convents, bosom'd deep in vines,
Where slumber Abbots purple as their wines.

POPE

For Alfred Newman Gilbey

Introduction

Monks in a vineyard, from a woodcut of 1513.

This book is for everyone who enjoys monasteries, whether ruined or inhabited, and who likes to drink nearby. It is a sad waste to drive past an abbey or friary in France, Germany or Austria, in Spain, Portugal or Italy, in the Old World or the New, without realizing its association with the local wine or liqueur one has just been drinking.

Very unfairly, literature is full of hard-drinking monks. There are Peacock's "bottle-cracking" Brother Michael and the boozy abbots and priors of *The Ingoldsby Legends*. Rabelais' Friar John, who accompanied Pantagruel in his quest for the Oracle of the Divine Bottle, told his abbot: "Never yet did a man of worth dislike good wine, it is a monastical apophthegm." Then there is Alphonse Daudet's immortal inebriate, Canon Gaucher, whose elixir was sold in a bottle bearing a monk in ecstasy on its label.

Yet there is a very real and a very important link between monks and wine. One of monasticism's greatest services to Western civilization has been its contribution to wine-growing and to the distillation of strong waters. "No man of the world will scoff at monks' liquor," wrote the atheist Norman Douglas in *Siren Land*. This agreeable byway of cultural history can be very pleasantly explored without having to make too serious a study of either monasticism or wine.

Abbeys, especially when ruined, have always possessed a curious fascination. Dilettantes, from John Evelyn to William Beckford, from Augustus Hare to Rose Macaulay, have taken a melancholy delight in

13

them. They inspire a sense of awe and mystery, a regretful nostalgia—
"Bare ruined choirs where late the sweet birds sang." On seeing the
remains of Netley Abbey in Hampshire, Horace Walpole exclaimed,
"Oh! The purple abbots, what a spot had they chosen to slumber in!"
Gothick novels and Romantic verse are filled with crumbling, haunted
priories—"the pointed ruin peeping o'er the wood". Nor is this fascination confined to ruined abbeys. One returns to the Middle Ages in modern
monasteries when confronted by the black habits of the Benedictines, the
black and white of the Cistercians or the white of the Carthusians, which
are the same as those of the long-dead brethren who once inhabited the
old ruins. It is hard not to feel a sense of eternity when listening to the
timeless, bell-like cadences of the Gregorian chant.

For most people wine is a more obvious pleasure. Its praises have been
sung by poets from the very earliest times, and it has its own modern
literature—delightful studies by George Saintsbury, André Simon,
Morton Shand, William Younger, Patrick Forbes, Hugh Johnson, with
evocative titles like *Blood of the Grape* or *Gods, Men and Wine.* As Hugh
Johnson says: "Wine is the pleasantest subject in the world to discuss."

Wine also has something sacred about it—"Wine that maketh glad
the heart of man." Noah first planted a vineyard and many of the
Prophets refer to wine in the Old Testament. "For the vineyard of the
Lord of hosts is the house of Israel," says Isaiah. Wine was the subject
of one of the most beautiful miracles in the New Testament, while
Christ Himself made frequent use of the imagery of vine-growing in His
parables. Indeed He actually called Himself "The True Vine", and on
one occasion said, "I will not drink of the fruit of the vine until the
Kingdom of God shall come." He also speaks of the Kingdom as a vineyard in which we must labour. Wine is of course one of the two elements
of the holiest sacrament of the Christian Church.

Roman Catholics seem particularly aware of this mystic quality, even
in casual drinking. As Hilaire Belloc put it:

> *But Catholic men that live upon wine*
> *Are deep in the water, and frank, and fine;*
> *Wherever I travel I find it so,*
> *Benedicamus Domino*

In a less exalted though no less fervent mood, the Anglican High Churchman George Saintsbury claimed: "Everyone knows or may know if he
chooses, instances of moderate drinkers who have reached ages far
beyond the average age of man, in a condition of health which compares
with that of most, and of intellectual fitness which would shame that of
nearly all teetotallers."

Indeed Pasteur believed that "*le vin est la plus saine et la plus hygiéi
nique des boissons*". More recently Hugh Johnson has emphasized the

medicinal properties of wine, pointing out that it can be particularly helpful in cases of diabetes, anaemia and heart trouble.

St Benedict, as ascetic if ever there was one but also a thoroughly practical man, allowed his monks to have wine every day. However, it is only fair to add that the Benedictine rule limits the brethren to a half a pint of wine a day, while in modern England they seldom taste any at all.

What is a monk? In the West he is simply a Christian who in his search for God lives apart from the world, under vows of poverty, chastity and obedience, either alone as a hermit or in a community. For centuries the model for Western monasticism was the Benedictine rule, but in the later Middle Ages and at the Counter Reformation new types of monasticism emerged—Canons Regular, Knights Hospitaller, friars, clerks regular and Jesuits—and even today Western monasticism is still developing. In this book the word "monk" is used in its widest sense.

The extent of monasticism's contribution to wine-growing and distilling is rarely appreciated. Monks largely saved viticulture when the Barbarian invasions destroyed the Roman Empire, and throughout the Dark Ages they alone had the security and resources to improve the quality of their vines slowly and patiently. For nearly 1,300 years almost all the biggest and the best vineyards were owned and operated by religious houses. It was the abbey of Romanée-Saint-Vivant which supplied Louis XIV's burgundy, while the largest vineyard in Burgundy, Clos de Vougeot, belonged to the Cistercians, whose fourteenth-century wall still encloses the vines. In Germany monks created hock and moselle; on the Rhine Johannisberg was the work of Benedictines and the Steinberg at Hattenheim of Cistercians. Most Austrian vineyards are of monastic origin—it is said that where the monks' wine was good there was no heresy. The brethren toiled no less fruitfully in Italy and Spain. The princely abbeys of Switzerland and Hungary, dissolved by Calvin and the Communists respectively, all cultivated the grape. Even in England monks made wine until the Reformation.

The excellent wines of California, too. little known in Europe, owe their beginnings to the vineyards of the Franciscan mission stations, whose tradition is worthily continued today by the Christian Brothers of Napa Valley. In the Antipodes, Spanish Benedictines grew wine in Western Australia for over a hundred years. The most successful vineyards in East Africa are those planted by German Holy Ghost Fathers.

The monks' greatest technical triumph was to perfect sparkling champagne by the introduction of the bottle cork. Before Dom Pérignon discovered the secret about 1700 the Champenois (including many monastic growers) drank still wines and did not know how to exploit the wonderful second fermentation. The cork later enabled growers all over the world to age their wine properly in bottles. The Benedictines also seem to have created the legendary Château Chalon, while it is just possible that the Carthusians were the first to fortify sherry.

Whenever a monastery of any age is in a vine-growing area, one can be fairly sure that it once owned and worked vineyards nearby, even though the best clos may not have belonged to it invariably. It is only reasonable to suppose that the monks followed the local pattern of husbandry and grew the same crops as everybody else in the district. Frequently a vineyard's name reveals that it has been the property of monks or nuns. Roches-aux-Moines, Clos des Pères, Bonnes Mares (Mères) are three good examples from France. In Germany, where the orders were the first to produce practically all the great wines, there is a particularly large number of such names, e.g. Graacher Mönch, Mönchsgewann, Eltviller Mönchhanach, Abtsberg, Eitelsbach Karthäuserhofberg, Nonnholle, Nonnenberg and even Förster Jesuitengarten. Throughout Germany and Austria innumerable vineyards named *Kloster* (Cloister) once belonged to the brethren. (Alas, many of the historic German names have disappeared since the Federal Republic's wine law of 1971, which allows only sites of more than five hectares [12.35 acres] to be registered.) Monkish names are also to be found among the wines of Spain and Italy, of Switzerland and Hungary. Nevertheless, in the majority of cases the presence of the monks in times past is not necessarily revealed by the name. Several hundred fine-quality wines are known to have had monastic associations at some period.

When the art of distillation was discovered in Europe in the twelfth century, it was the monks who—for medical purposes—first made *aqua vitae*. There have been countless monastic *eaux-de-vie*, each one with a jealously guarded secret formula. The most famous is of course Chartreuse, whose receipt was given to the monks by Marshal d'Estrées, the brother of Henri IV's mistress; they still make the liqueur themselves near the Grande Chartreuse and still keep the secret. Benedictine is now an entirely secular production, but the formula comes from the abbey of Fécamp—handed down by the family of one of the monks after the monastery was destroyed at the French Revolution, until it was distilled once again nearly 70 years later. Yet a surprisingly large number of liqueurs are still made by monks. Even the first maker of Scotch whisky known to history was a friar.

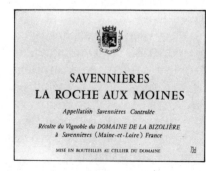

Most monasteries lost their vineyards and their stills in the great dissolution which followed the Revolution and the Napoleonic wars. None the less, even today a number of monastic houses continue to cultivate the vine. There are those in France, Austria, Italy and Spain who produce wine both for their own consumption and as a source of income, houses where one may still see habited figures harvesting the grapes at the vendange. There are also the new monastic vineyards in North and South America, in New Zealand and Australia, and in Israel and the Lebanon. At least 80 different—and excellent—wines are still grown by religious orders.

A book of this size cannot, unfortunately, attempt to be comprehensive and cannot tell the story of every wine or liqueur which is known to have been produced by the brethren. There have to be gaps; the field is so vast that one must be selective. I have been guided by two overriding considerations. The first is the quality of the wine, the second the beauty of the monastery. For monastic architecture is among the loveliest and most inspiring in the world. It includes the Romanesque abbeys and priories of France, of Spain and of southern Germany; the puritan grace of the early Cistercians; the *flamboyant* Gothic of the later medieval French monasteries; the Burgundian and Renaissance glories of the great charterhouses; the Baroque and Rococo of the mighty Benedictine, Cistercian and Premonstratensian houses of Bavaria, Austria, Czechoslovakia and Hungary; and the charming Franciscan mission stations of California. Nor should one forget the mournful relics of the old English monks. Many of the loveliest of the monasteries which survive have, or have had, vineyards, and many romantic ruins are to be seen among the vines.

This book approaches its subject from the monks' point of view—where practical, order by order. Such a method makes it at least possible to convey something of the spirit of the men who made the wine; to know even as little of their rules and how rare was the appearance of their own vintages in their austere refectories, can add to one's appreciation of both their buildings and their wine.

Seeking out monasteries associated with a vine or a liqueur can be a most agreeable pastime, especially in the spring when the grapes are in blossom. Writing of the sweetness of "the breath of flowers", Sir Francis Bacon gave it as his opinion that "the flower of the vine" ranked after only the rose, the violet and the musk rose. A Trappist once told the author that one of the joys of Cîteaux—the mother house of all Cistercian abbeys—is the scent of the vines in blossom at Clos de Vougeot drifting down on the spring wind. The autumn is also a pleasant time for such a pursuit, with the aromatic bonfires of discarded vines. Anyone with a taste for the quieter pleasures of life, particularly those who have a nostalgia for the Middle Ages, is susceptible to the tranquil charm of the monastic world. The dwellings of the monks appeal to believer and non-believer alike, to antiquarian and dilettante, to pilgrim and tourist. In *A Time to Keep Silence* Patrick Leigh Fermor writes that even a stranger, when thrown by chance into contact with monasticism, "can glean from it much of the healing and mysterious enchantment for which, among other purposes, monasteries were built". Monasticism is still very much alive, but since the Second Vatican Council (1962-65) it has been changing rapidly. The picturesque dress of 14 centuries ago may perhaps vanish for ever; already it is giving place to jeans and dungarees. As for "sweet birds" singing in the choir, Latin has almost gone and the Gregorian chant is heard less and less.

Wine tours are increasingly popular, especially if they have a theme, usually the wines of a particular region, and when combined with visits to places of architectural and historical interest. Monks and wine can provide an outstandingly varied and satisfying theme. It is only fair to point out that as men who have fled the world, the monks do not welcome visitors unreservedly, though often are only too pleased to see them—Heiligenkreutz in the Vienna Woods actually has a restaurant.

Chapter 1
The Coming of the Monks

C'est mourir tous les jours que de vivre sans vin.

HENRI REGNARD

*In that day sing ye unto her, A vineyard of red wine.
If the Lord do keep it; I will water it every moment:
lest any hurt it, I will keep it night and day.*

ISAIAH

The two greatest achievements of the ancient Egyptians were the building of the Pyramids and the invention of Christian monasticism. When the message of the Gospel finally convinced that strange people they could not take their treasures with them to the next world, they invented an equally extreme form of insurance against mortality by going out into the desert and leading lives of prayer and self-denial.

The first monk (Greek *monos*, "solitary man") was the Copt St Anthony, who about AD 271 left the tomb in which he was living and moved into the hilly wilderness between the east bank of the Nile and the Red Sea. Others followed and by 300 he was ruling a little community of hermits. Many of the men and women who came later preferred a more communal or "cenobitic" way of life and by the middle of the fourth century the Wadi el-Natrun, a desert valley which had become the centre of the new monasticism, contained groups numbering as many as a thousand souls. The first written monastic rule was that of Pachomius, who gathered these enormous communities into monastery towns that often had 2,000 brethren and sisters under a single abbot; at Oxyrrhynchus there were 30,000 religious, more than half of them nuns. Such monastery towns supported themselves by their produce, which they sent down the Nile to be sold at Alexandria; they may well have cultivated the vine which was then grown in Egypt.

Many Desert Fathers practised alarming austerities, like Macharius of Alexandria, who once spent six months sitting naked in a swamp where mosquitoes as big as wasps bit him until he appeared to be suffering from elephantiasis. He was not without compassion for his fellow creatures, however—on one occasion he restored the sight of a blind hyena. A more engaging figure was abbot Paphnut, who when he wished to cross a canal would hail a passing crocodile as if it were a taxi and order it to ferry him over on its back. *The Sayings of the Fathers*, a contemporary collection of anecdotes, tell us that some of those desert monks drank wine and speak of "the first of the new vintage", but also say that many abstained; when the great Macharius was offered wine he would always accept, to punish himself—for every cup that he drank he would drink no water for a whole day. None the less, some hermits were sufficiently hospitable to keep a jar for visitors.

It seems likely that St Athanasius, the Pope of Alexandria after whom the Creed is named and friend and biographer of St Anthony, established the first Western monastery at Trier in south Germany during his banishment there in 335-37. St Augustine, writing (in his *Confessions*) of Milan in about 380-90, says that there was a monastery "outside the walls, full of good brothers" and under the direction of St Ambrose. Augustine established his own form of monastic life at Hippo, in what is now Algeria, where he was bishop from 397 until his death in 429. Although he considered that "immoderate drinking foments lust", he allowed his brethren a daily modicum of wine with their meals—he also gave communal means a sacramental symbolism, associating all eating and drinking with the Last Supper.

The first Western monk who is both a recognizable personality and a known viticulturist was St Martin of Tours. He was born in Roman Pannonia (modern Hungary) in about 316, the son of a pagan legionary. Martin himself joined the Roman army, and it was when he was garrisoned at Amiens that there took place the incident beloved by painters: one bitter cold day a beggar asked the young centurion for alms, whereupon he tore his own red cloak in two and gave the man half; that same night Christ came to Martin in a dream, wearing the missing piece. Next day he left the army and was baptized, and, after first returning to Pannonia to convert his mother, became a hermit on an island off the Ligurian coast. Eventually, he decided to go back to Gaul.

By about 360 Martin was living as a hermit at Ligugé just outside Poitiers, where he was soon ruling a small community. (Ligugé is still a monastery, and the foundations of Martin's abbey may still be seen—until the late 1960s its Benedictines produced an excellent red wine.) In 372 the people of Tours made Martin their unwilling bishop by force, bringing him to their city under armed guard. He found a compromise by carrying out his episcopal duties conscientiously but also slipping away from time to time to a new monastery of hermits which he had established on the banks of the Loire at Marmoutier.

His biographer, Sulpicius Severus, says that Martin always retained his desert ideals and that his dirty appearance, shabby clothes and uncombed hair horrified the Gallo-Roman noblemen who were his fellow bishops. None the less, during his 26-year episcopate Martin was brilliantly successful in evangelizing the hitherto neglected pagan countryside, destroying temples and idols and building churches all over Gaul. When he died in 397 his funeral was attended by 2,000 monks and he was acclaimed as a saint. The red cloak was kept at Tours and became the most sacred relic in France; in the early Middle Ages the great Capetian dynasty derived their name from Hugues Capet's possession of it (Latin *capa* = cape or cloak). Today little remains of the once mighty abbey of Saint Martin at Tours. However, the beautiful thirteenth-century Tour du Tresor and a most impressive and unusual cloister, half French *flamboyant* and half Italian Renaissance, still convey something of the abbey's former glory. In the neighbouring thirteenth-century abbey of Saint Julien an ancient wine-press has been most fittingly placed in the cloister.

The cheerful Tourangeots continue to celebrate Martin's *fête* even today, at the end of January (although his actual feast day in the Roman Calendar is 11 November), with much merry-making and plenty of drinking. They call drunkenness "St Martin's sickness", while to tipple is *martiner* and until quite recently to tap the barrel in Touraine was *martiner le vin*. Many miracles have been performed at his shrine. The Frankish chronicler Gregory of Tours informs us that when a nun placed an empty wine jar next to Martin's tomb it was replenished each time a single drop of holy water was poured into it. The patron saint of innkeepers, Martin has a well-attested interest in viticulture. In 1096 Pope Urban II—fresh from summoning the First Crusade (and a lover of the champagne of Ay, which he declared the best wine in the world)— saw at Marmoutier a venerable vine planted by Martin and surrounded by a vineyard of flourishing descendants. The saint is credited with domesticating the wild grapes of the Touraine forest and developing the Chenin Noir grape from the wild Chenin, the black grape which in turn became the Chenin Blanc (or Pineau de la Loire) and which is now the cépage most widely used for the white wines of Touraine and Anjou— the grapes are sometimes called *pattes-de-lièvre*, hare's feet. One wine in particular is said to owe its origin to him—he is credited with planting the first Vouvray vineyard, on a slope by Marmoutier. Finally, for the vignerons working in the autumn, burning vines and replanting, the abbot had a last gift—some sun. Even in England his miraculous little late summer is still sometimes called Martinmastide.

So great was St Martin's contribution to wine-growing that one legend actually credits his donkey with the invention of pruning. Left tethered in a vineyard, the brute ate everything in reach, leaving only the grapes which grew below the level of its knees. Much to their astonishment, its master's despairing monks then made the best wine of their lives. To this day the grapes of Touraine are never grown far off the ground.

St Martin is also remembered in Germany, where he is a popular patron of the wine-growers along the Moselle. He is said to have visited

Trier on a number of occasions, working several amiable miracles. His feast is celebrated just as cheerfully as on the Loire, being the day when the young wine is first tasted. It was once the day when the peasants paid the monks their tithes of grapes or wine.

It is not known what rule was followed in St Martin's monasteries, though it must have been essentially eremitical and was probably very like that of the Desert Fathers—it would have had more in common with that of today's Camaldolese or Carthusians than with those of the Benedictines or Cistercians. The early monks of the West followed a number of rules. That of the Irish St Colombanus—who changed water into wine on several occasions—was characterized by ferocious penances which included flogging and starvation. Nevertheless, certain of the more extreme Eastern practices did not appeal to the West. When the deacon Walfroy, a would-be stylite (pillar hermit), set up his pillar in the Ardennes in 585, the local bishop made him come down at once and demolished his perch. The *Rule of the Master*, compiled by an anonymous Italian abbot in the first half of the sixth century, provided a comparatively balanced way of life, which was later simplified and adapted by St Benedict.

Benedict of Nursia (*c*. 480-547), "Patriarch of the Monks of the West", was the real founder and genius of Western monasticism, and culturally one of the most important figures in European history. Curiously enough, he obviously possessed many of the traditional virtues of pagan Rome—in particular *gravitas*, that seriousness of mind so much recommended by the ancient philosophers. He probably came from a family of land-owning patricians and had undoubtedly received an excellent classical education, which included study at Rome. As a very young man he felt the call to be a hermit and spent three years in a grotto near the ruins of Nero's palace at Subiaco. He was an exemplary solitary and in consequence was rashly invited by some neighbouring monks to be their abbot. His discipline proved more severe than they had expected, so someone poisoned his wine; however, when the glass was taken to him

to be blessed according to the custom of the monastery, it shattered at the very moment when he made the Sign of the Cross.

Eventually Benedict succeeded in establishing a more obedient monastic family at the hill-town of Cassino. (The Benedictines have always shown a certain preference for building their houses on mountains, especially in Italy.) The first Benedictine abbey consisted of from 12 to 15 monks—very few of them priests—who lived in a simple one-storey building that contained an oratory, a refectory, a communal dormitory and a reading room. What made its monks so different from their contemporaries was the rule given to them by their abbot.

It was not a truly original rule. St Benedict synthesized and harmonized the monastic ideals which already existed into a short code of about 12,000 words, largely based on the untidy and verbose *Rule of the Master*. Benedict's rule was practical, moderate and humane. Instead of singing the entire 150 psalms every day, the brethren were given a week in which to do so. They received adequate food and clothing and were allowed reasonable hours of sleep. The basic rhythm of their life was a threefold division of the day's work into prayer, study and manual labour. The emphasis on agricultural work, the most important activity after prayer in the monks' day, made it inevitable that they would cultivate the vine. Then as now, agriculture in the Mediterranean lands was based on the hallowed trinity of corn, oil and wine. Nowhere is the spirit of the rule better illustrated than in Chapter 40, "The Measure of Drink":

> Each man has his own gift from God, one this and
> another that. We are therefore hesitant in deciding how
> much others should eat or drink. Keeping in mind the
> weakness of the less robust, we consider that half a pint
> of wine a day is sufficient for everyone. None the less,
> those to whom God has given the gift of abstaining
> should know that they will be rewarded. But in a case
> where the locality or the work or the heat of summer
> may make a larger allowance necessary, the abbot must
> decide, taking care that there is no excess or drunkenness.
> Indeed we read that wine is not a drink for monks, but
> since monks cannot nowadays be persuaded of
> this, let us at least agree to drink sparingly and not to
> take our fill, as "wine maketh even the wise to fall away".

What wine did these first Benedictines drink? Presumably their own regional vintages, red or white (somehow, wrongly, one thinks of monks drinking nothing but red), which must have resembled the modern vintages of the Campania, famed for quantity rather than quality—no great wine is produced near Monte Cassino. Perhaps on feast days they drank the delicious white Orvieto, brought from Umbria like their abbot.

For all his reservations St Benedict obviously took the occasional glass of wine. He was not above receiving gifts of it. When a local worthy sent him "two wooden flasks of wine"—probably small barrels—the lay brother who was bringing them (and whose name was almost unbelievably Exhilaratus) kept one for himself. After telling him to thank the donor, Benedict warned Exhilaratus to be careful with the other flask, and when the poor monk opened it a snake crawled out.

Women as well as men are of course drawn to monasticism. By the seventh century there were Benedictine nuns leading a very similar life to that of the monks of Monte Cassino. Benedict's sister, St Scholastica, "a consecrated virgin", became the patroness of Western nuns. These women would also make an important contribution to vine-growing.

Benedict had been born in 480, only four years after the deposition of Romulus Augustulus, last Emperor of the West, and though for a time the barbarian conquerors ruled through Roman civil servants, the dissolution of what remained of Roman order and civilization continued at an ever-quickening pace throughout the saint's life. The Germanic invaders steadily took over the *latifundiae*, the great agricultural estates, ejecting the owners and moving into the villas in their place. They became a new ruling class of warrior lords, who guarded the slave labourers in return for a large share of their produce—which meant, basically, food and wine. This crude protection racket eventually formed the economic basis of feudalism. Meanwhile, even at the height of Ostrogothic rule, Italy was convulsed by local wars between its chieftains and other barbarians who had arrived late. Ironically the peninsula's final ruin was brought about by its reconquest by the Eastern Roman Empire during the second quarter of the sixth century, a period which coincided with Benedict's last years. The result was the total collapse of what remained of Roman civilization and technology. Italy was depopulated, its trade and communications destroyed—even the Eternal City itself was completely abandoned for a time.

As the late Dom David Knowles put it:

> All was tending to fall apart, in greater or less degree,
> into the smallest possible self-supporting units. Such a
> unit, such a cell was the monastery of the Rule.
> Economically, spiritually, functionally, it was self-
> supporting. . . . Monasteries of this type, especially
> those in Mediterranean lands where the trinity of wheat,
> vine and olive could be cultivated within a single ring-
> fence, almost within a single enclosure, were vulnerable
> only at the hands of an armed force moved by a deliberate
> design to exterminate the whole community. All other
> forms of higher organization might dissolve, whether in
> empire, province or diocese, but this family would survive.

Chapter 2
Monks and Wine in the Dark Ages

Le vin pris avec temperance est une seconde vie.

TRISTAN L'HERMITE

They shall build the waste cities,
and inhabit them; and they shall plant vineyards
and drink the wine thereof.

AMOS

The claim that monks saved viticulture during the fall of the Roman Empire and the ensuing Dark Ages was first made in the 1860s by the Comte de Montalembert in *Les Moines de l'Occident*. Although the Count, a Catholic apologist rather than an historian, advanced little evidence his claim was widely accepted. However, it has recently been challenged by the late William Younger in *Gods, Men and Wine*. In Younger's view "wine-growing was brought over the Dark Ages by private enterprise". His argument, that the secrets of viticulture were preserved not in dusty monastic libraries but by the vignerons in the field, does not stand close examination—in many cases monks *were* the men in the field and if they were not they took care to employ the best vignerons available. Younger's one apparently solid piece of evidence is that for a brief and comparatively late period English vineyards were in lay rather than clerical hands, but England can hardly be cited as a typical example of a wine-growing country.

In fact, insufficient evidence survives from the Dark Ages to prove or disprove Montalembert's claim. Nevertheless, as will be seen, the circumstantial evidence is very strongly in his favour—in particular the sheer size and effectiveness of the monasteries as economic units. Moreover, Professor Roger Dion, the author of the only scholarly historical study of French viticulture, seems to support Montalembert. "Until the very end of the Ancien Régime compliment after compliment was paid to the perfection of monastic viticulture," says the Professor, who supplies an impressive list of tributes from contemporary vignerons; as late as 1762 it was reported from Laon that the vines there were excellent "and belong largely to men of the Church who are in a condition to tend them properly".

The most telling argument in Montalembert's favour is that when the monks were at their prime and possessed their most considerable work force they made famous wines from vineyards which, since their passing, have been totally eclipsed. Among the most sought-after vintages of thirteenth-century France were those produced by the abbeys of Souvigny and Château-Chinon, now completely forgotten. If Saint-Pourçain is enjoying a mild revival, it is hardly the wine Kings of France served at their banquets and medieval Parisians valued so highly.

During the collapse of the West most barbarians left the monasteries alone, fearing the monks as miracle-workers and magicians. The story of the visit of the Ostrogoth Chieftain Totila to St Benedict shows this very clearly. Totila sent a companion ahead of him, dressed in his robes, to test the abbot's powers. Benedict at once told the man, "Take off those clothes—they don't belong to you." Totila was so shaken that he threw himself at the feet of the saint, who warned him, "You have already done enough evil and you are going to do much more! Cease your wickedness. I tell you that you will enter Rome, you will reign for another nine years and in the tenth you shall die." Benedict proved gratifyingly accurate in his prediction, and such a reputation won his monks a certain measure of protection—they were probably the only tillers of the soil who could expect to be left in peace. This security was of vital importance in their work as farmers and vignerons.

During the sixth and seventh centuries more and more men, and later women too, were attracted to the monastic life—to its search for God; its arduous happiness and security; its ritual yet simple courtesy; its temperance and kindliness; its balance and rhythm and all the other benefits of this voluntary communism. New abbeys were founded throughout the West; in Italy, in Spain, in Gaul, in south Germany, in Britain and in Ireland. In 610 we find St Columbanus at Nantes shipping wine to his brethren in Ireland. The monks continued to follow a number of rules, but by the end of the period most had changed to that of St Benedict. The effect of this monastic expansion on viticulture may be judged from the fact that by 643 the abbey of Bobbio in the Apennines (founded by Columbanus, who died there in 615), with 28 farms and 150 monks, was producing 800 amphorae of wine a year.

Almost certainly lay vignerons swelled the monks' labour force. Since the general flight from the towns, which had begun in the Western Empire in the first century, country temples and then churches had, like villas, been the nuclei for agglomerations of industries and handicrafts. Artisans joined the *coloni* in settling round the monasteries.

Undoubtedly those monks who had read St Augustine's *City of God* believed that they were rebuilding the world. For many the collapse of the cities and the end of civilized life would have recalled those pages in

Christ in the wine-press, a drawing c. 1250.

the Old Testament which tell not only of the Babylonish conquest of Jerusalem and the miseries of the captive Israelites but also of God's forgiveness and the rebuilding of Israel. From the Old Testament too they learnt that corn, oil and *wine* are the unmistakable marks of God's favour. Prophecies like those of Amos must have seemed peculiarly relevant—"they shall build the waste cities, and inhabit them; and they shall plant vineyards, and drink the wine thereof."

However, even in Italy the monasteries began to suffer from the continuing disruption of society. In the latter half of the sixth century another wave of savage Germanic invaders, the Lombards (or "long-beards"), who were Arian heretics and "whose friendship was a punishment from God", swept over the Alps. They soon wrested the exhausted peninsula from the Byzantines, who had only just reconquered it, and divided it into little duchies and counties which warred endlessly with each other. The new rulers of Italy were no respecters of the abbeys and in 589 they sacked Monte Cassino itself. It would be many years before the Lombards were converted to Catholicism.

The chaos and bloodshed were no less dreadful in the other lands of what had once been the Western Empire. In Gaul the Franks, Burgundians and Visigoths had brought devastation and continued to wreak havoc with their dynastic wars. In Spain the religious conflict between Catholic and Arian Visigoths was equally destructive. Then in the eighth century the Arabs conquered both Spain and North Africa. Mediterranean trade was ruined as a result, while at the same time almost the last vestiges of internal trade in western Europe disappeared as roads and waterways fell into disuse.

But the monks and most of the monasteries survived—Monte Cassino was rebuilt in 717. Every abbey cultivated the grape if it was at all possible, whatever the obstacles of soil or climate; Bede reports that vines were even grown in Ireland. As the monks spread northwards they took the vine with them, to Ghent and Limbourg and later even to Poland and Pomerania.

Slowly agriculture recovered. Arable land that had been neglected for decades and even centuries was steadily cleared of brushwood and reclaimed. By the eighth century new land was necessary and for this the forest had to be felled. Monastery after monastery was built in the totally uninhabited wooded areas, which the monks had to clear for themselves. In Cardinal Newman's words, "Silent men were observed about the country or discovered in the forest, digging, clearing and building."

Wherever they cleared the forest they also planted vines. These pioneer monk vignerons are commemorated by a number of legends. St Ermeland, who founded a monastery near the mouth of the Loire in about 670, is said to have planted the entire island of Indret with vines. In the sixth century the great abbot St Carilef (St Calais) had established a community at Anille, on the banks of the little river of that name, some 30 miles south-east of Le Mans and, in those days, deep in a vast forest. Here he discovered "a little vine bathed in mysterious light", which yielded so much wine that when the abbot met King Childebert hunting he was able to entertain the monarch and his entire court.

Trade and communications were so broken that everyone depended on local vintages. Throughout the Middle Ages the wines best known to Parisians were those from long-forgotten vineyards in the Île de France and other unlikely places:

> *And the wine that's clear and green,*
> *Orléans, Rochelle, Auxerre.*

The accounts of the abbey of Saint Germain des Prés in Paris in about 814 (the year in which Charlemagne died), the so-called Roll of Abbot Irminion, tell us of vineyards owned by the monastery in such localities as Rambouillet, Fontainebleau, Dreux, Sceaux and Versailles. In the ninth century Saint Denis, the royal mausoleum just outside Paris, had a vineyard in the abbey precincts together with a whole string of wine-growing estates in the Île de France.

Some monastic wine was very bad indeed; the wine of the abbey of Saint Wandrille in Normandy (part ruined but still inhabited by Benedictines) was a byword for nastiness. However, the monks had beehives, orchards and herb gardens to supply the additives which could make the sourest vintages reasonably palatable. Colour and clarity were all-important in the medieval world, so red wines were fined with white of egg and white wines with isinglas, while sometimes blood or milk was added. Inferior wine was turned into vinegar while grapes from which it was not possible to make wine were a useful crop in themselves. The rejected fruit could be eaten or turned into verjuice for pickling ham and cheese, the residue making good manure. Oil for soap could be derived from the pips, which might also be employed to flavour cheese or as chicken feed. The leaves provided an excellent autumn cattle feed, and vine wood made a most agreeable and aromatic fuel.

From the very beginning it was accepted that monks contributed to the well-being of society as a whole. They were the recognized restorers of civilization and the outstanding colonizers of the wilderness. They provided the age's social and cultural services; dispensing charity, keeping the only hospitals and schools, and even having safe deposits. In the most remote areas, where churches were few and far between, they had a pastoral function, providing christenings, marriages and consecrated burial ground as well as Mass and confession.

Monasteries also served as hotels or hospices for travellers, both rich and poor. St Benedict had said specifically in Chapter 53 of his rule—"Of the Reception of Guests"—"Let all guests that come be received like Christ for He will say 'I was a stranger and ye took me in' "; the same chapter orders the provision of "a separate kitchen for the abbot and guests, so that the brethren may not be disturbed". In the mid-eleventh century at the abbey of Farfa, to the north of Rome, a *palatium* 135 feet long was constructed for guests, with 40 beds for noblemen on one side and 30 on the other "for countesses and gentlewomen". Another building accommodated less distinguished visitors, while there was also "a place where all such men as arrive not in a retinue [only the very poor or outcasts travelled alone] may foregather and receive charity in the form of food and drink, as much as shall seem fit to the brother almoner".

The usefulness of monks was fully recognized by rulers and magnates who encouraged the foundation of new abbeys by large gifts of land. In addition, everyone valued the monks for their spiritual contribution—it was their prayers that warded off plague and famine. Heaven and Hell were terrifying realities in that age of simple faith, and great lords tried to buy salvation by endowing the holy men who would pray for them.

The documents of the abbey of Lorsch, which go back to the eighth century, show the magnitude of such endowments. The monastery of St Nazarius of Lauresham, usually known as Lorsch, was founded in 764 during the reign of Charlemagne's father, King Pepin the Short. The following year it acquired great prestige by obtaining the relics of a holy martyr, hitherto housed in a church at Milan named after him, San Nazario—henceforward most benefactions were made in his name. Lorsch is in Hessen, not far from the university town of Heidelberg and in the plain below the Bergstrasse hills, which are still a wine-growing area. Its Carolingian "royal hall", with Corinthian columns and patterns of fluted pilasters, dates from 800, and has miraculously survived. The *Codex Laureshamensis* lists strings of vineyards all over south Germany, presented to Lorsch by emperors, kings and noblemen. In the year of its foundation the abbey was given vineyards at Oppenheim by two landowners there, Folcred and Berticus. In 765 it received vineyards at Bensheim in the Bergstrasse (the earliest documentary evidence of viticulture in these hills) from Udo, son of Lando. The following year it was presented with another vineyard at Bensheim by the nobleman Stalan. In 773 it was given the large estate of Heppenheim by Charles, the future Emperor Charlemagne, a gift which included houses, farms, woodland, pasture, watermills and serfs, not to mention vineyards. The following year Charles attended the consecration of St Nazarius's new church at Lorsch and presented the monks with the entire crown estate at Oppenheim. At Dienheim nearby they received nearly a hundred vineyards between 765 and 864. By the thirteenth century Lorsch owned 189 villages in Rheinhessen alone, but this was not the only area where they possessed vines. The codex contains the deed of gift of vineyards at Heitersheim in the Markgräflerland, not far from Freiburg, by Starafried and his son Egilbert in 777, "to the holy Nazarius, martyr of Christ, whose body rests in the monastery of Lauresham". Six similar endowments were made to Lorsch in the same locality shortly after. Lorsch owned vineyards in many other regions as well.

The great abbeys of Fulda and St Gall were no less richly endowed with vineyards through Germany, reaching farther northwards as Christianity advanced. All these monasteries built granges (abbey farms) staffed by lay brethren, wherever they possessed a large concentration of wine-growing properties. Among other great abbeys that were producing wine in Germany during the Dark Ages one might mention Reichenau on its island on Lake Constance, Prüm in the Eifel hills, and Hirsau and St Blasien in the Black Forest.

The relationship between the abbeys and the *pagani* (as the country people were still called in vulgar Latin) was of particular importance to their effectiveness as economic units. A peasant would surrender his freedom to obtain the monks' protection and henceforward hold his land in return for "dues of labour—working on the abbey farms on specified days—and of kind". In vine-growing areas the latter invariably included grapes or wine, and as the monks were nearly always the biggest land-owners in their region they held the largest stock of the local vintage. Sometimes they divided distant vineyards with the peasants, keeping half the produce. The *pagani*, no longer pagans but Christians, were understandably awed by the monks' skills.

Not only did the holy men produce good wine but, according to Montalembert, they discovered the secret of brewing beer with hops, just as later they would be the first to distil *eau-de-vie* and whisky. It is possible that they also invented a method of inseminating fish artificially in their great stew ponds. The monks were the best fruit-farmers and the best beekeepers of their time, while countless delicious cheeses owe their origin to them, including Parmesan.

Villages sprang up around the abbeys throughout the Dark Ages and the monks made viticulture part of the peasants' life, with blessings of the grapes and even exorcisms of vine disease. The text of a sixteenth-century Burgundian exorcism has survived and although much later in date, it conveys the spirit of the prayers used by the early monk vignerons.

> I summon, and armed with the shield of faith and by
> the power of the Holy Cross, I command and conjure a
> first, a second and a third time all those flies which are
> called *escrivains, urébères* or *uribères* and all other
> maggots harmful to the fruit of the vine, to cease
> immediately their ravaging, eating, destroying and
> annihilating of the branches, buds and fruit, to
> abandon such power henceforward, and to withdraw
> to the depths of the forest where they can no longer
> harm the vines of the faithful.

The exorcist continues that if they still follow Satan's counsel and persist in their ravages, "then I curse and call down a sentence of malediction and anathema".

In those days the Catholic laity received Communion in both kinds, the villagers drinking from the chalice like their priests. After Mass there was often a distribution of unconsecrated wine as well as *pain bénit*; in medieval England such wine was considered a sovereign remedy for sore throats. Wine was also needed for salving cuts and wounds, just as in the case of the Good Samaritan, being the only known disinfectant. In fact it was a universal medicine.

Medieval man was no less conscious of the magic quality of wine than the ancient Israelites. Sometimes his awareness resulted in a startling and terrifying and seemingly almost blasphemous symbolism; certain German miniatures from the twelfth to the fifteenth centuries depict Christ in his Passion as a crucified and crowned vine-dresser treading out the grapes, the blood spurting from his wounds to mingle with the grape juice (see p. 104). This is a picture originally suggested by Isaiah: "Who is this that cometh from Edom, with dyed garments from Bozrah? . . . Wherefore art thou red in thine apparel, and thy garments like him that treadeth in the winefat?" The image was taken up by such Church Fathers as St Augustine and St John Damascene. As late as the seventeenth century a sober Anglican divine, Lancelot Andrewes, bishop of Winchester (and a leading translator of the Authorized Version of the Bible), preached a sermon on this strange theme before King James I. "He [Christ] was himself trodden and pressed: He was the grapes and clusters Himself. . . . The press He was trodden in was His cross and passion. . . . The wine or blood (all is one) came forth at all parts of Him . . . before He came to be wine in the cup." Even in eighteenth-century France "Our Lord in the Wine Press" was a far from forgotten theme in popular religious art.

By the reign of Charlemagne (771-814) many abbeys had declined from their original ideals. The Emperor encouraged the great abbot St Benedict of Aniane to bring about a reform. In 817 Charlemagne's son, Emperor Louis the Pious, summoned a meeting of monks at Aachen to discuss a constitution that would unite all abbeys within a single organization. The plan failed but several decisions had a lasting influence. One was that agricultural labour was not fitting for monks since for many years the majority of brethren had been priests, unlike the first Benedictines; in consequence the abbeys acquired more serfs and grew larger than ever. Indeed the monks themselves were often forcibly recruited, compelled to enter religion by their lords. Nevertheless, as the "school-masters" of the Carolingian renaissance they received new respect, and rulers and magnates who had already been generous enough became even more prone to endow them or to found new houses as centres of order and civilization. The abbeys were pioneers not only in science and agriculture but, until the rebirth of city life in the eleventh century, in industry and commerce as well.

They were now almost like cities themselves. Their great churches and courtyards were surrounded by a complex of supernumerary buildings, such as infirmaries and guest houses, and also by entire streets of dependants, protected by a ditch and a stockade which later became a moat and a wall. Professor Bautier of L'École des Chartres tells us that, "In the monastic borough of Saint Riquier, these were artisans grouped in whole streets according to trade (blacksmiths, shield-makers, shoemakers, carders, fullers, farriers, etc.); they evidently carried on a fair amount of business both on behalf of the abbey and on their own account. The same feature is found in northern Italy and along the Rhine." He also says that some abbeys "sold the surplus wine from their vineyards far and wide". Saint Riquier was sumptuously rebuilt by Abbot Angilbert, Charlemagne's son-in-law, with three churches—only one remains, rebuilt in turn in the thirteenth and fifteenth centuries, but still well worth a visit.

Enormous quantities of wine were needed for these monasteries. Their population, including brethren, servants and pupils or child-monks— boys whose parents had chosen a monastic life for them—together with the serfs and artisans and their families might amount to several thousand souls. Saint Riquier had 300 monks and 100 pupils, while at Tours the abbey of Saint Martin ruled the town, constituting a monastic state of 20,000 human beings. In addition guests and travellers had to be accommodated. It has been estimated that a modern English monastery with 30 priest-monks uses about 155 gallons of wine a year for sacramental purposes alone. In the early Middle Ages, it must be remembered, every adult man and woman communicated in both kinds three times a year and received additional unconsecrated wine after Mass every Sunday and feast day, while priests communicated each day. One can therefore understand why, in the ninth century, Saint Germain des Prés was producing over 11,000 gallons a year in its various vineyards.

In the ninth and tenth centuries Western society again collapsed beneath the onslaught of invaders—Saracens, Vikings and Magyars. Even when the invasions finally ceased, centralized government was practically non-existent and most of western Europe was ruled by robber barons. Where they survived the abbeys were once more oases of security and prosperity, though many had been sacked, including Saint Martin at Tours and Saint Germain des Prés.

By the end of the Middle Ages the monks had become the chief producers of wine, enjoying a far larger selection of grapes and a far larger quantity than any modern grower or co-operative. Despite bad roads and dangerous waterways they somehow managed to sell their vintages

in surprisingly distant markets. They alone had large, centralized labour forces. They alone kept proper calendars, could count the days of the year and not be deceived by unseasonable weather. They alone had the time, the records and the organization to improve a vineyard systematically; they were the first to use marl to change the soil and to plant and replant vines on a large scale. They alone possessed the cellars and store-rooms in which to mature wine, unlike peasant producers, who had to drink their wine within a few months. Considerable patience is required to create a new wine from a new combination of grapes—even nowadays it usually takes at least five years before a grower can taste the wine from newly planted vines.

Viticulture is indeed a science of daunting complexity. The grower has to know what proportion of different types of grape there should be in a vineyard; how to exploit the soil, how to use sun and climate, when to replant; and then how to rack off, how to fine and how to mature. The foundation charter of Muri, an abbey established near Zürich in the eleventh century, actually lays down a programme—manuring, pruning and hoeing over before Easter; binding up vine-shoots and removing leaves which might keep the sun off the grapes, and if necessary hoeing over young vines every month. (Muri still stands, although it is now a lunatic asylum, and the magnificent abbey church begun in 1064 but largely Baroque is worth a visit. Its community survives at Muri-Gries in the Italian Tyrol, where it continues to make wine—see p. 178.)

The close association in the peasants' mind between monasteries and wine is shown by the attributes of so many monk saints. Admittedly, vine-growers have a few patrons who were not monks, like the fourth-century Spanish martyr St Vincent, but they are easily outnumbered by the brethren. One of the earliest of these monastic patrons of wine and its producers was the hermit St Goar (*d.* 575), who is venerated in Aquitaine, Oberwesel and the Rhineland, and who still has a church dedicated to him—St Goar-am-Rhein. The patron of wine-growers in Franconia is the Irish monk missionary St Killian, who was martyred in 689. St Omer (*d.* 670), bishop of Therouannes, who was born near Coutances and became a monk of Luxeuil, is often represented holding a bunch of grapes. St Gualtier of Pontoise, once abbot of the monastery in that town, is not only a patron of vine-dressers but is frequently invoked against fever, rheumatism and diseases of the eye. His contemporary and fellow Benedictine St Morandus (*d.* 1115), a Rhenish nobleman who fasted on a single bunch of grapes throughout an entire Lent, is the patron saint of Alsatian wine-growers; he is customarily depicted either holding grapes and a pruning knife or standing in a vat, treading out the grapes. In Badia and Ripoli in Tuscany there are similar representations of a Vallombrosan abbot, Blessed Benedict Cerretani (*d.* 1215), whose statues show grapes hanging from his crozier. The Franciscan St Roch (*d.* 1327), a native of Montpellier, was once better known for healing any plague-stricken person who invoked him, but he is also a patron of wine-growers; along the Rhine and the Nahe his statue is still garlanded with grapes on his feast day, 16 August, when an annual pilgrimage is made to his shrine at the Rochusberg near Bingen. In Umbria there may still exist the cult of a fourteenth-century Camaldolese hermit who had the estimable gift of changing water into wine (see p. 111) and who was unually represented carrying a pitcher.

By the time of the Renaissance of the twelfth century, when the towns had begun to expand and civilization entered into the High Middle Ages, not only were the monks the largest producers of wine but their vintages were usually the cheapest as well as the best. This was in part due to feudalism, which gave the monks considerable advantages; the peasants had to give a tenth of their entire crop to their monastic landlords and were not allowed to sell their wine until the monks had sold theirs. Besides this "*droit de banvin*", the brethren were exempt from any sales tax on wine. Moreover, in many places they enjoyed a monopoly of wine-pressing, as did the abbey of Marmoutier at Boire in Anjou in the twelfth century; every local grower, whether lord or serf, had to take his grapes to the monks' press. Perhaps this monastic supremacy was not always beneficial to viticulture; peasants who had to pay tithes deliberately grew vines which yielded quantity rather than quality, and sometimes this resulted in inferior wine. Nevertheless it is beyond dispute that the monks laboured ceaselessly to improve their own vines.

If some vines were never in monastic hands, it is indisputable that the monks owned most of the best vineyards. To say the least, without their contribution viticulture would have taken far longer to develop. As Hugh Johnson observes, we owe to the Church "the whole of the long wine-making tradition which is continuous from the Roman to the twentieth century". And, so far as wine was concerned, it is not too much to claim that the monks were the Church.

Chapter 3
The Benedictine
Wines of France

*And Noah began to be an husbandman
and he planted a vineyard.*

GENESIS

*Blessed be God, Who prosper'd Noah's vine
And made it bring forth grapes, good store;
But much more Him I must adore
Who of the Law's sour juice sweet wine did make
Even God Himself being pressed for my sake.*

GEORGE HERBERT

The Black Monks are, after the Papacy, the most venerable institution in western Europe. They are the heirs of the original monks of the West. For 500 years the Benedictine Rule was the only monastic rule in the West, having superseded all its rivals; Charlemagne had never heard of any other. Helen Waddell called them "the Benedictine order that kept the gates of knowledge for Europe". For the Black Monk skills are letters and the liturgy; they were the first savants as well as the first great chroniclers of the medieval world, while even today no one sings the Office more beautifully or celebrates the Mass with more dignity. Yet they also converted Holland, Germany and Scandinavia and began the conversion of England and Poland. Furthermore, they have always been excellent farmers. It was the Benedictines too who evolved the classical form of Western monastery with all its distinguishing features: cloister, developed from the Roman *atrium*; chapter- or meeting-house; refectory or communal dining-room; and dormitory—though later they abandoned dormitories (which were only a rationalization of the sleeping arrangements in any early medieval hall) for cells. At their zenith they possessed several thousand monasteries and they have built the most magnificent of all abbeys whether Romanesque or Gothic, Baroque or Rococo. In addition they have owned, and in many cases created, a large number of the world's greatest vineyards. Above all, Benedictines have retained throughout something of the Roman moderation of their founder and are the most human and tolerant of monks.

In the twelfth century the Benedictines lost their monopoly of Western monasticism. New orders appeared—Carthusians, Cistercians, Canons Regular, Templars and Hospitallers. In the thirteenth century came all the friars. Nevertheless, the Black Monks held their own, at their steady, stately pace. It has been said with some truth that the Benedictines are the spine of Western monasticism.

From a very early date the Benedictines had six monasteries in the diocese of Reims and they owned many vineyards in Champagne. Also in Champagne, though not in the Reims diocese, is a Benedictine nunnery which was founded in 630 and which still belongs to the nuns. Mr Patrick Forbes tells us that, "At the outbreak of the French Revolution, at least half of the really great vineyards in the Champagne district were in the hands of monks." However, the glorious role of Dom Pérignon must wait for a later chapter.

Bishop Bossuet, the Eagle of Meaux who was born a Burgundian, considered that "*le vin a le pouvoir d'employer l'âme de toute vérité, de tout savoir et philosophie*". No doubt he was thinking of burgundy. Indeed the Black Monks' association with "the foaming grape of eastern France" dates from a very early period. Burgundy takes its name from the tribe of Germans who conquered it in the fifth century, but its vineyards date from Roman times. They seem to have remained in production despite the barbarian invasion, and in his chronicle Gregory of Tours—who died in 594—says that, "To the west [of Dijon] the hills are covered with fruitful vines which yield a noble Falernian-type wine."

But before discussing the monks' contribution, it is necessary to know something of Burgundy's geography. The red wines are grown on a long sequence of low hills, the first range being the Côte d'Or, which runs south-west from Fixin, just south of Dijon, almost to Chalon-sur-Saône; the Côte d'Or is divided into the Côte de Nuits and the Côte de Beaune. The greatest red burgundies come from these hills, which run for 36 miles. Farther south are other ranges which grow lesser but excellent wines, the Côte Chalonnaise, the Côte Mâconnaise and the hills of the Beaujolais. However, some of the best white wines come from Chablis, north-west of the Côte d'Or, though the greatest white burgundies come from the Côte de Beaune.

In 587 King Gontran of Burgundy gave "lands with vines" at Dijon to the monks of the abbey of Saint Benigne. (St Benignus, the apostle of Burgundy, had been martyred in AD 179 during the reign of the Emperor Marcus Aurelius and the abbey was founded at his shrine; today one may see a Gothic church built between 1281 and 1325 and also a magnificent thirteenth-century monks' dorter or dormitory.) In 630 Duke Amalgaire of Lower Burgundy gave the abbey of Bèze, near Gevrey, vineyards at Gevrey, Vosne and Beaune. (Later there were to be no less than 20 religious houses at Beaune, though not all were Benedictine.) Bèze, two towers of whose church still stand, also had vineyards at Chenove and

Marsannay north of the Côte d'Or at a very early date, while even today Clos de Bèze is the name of a very fine wine from vines next to the old abbey. In 775 Charlemagne gave the monastery of Saulieu his vineyards at Aloxe-Corton, at the top of the Côte de Beaune, though he retained a few acres for himself and his court; ironically, Corton was to be the favourite and indeed indispensable wine of Voltaire, deadly foe to all monks. A fine barrel-vaulted church, with interesting carvings, dating from 1143 can still be seen at Saulieu. In the ninth century the Emperor Charles the Bald gave vineyards at Chablis to his brother Eudes, who was the abbot of St Martin's old monastery at Tours.

Even in those days red burgundy was almost certainly considered to be the greatest of all wines, a claim which was undisputed until the advent of sparkling champagne in the eighteenth century. (The virtues of claret were not sufficiently appreciated outside Gascony; the Duc de Richelieu once brought Louis XV—whose favourite wine was Beaune—the best bordeaux he could find; the monarch sipped it, muttered "*potable*" and never touched it again.) Shakespeare's King Lear refers to "The vines of France, and milk of Burgundy". Brillat-Savarin believed that "*Le Bourgogne est la plus belle louange de Dieu*". Even now it retains the title "The King of wines".

The monks' burgundy—and indeed most of their other wines—was somewhat different from what we drink today. Until the end of the eighteenth century nearly all wine was drunk from the wood, being bottled for almost immediate consumption from huge butts which had to be steadily topped-up. While 1811 was the first year when a significant number of French wines were bottled for maturing, the process seems to have been introduced in Burgundy as early as 1795. Before that date wines were much less full-bodied and lighter in colour—even the great burgundies must have resembled a modern dark rosé. The qualities which were prized were a gentle, fruity flavour, and clearness (hence *clairet* from which claret is derived); to procure them, white and red were often blended. The implications of Dom Pérignon's discovery of the bottle cork and its role in maturing wine and preventing evaporation were not understood for many years; until the invention of the cork-screw wine in bottles was sealed with wax, which quickly turned it to vinegar. Wines were therefore drunk much younger than they are today, and were also much weaker with a smaller alcoholic content.

The rise of the Burgundian abbey of Cluny during the tenth century was the most important development in Western monasticism since the introduction of the rule of St Benedict. During the reign of only five abbots, spanning the immense period from 927 to 1157, Cluny's two most striking features were a scrupulous and magnificent performance of the ceremonies of the Church—eight hours a day were devoted to the liturgy —and the foundation of a network of nearly a thousand daughter houses all over Europe. Apart from certain abbeys who submitted to

Cluny's reforming yoke, these houses were priories instead of abbeys and depended on the mother house in a kind of monastic feudalism; every prior was appointed by the abbot of Cluny and every monk was technically a monk of Cluny. The enormous Romanesque church at Cluny, with its nave of 11 bays, "coronet" of radiating chapels, and seven bell-towers, would still be one of the wonders of the world had it not been destroyed—save for a tower and a few fragments—during the French Revolution; it was larger than any cathedral anywhere until, in the sixteenth century, St Peter's was deliberately designed to surpass it, though only by a few feet. Nor was Cluny's expansion confined to full-scale daughter houses. Like all Benedictine abbeys she set up "cells" to administer distant properties. Some of these cells were miniature monasteries with five or six monks, whereas others were no more than a cottage with a chapel, and contained only one or two brethren or, occasionally, just a solitary individual. An even smaller monastic dependency was when an abbey owned a parish church and appointed a monk as parson. Many vineyards were administered by cells or monastic rectors, constituting a network which enabled the brethren to control mile upon mile of vines.

In the always profound words of Morton Shand: "In the Middle Ages the more delicate husbandry of vineyards and the vintaging of fine wines were monopolies of the great monasteries. The great Abbey of Cluny, situated in the very heart of the Mâconnais, which played such a predominant part in the intellectual resurrection of Europe, had just as profound an influence on its agricultural development, and especially in improving the prevailing standards of viticulture."

Cluny lies between Beaune and Mâcon and was the biggest landowner in Burgundy. It early acquired estates in the Côte de Nuits and by 1275 owned all the vineyards round Gevrey, including the splendid Clos de Bèze. The monks are still commemorated by a vineyard at Gevrey-Chambertin (the suffix was added in 1847) called Combe-aux-Moines. (However, one vineyard at Gevrey which the monks did not own was the original Chambertin, though they could claim to have inspired it. A peasant named Bertin who owned a little strip of land at Gevrey was so impressed by the brethren's skill as vignerons that he planted it with

vines and copied their methods; the vintages of *Campus Bertinus*—Chambertin—are considered by some to be the greatest of all burgundies, and after he became Emperor, Napoleon never drank anything else.) Yet Cluny was responsible for some rather undistinguished wines, such as the red wine of Avallon in Lower Burgundy. This only deserves mention because some of it is still made from vines which grow around the old Cluniac priory of St Mary Magdalene at Vézelay. The tympanum over one of the doors of the beautiful Romanesque basilica is exquisitely carved with intertwined vines, and Sir Sacheverell Sitwell has called the church "one of the major architectural sensations of the western world". Here St Bernard preached the Second Crusade before Louis VII and all his knights. As for the wine, Mr H. W. Yoxall, in his delightful book *The Wines of Burgundy*, says that it may be bought at an *estaminet* opposite the church and is "at any rate strong".

Cluny did not have a monopoly of Burgundian monastic vineyards. Undoubtedly the Burgundian monastery with the most precious vines was the abbey of Saint Vivant at Vosne, which owned the fabulous vineyards of Vosne-Romanée on a ridge of the Côte de Nuits; they included Romanée-Conti, La Romanée, La Tâche, Richebourg and Romanée-Saint-Vivant. These were all bequeathed to the abbey in 1232 by the Duchess of Burgundy and, although the monks gradually parted with the finest jewel of their bequest in the fifteenth century when they sold the four and half acres of Romanée-Conti to the Cronembourg family (who sold it to the Prince de Conti in 1760), they kept the vineyard now known as Romanée-Saint-Vivant until 1789. At the Revolution the abbey and its vines were put up for auction as a confiscated *bien national* and the purchaser at once razed the buildings to the ground. If generally ranked as one of the less magnificent of the Vosne-Romanée wines, Romanée-Saint-Vivant was nevertheless prescribed by Dr Fagon for Louis XIV—"Tonic and generous, it suits, Sire, a robust temperament such as yours." This abbey also owned the vineyards of Flagey-Echézeaux; Les Grands Echézeaux is a soft and delicate burgundy, which enthusiasts say has a hint of truffles in its bouquet.

Joris Karl Huysmans, the author of *A Rebours* (which inspired Oscar Wilde's *The Portrait of Dorian Gray*) and also a lover of Benedictine monasteries, wrote of a vision seen by one of his characters: "Romanée and Chambertin, Clos Vougeot and Corton paraded before his eyes abbatial pomps, princely feast days and the opulence of vestments heavy with gold and gleaming in the sun." (Though Clos Vougeot, as will be seen, was a Cistercian creation.) Such vintages must indeed have made for the happy convents of which Pope sang in the *Dunciad*.

Another great Burgundian vineyard which belonged to the brethren was on the Côte de Beaune at Pommard, that agreeable little town on the banks of L'Avant Dheune. (It is said that when Erasmus was rebuked by a certain prelate for drinking Pommard on a fast day he replied, "My heart is Catholic but my stomach is Protestant.") In Beaune the offices of the well-known firm Pierre Ponelle are in what is left of the old Abbey of Saint Martin. The monks are also said to have grown fine wines at Auxey in the thirteenth century, and they had vineyards at Santenay at the southernmost end of the Côte de Beaune; there are the remains of a monastic building in the village.

Santenay is not far from the abbey of Tournus on the banks of the Saôns. Tournus was founded in the sixth century on the tomb of the martyr St Valerian (*d.* 177) and in 875 became the refuge of the monks of Saint Philibert at Noirmoutiers who had fled from the Vikings. A mighty Romanesque church, which their successors built in the eleventh century and dedicated to St Philibert, still stands over Valerian's tomb and is remarkable for its nave with enormously tall pink columns, and two great towers which dominate Tournus. A Gothic chapter-house and an abbot's lodging also survive. The town plan has remained unchanged since the Middle Ages, when it was a monastery village of the sort mentioned in the previous chapter; the abbey lay to the north, forming a kind of citadel under whose southern walls a colony of artisans and tradesmen settled—both abbey and town were eventually encircled by a defensive curtain wall. The abbey was fittingly celebrated for excellent wines. Today Tournus is one of the very few French towns of monastic origin to preserve something of its original character.

Some of the best wine of the Côte Chalonnaise in southern Burgundy is that grown around the pretty little seventeenth-century town of Givry. Both red and white are notably fresh and light. One of the commune's best vineyards is Cellier aux Moines, though it is not known whether this was created by Tournus or by Cluny.

The Benedictines were very active along the Loire and its tributaries. As has already been seen, they were planting vines near the Loire estuary in the seventh century. Later they brought the Melon de Bourgogne grape to the Nantes region, where, known as the Muscadet, it make the light, dry white wines of that name including Château la Moinerie.

La Roche-aux-Moines is a wine that comes from farther up at Savennières on the Coteaux de la Loire, on the hills which overlook the river south-west of Angers—that beautiful little medieval town which still keeps its walls and is the capital of Anjou. La Roche-aux-Moines is a strong white wine made from the white Chenin grape. Although dry it is considered a dessert wine, one of the best of the Coteaux de la Loire. It takes its name from the men who made it in the Middle Ages, the monks of the long-vanished abbey of Saint Nicolas at Angers. (However, Angers preserves much of the eleventh-century abbey of Saint-Aubin, which now houses the prefecture.)

Anjou wine has always had its admirers. Milady tried to poison d'Artagnan and the Three Musketeers by sending them a doctored case when they were besieging La Rochelle. A famous ninth-century abbot of Angers, about whom there is a famous drinking song, may well have been an admirer of La-Roche-aux-Moines when he was not swallowing red wine. Helen Waddell translated the song, probably written by a wandering Irish monk, which tells us how this splendid churchman was indeed "a purple abbot", his skin being dyed with wine and his body so soaked in it that his flesh became incorruptible. It adds that the townsmen of Angers will never see his like again for steady drinking.

Farther up the river still is Saint-Nicolas-de-Bourgueil, which produces a pleasant, reliable red wine of Touraine, *said* to smell of wall-flowers. The town of Bourgueil and its vineyards grew up around the monastery founded in 990 by a daughter of Count Thibaud le Tricheur of Blois, the phantom huntsman who still haunts the Sologne with his ghostly wolf-hounds. In the eleventh century the monks boasted that their abundant wine "brought rejoicing to sad hearts". Their memorial is Clos de l'Abbaye—alas, no longer the most renowned Bourgueil.

From the upper reaches of the river at the pleasant little town of Pouilly-sur-Loire comes the delicious dry white Pouilly Fumé with its distinctive taste (largely derived from a chalky soil), which is sometimes compared to the tang of gun flint and sometimes to a hint of truffles, though it is hardly smoky. Oddly enough it is made from the Sauvignon grape, which produces so much sweet wine in the Bordeaux region. Among Pouilly Fumé's most famous growths is the revealingly named La-Loge-aux-Moines. Pouilly Fumé owes its creation to the monks of La Charité, a monastery founded by St Loup in 700 which later became Cluniac, around which a town grew up as at Bourgueil. The abbey church of La Charité, Sainte Croix Nôtre Dame, is a perfect example of twelfth-century Burgundian Romanesque—it was the largest in France after Cluny, though only a small but magnificent section survives today.

At sometime during the sixth century St Pourçain founded an abbey on the banks of the river Sioule in the Loire basin in the centre of what later became the Bourbonnais—now the department of Allier. The abbey vineyards, sloping down to the banks of the rivers Sioule, Allier and

Bouble in a long strip that ran for miles, produced one of the most esteemed wines in medieval France. In 1241 when King Louis IX (the great St Louis who built Sainte Chapelle in Paris) gave a banquet at Saumur for his brother, Alphonse of France, the vintage which the chronicler remembered was Saint-Pourçain. In the fourteenth century it was fetching high prices in Paris and later it was a favourite of François I. Alas, over the years the wines of Saint Pourçain-sur-Sioule gradually declined in quality and repute, a falling off that was accelerated by the expulsion of the monks at the Revolution and completed by the phylloxera. Only a handful of growers continued. Yet a legend persisted, of a few small but excellent cuvées produced by one or two farmers. In recent years a tremendous effort has been made to restore the glories of the past and the wines have undoubtedly shown a steady improvement since the establishment of a co-operative in 1952, which rigorously excludes all inferior grapes. The wines include a red, a rosé, a white and a *gris* (made from equal proportions of black and white grapes). The cépage for the red and the rosé is the Gamay Noir-à-jus-blanc and the Pinot Noir, and to a lesser extent the Gamay Teinturier. The cépage for the white is more elaborate—Tressalier, Saint Pierre Doré, Chardonnay and Sauvignon. Most people who have drunk the wines of Saint-Pourçain prefer the white, which some say has a bouquet of apples. This is undoubtedly the best; a wine to watch as the co-operative continues to make progress. (It is still not yet entitled to the AC certificate—the *Appellation Contrôlée* —but to the lower ranking VDQS—*Vin Délimité de Qualité Supérieure*.)

Saint-Pourçain is a most attractive little town which repays a visit. The great abbey church has survived and contains a bewildering mixture of architectural styles, ranging from the eleventh to the eighteenth century. However, nothing remains of the monastery except the fifteenth-century cloister.

Curiously enough, the monks of all orders as well as Benedictines seem to have had far less influence on the wines of Bordeaux than they had on those of Champagne, Burgundy or the Loire. A possible explanation is that scientific viticulture was not applied to their extremely subtle and delicate cépage until a much later date; moreover, the Médoc was once marshland which was not completely drained until the eighteenth century. Indeed many of the early medieval wines for which Gascony was renowned seem to have come from outside the Bordeaux area. In 1206 and 1207 King John of England bought large quantities of wine from the monks of Moissac, the Cluniac monastery on the river Tarn. Moissac's graceful Romanesque cloister and its famous tympanum's sinuously majestic figures are still perfectly preserved.

It is an exaggeration to suggest with Alexis Lichine that the Benedictines were to the Médoc almost what the Cistercians were to the Clos Vougeot in Burgundy. During their stewardship of vineyards in the area none of the Black Monks' wines enjoyed anything like the reputation of

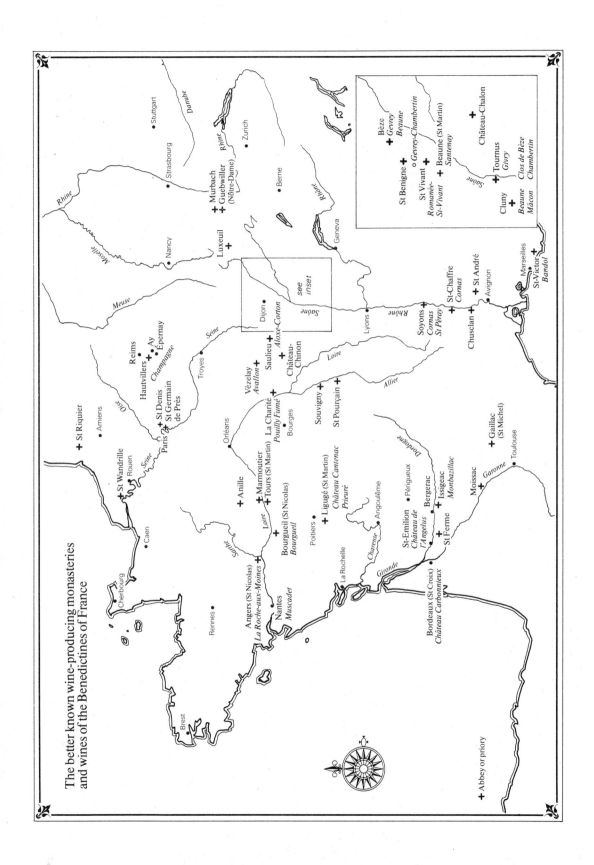

The better known wine-producing monasteries
and wines of the Benedictines of France

Clos Vougeot in its Cistercian heyday. Admittedly they possessed some fine vineyards, like Château Cantenac Prieuré (which also owned Château Pouget). In the eighteenth century Château Prieuré had an annual income of 24,000 livres—just over £1,000 in contemporary English money. This was re-created in the 1950s by M. Lichine, as Château Prieuré-Lichine, after some 40 purchases of the little plots into which the monks' vineyard had been fragmented since the Revolution. Two pleasant clarets that may have had Benedictine associations are Château les Moines (Pomerol) and Château de l'Angelus (Saint-Emilion), a Grand Cru Classé. One might also mention Le Prieuré-Saint-Emilion, which is another Grand Cru.

In 1740 the Benedictine abbey of Sainte Croix, in Bordeaux, bought for 120,000 livres (£5,000 in English money of that period) the very famous vineyard of Château Carbonnieux in the Graves. Since the seventeenth century they had been experimenting with cépages elsewhere and at Château Carbonnieux they triumphed, producing the most distinguished of the dry white Graves. This wine was once in great demand, but in recent years many people seem to have lost the taste for it. Thomas Jefferson, the future President of the United States who was American envoy in France from 1785 to 1789, reported that the monks made 50 tonneaux each year. They kept this for three or four years and then sold at £800 the tonneau. There is a dubious story of how the good Fathers, by labelling their wine *Eaux Mineralés de Carbonnieux,* smuggled barrels through the customs' houses into Moslem Turkey and made a fat profit. There is also a legend that this wine was introduced to Constantinople by a beautiful young Bordelaise, who had been captured by a corsair and given as a present to the Sultan. Cocks et Feret, that bible of the Bordeaux négociants, report that *"l'eau minérale calmait les nerfs de la capricieuse odalisque"*. The Turks wondered, "How can Christians drink wine when they have such wonderful water?"

English tax exiles in the Dordogne are well acquainted with the region's best wine, Monbazillac, grown near Bergerac. Few of them realize that they owe it to monks who in the sixteenth century, to avoid excessive taxation, first cleared the wooded slopes above the plain of the Dordogne and planted vines. It is not quite certain where these monks came from, but it may have been the neighbouring abbey of Issigeac, once the residence of Fénélon. Sometimes called "The poor man's Sauternes", Monbazillac is a sweet—but not too sweet—yellow wine with plenty of body, made from Muscadelle, Semillon and Sauvignon grapes which are left to rot on the stem until *pourriture noble* sets in. Modern improvements have enhanced its quality and, especially when old, it can be compared to a good Barsac. It used to be a traditional favourite in Holland, where it was brought in the seventeenth century by Huguenot exiles. Monbazillac is now beginning to be appreciated in England, though it is usually drunk too young.

In the tenth century much of southern France was ravaged by Moors, whose unwelcome presence is still commemorated by the Montagnes des Maures. True to their prophet, they uprooted the heinous vine wherever they met it; according to the Koran, "There is a devil in every berry of the grape." Among the vineyards to suffer most were those in the Tarn basin. However, in 960 Count Raymond I of Toulouse founded the abbey of Saint-Michel at Gaillac. Here the monks quickly embarked on a programme of replanting. Viticulture recovered for miles round about, while a little town grew up around the abbey, the townsmen recognizing the abbot as their seigneur. Soon the Gaillaçois were shipping their wines down the Tarn to Bordeaux and from thence to England, to Germany, and even to the remote and barbarous land of the Scots. The English liked in particular a dark red, almost black, vintage which a sea-voyage was supposed to transform into delectable *clairet*. There were also prized sweet white wines, one of which was a natural *mousseux*. Alas, Gaillac lost first its popularity and then its quality, suffering terribly from phylloxera and from injudicious replanting. The long road to recovery began in 1903 when a co-operative, the first in France, was established in the little town and recent years have shown a steady improvement. The cépage of the sweet white Gaillac is mainly Mauzac, Sauvignon, Semillon and Muscadelle. The dry whites are better ignored, though there is a rough red which is not too bad. Fittingly, the Gaillac co-operative is installed in the old abbey of Saint-Michel, which dates mainly from the twelfth and sixteenth centuries.

The Moors also ravaged the vineyards of Provence which had been planted as early as 600 BC by Greek colonists. The monks seem to have performed the same service for the wines of Bandol as they had for those of Gaillac. In 1023 a certain Stephanus gave the abbey of Saint-Victor vineyards at La Cadière, north of Bandol (a town some miles west of Toulon). This is the first mention of the wines of Bandol, which include red and rosé and a few white. The latter are made from the Clairette,

Ugni and Sauvignon grapes, while the red and rosé of which the region is prouder are from the Mourvèdre, the Cinsaut and the Grenache. Mr Julian Jeffs describes the red Bandol as "a fine, vigorous red wine that can be compared with a Châteauneuf-du-Pape and which, at its best, is every bit as good". There is also an unusually light, excellent red wine, Domaine Templier, and some of the Bandol rosés are well worth drinking.

In the ninth century Black Monks were given two small vineyards on the Rhône, on a hill opposite the celebrated town of Valence. These were Cornas and Saint-Péray. The Benedictines held them in return for a due of an annual dinner whose main dish had to be a large and locally caught fish. The red wine of Cornas is made from the Syrah grape (said to have been brought back from the Crusades) and, according to some, has a taste of raspberries. It is, in fact, a poor relation of Hermitage but does not keep so long. The cépage of Saint-Péray is a mixture of Roussan and Marsanne. As a still, golden wine, Saint-Péray was enjoyed by Pliny centuries before it belonged to the monks. There is also an excellent sparkling wine made by the champagne method, which locals claim was invented long before Dom Pérignon's time. That very knowledgeable wine writer Mr Vivian Rowe pays the Saint-Péray *mousseux* the following tribute: "I believe it to be the most attractive sparkling wine in France after champagne. Others may prefer Vouvray or Saumur, Gaillac or Blanquette de Limoux, but I find this mousseux of Saint-Péray—light, dry and beautifully limpid—to have a more delicate flavour than its near rivals." None the less, it has to be admitted that sparkling Saint-Péray is heavier than any champagne. The monks who once grew these wines probably came from the monastery of Soyons just south of Valence, where the curious eighteenth-century church has survived—an odd Rococo building in the "pompadour" style. However some Cornas vineyards belonged to the abbey of Saint-Chaffre, in the diocese of Viviers, which acquired them as early as 993.

Among the Côtes du Rhône villages are the excellent vintages of Chusclan, from whose co-operative come a strong red, a light red, a rosé and a pleasant white. From the tenth century until the Revolution, a Benedictine priory dominated wine-production at Chusclan. Another good Rhône wine is Gigondas, which is rather like Châteauneuf-du-Pape. It was produced by—among others—the nuns of the abbey of Saint André on the banks of the river Ouvèze. Their best customers were the vineless monks of Montmajour near Arles.

The Black Nuns were the creators of the famous *vin jaune* of Château-Chalon, a remote village in the Jura, south of Arbois and between Menétru and Voiteur. The abbey of Château-Chalon dated from the ninth century. During its prime admission was restricted to ladies of birth; would-be novices had to show 16 proofs of nobility. The nuns were renowned for producing a curious sweetmeat which was a kind of caramel baked in a *bain-marie*—a cousin of Nun's Incense. However, their true fame rested upon their wine. The abbess always supervised the vineyards herself and retained the privilege of deciding and announcing the date when each year's vendage should begin. Although Château-Chalon is in Franche Comté, which did not become part of France until Louis XIV's reign, its wine was popular at the court of François I. Marshal Biron (who lost his head for plotting to betray Henri IV) was said to have been crazed by overindulgence in it. By the time of the Revolution the nuns and their last abbess, Mme de Stain, were leading a notably relaxed life; each one living in a separate house with her own staff of servants. If they had unlimited access to their wine, it must have been a far from disagreeable existence in the depths of a wild and lovely countryside. The abbey was dissolved in 1790 and today nothing is left of it except the vineyards and the nuns' cellars.

The cépage of Château-Chalon is the white Savagnin, whose ancestor may have been the Traminer grape, though there is a picturesque tradition that it is a Tokay brought back by a local worthy on his way home from the Crusades. In the fourteenth century one of the abbess vignerons ordered her labourers to pick the grapes as late as possible, when they were overripe, if feasible not until December. Her inspired precedent has been followed ever since. After pressing, the must is fermented in vats hewn out of the natural rock; it then stays in casks for at least six years, and sometimes ten. During its period in the cask it is covered with a yeast film which is similar to the *flor* of sherry. It is the only French wine which seeks rather than avoids *maderisation*. The result is a very strong wine, dark yellow in colour, which is sometimes unhelpfully compared to sherry, and which has extraordinary powers of longevity; in 1921 the French President was given a bottle dated 1772 which was in perfect condition, and it has been said that to drink a bottle is like parting with a precious heirloom. The wine has a most powerful and individual aroma in which some experts profess to detect a flavour of nasturtium leaves. It is bottled in curious flasks which look rather like squashed, flat-shouldered claret bottles and which date from the days of the nuns. Château-Chalon is generally accepted as one of the classic wines of France, especially by the English and Americans who have discovered it in recent years, with a consequent increase in price. Unfortunately very small quantities are produced and most is drunk locally. It is said to go particularly well with oysters.

Château-Chalon also makes a *vin-de-paille* from the Savagnin grape. It too is believed to be the invention of that great fourteenth-century abbess who first made her vignerons pick the grapes for the *vin jaune* as late as possible. To make *vin-de-paille* grapes are laid on straw mats for several weeks in the winter sun to reduce their moisture while concentrating their sugar content; the juice is then fermented in the same sort of vats as the *vin jaune*. This "straw wine" is very sweet, better suited to the sugar-starved palates of our medieval forefathers than to our own, and is better drunk as a liqueur than as a dessert wine.

There were other medieval abbeys which recruited their members exclusively from the nobility. At Murbach in the southern Vosges of Alsace, founded in 727 by Saint Fermin with lands that eventually extended far north of the Rhine, not only did every choir monk later have to prove 16 quarterings but the Prince-Abbot had to be a Prince of the Holy Roman Empire by birth, and was popularly believed to rank after the Emperor himself. The last of these semi-regal prelates was Casimir von Ratmanshausen who built the church of Nôtre-Dame at Guebwiller in 1765, even though the abbey had been secularized the previous year by Louis XV. The Alsatians did not mourn the passing of the monks. The abbey's achievement of arms included a hound argent and there was a local saying "as proud as the dog of Murbach". But the monks were detested by the peasants not so much for their pride as for their feudal dues, which they exacted until the very end. Admittedly, they had been the first to plant vines at the now famous wine-producing town of Guebwiller, but for centuries their men-at-arms had cowed the townsmen, with the point of the sword if necessary. At the Revolution the abbey's buildings went down amid general rejoicing. Today, in the exquisite Florival (vale of flowers) one can still see part of a Romanesque church with two imposing towers and some fine carvings—all that is left of proud Murbach. A renowned modern vineyard which once belonged to Murbach is Clos In Der Wanneri.

Murbach was not the only Benedictine abbey to own vineyards in Alsace. Münster owned Turkheim, and even today Turkheim is one of the most reputable Alsatian growths. Until the Revolution the best wines on the hill of Sigolsheim belonged to Ebersmunster—as early as the ninth century a monk of St Gall in Switzerland was praising the fine wines of Sigolsheim.

These are some of the outstanding instances of associations between great French Benedictine abbeys and great French wines. Countless other Black Monk monasteries had links with lesser wines. In some cases the connection cannot be established but is extremely likely, if only from the sheer proximity of the monks and the vineyards. A good example is that of the priory of Ambierle and the wines of the Côte Roannaise.

Chapter 4
Benedictine Wines
of Germany
and Other Lands

Boire du vin, c'est boire du génie.

BAUDELAIRE

*I went down into the garden of nuts
to see the fruits of the valley,
and to see whether the vine flourished
and the pomegranate budded.*

SONG OF SOLOMON

The Anglo-Saxons divide most German wines into hock and moselle, but the Germans themselves do not make this distinction for they both are *Rheinwein*. The river Moselle runs north-west, twisting like a corkscrew, from France to join the Rhine at Coblenz. Its best vineyards are between Trier and Coblenz. The Rhine's great vineyards are on its right bank, a strip of land some 20 miles long stretching from opposite Bingen to the Rauenthal hills. This is known as the Rheingau and includes certain tributaries of the Moselle. The area on the left bank is in Hessen and is known as Rheinhessen, though few of its wines can compare with those from the Rheingau. South of Rheinhessen and also on the left bank is the Palatinate, while farther north and east is Franconia. These are the principal wine-growing areas of Germany, and the Benedictines have left their mark on all of them.

The Emperor Probus is popularly supposed to have brought the vine to Germany in the third century. Not so long ago a Roman glass bottle of about that date was found at Speyer and contained traces of wine. In the fourth century, Ausonius (reputedly the original proprietor of that fabulous claret Château Ausone) wrote a poem about the Moselle—"its beauty and its variety, its wine and its trout and its grayling". Even in Ausonius's day the abbey of St Maximin in Trier, which later became Benedictine, had vineyards at Longuich, Detzem and Leiwen, while that

51

of St Eucharius had them at Bernkastel and Krettnach (and much later at Trittenheim, which is named after a fourteenth-century abbot).

St Maximin was to have a staggeringly long history of wine-growing. The will of an abbot who died in 636 mentions a vineyard at Lieser and the monks steadily increased their acreage under vines. In 783 they produced no less than 900 *fuder* (9,000 litres) of wine. In 996 the Emperor Otto II gave them yet more vineyards, and over seven centuries later the monastery was busy planting over 100,000 new vines at Maximin Grünhaus, where their grange survives and still produces delicious wine, though it was secularized long ago. There was a hierarchy of drinking at St Maximin: the abbot drank the best wine, Abtsberg, made from vines grown at the top of the hill; choir monks drank Herrenberg from lower down; novices drank Bruderberg, lower down still; and lay brethren had to be content with Viertelsberg, "fourth-rate" and from the bottom. As Milton observed, "Lords are lordliest in their wine."

Another notable abbey that owned vineyards on the Moselle was St Matthias at Trier. It is still inhabited by Benedictines but, sadly, they no longer cultivate the vine. During the second half of the eighteenth century it was the monks of the abbey of St Martin at Trier who planted the famous Scharzhofberg, the greatest vineyard of the Saar, a tributary of the Moselle; they also planted Martinshof (now called Josefshof) on the Moselle, as well as the neighbouring vineyards of Graacher Mönch and Graacher Abtsberg. Vineyards at Wiltingen, on the Saar, were given to the Benedictines of St Marian-ad-Martyres at Trier in 1030 by Archbishop Poppo.

Along the Rhine the monks of Hasbach near Strasbourg were planting vines in 613, while in 644 the monastery of Wissembach owned vineyards at Lautenbach, Grünnesbrunnen and 15 other places. The monks of Alsatian Wissenbourg also had large wine-growing estates at Westhofen from a very early date.

Writing in 1732 the great traveller Baron de Pollnitz said:

> you are to know that the Fashion of Wines alters, as well as of every Thing else. Formerly the Wine of Bacharach was most in Vogue, and the French have not disdained to celebrate it in their drunken Catches; but now that Wine is no longer in request by the Wine Conners, who are here so delicate, that if they do but wet their Lips, they can presently tell the Age and the Growth of any Wine that they taste. They say now that the Wine of Bacharach is worth nothing, in comparison with the Wine of Ridelsheim and of Johannisberg.

It is interesting that the Baron should mention the growing repute of Johannisberg at this time. For the Benedictines' greatest vineyard in

Germany was unquestionably Schloss Johannisberg in the Rheingau. In 1130 the Archbishop of Mainz gave the monks of the priory of St Alban in Mainz a hill called *Mons Episcopi* ("bishop's hill") above the village of Winkel, looking down on the Rhine. Here they built a priory and a chapel dedicated to St John—hence the name Johannisberg. They also planted a vineyard, though in the early centuries it does not seem to have been particularly notable. In 1563 the priory was dissolved and was managed by a steward of the Archbishop of Mainz, before passing into the hands of a Cologne bank from being mortgaged during the Thirty Years War. However, in 1716 the abbot of Fulda redeemed the mortgage and re-installed a community of monks, under Fulda's jurisdiction.

It was now that its vineyards began to be famous. The monks planted Riesling grapes, tried new sites and improved cellar methods—they were probably the first German vignerons to bottle their wines. It was a popular joke that when a bishop visited Johannisberg he could find no books, but that on asking for a corkscrew every monk produced one from beneath his habit. Undoubtedly these monk vignerons played a leading role during the eighteenth century in raising the quality of German wine. Hitherto production had concentrated on quantity rather than quality. They were more than successful and few will dispute the claim that Schloss Johannisberg is one of the most glorious of all hocks.

The priory was again dissolved in 1801, its lands eventually passing into the possession of Prince Metternich, whose descendants still own them. The monastery has disappeared but the schloss still occupies the same position on top of the great hill overlooking the river; at sunset, from a distance, Johannisberg still retains the air of an abbey.

The mighty abbey of Fulda, for a time Johannisberg's mother house, is the Monte Cassino of Germany. It was founded in 744 by a Devon man, St Boniface, who as well as being a missionary was also the first known importer of German wines into England. He is credited with planting a number of vineyards, mainly near Mainz. Most of Fulda's abbots were enthusiastic connoisseurs of wine, and it is said that one of them had a special cellar for his best Johannisberg, which was administered by a secret "cabinet"—hence the modern term *kabinett* for certain wines. The abbot was *ex officio* both Primate of the Imperial Abbots and Hereditary Chancellor of the Empire, and in 1752 became a Prince-Bishop as well. As independent ruler of a tiny clerical state, he lived with suitably regal magnificence. Baron de Pollnitz, who visited Fulda in the eighteenth century, noted that, "The Prince-Abbot has a Grand Marshall, a Master of the Horse, a Marshall of the Court, several Privy and Aulic Counsellors, a Number of Gentlemen, a Company of Horse Guards well cloathed and well mounted, a Regiment of Foot Guards, eight Pages, a Number of Footmen and several Sets of Horses." The monks, "all Gentlemen by sixteen descents", shared in this splendour—"The House they dwell in is more like the Palace of a great King than a

Convent." Obviously it was a very comfortable existence. " 'Tis my Opinion, things duly consider'd," commented Pollnitz, "that there's no need for any extraordinary Vocation to be a Fryar at Fulda; for those Gentlemen enjoy everything that a Man would wish for in a genteel Life."

Moreover, according to the envious Baron, "There are very few sovereigns in Germany whose Table is better served; for there is plenty of every thing, particularly delicious Wines of which they tipple to such Excess that in a very little time they are not capable of distinguishing their Liquor. They are, I believe, the hardest Drinkers here in Europe." The then abbot—who bore the Irish name of Butler—was no exception. Pollnitz commented acidly, "I should have lik'd his Reception of me very well, if he had not made me drink so hard." The monks, alas, went during the Napoleonic invasion of Germany, but the Prince-Abbots' *Residenz* still stands in the centre of Fulda, though today it is the headquarters of the region's local government. However, the brethren's truest memorial is the credit for a most momentous development in German viticulture.

The Prince-Abbot had ultimate control over all the monastic vineyards of the Rheingau, a jurisdiction which extended to choosing the date for the vendage. In 1775 a notoriously absent-minded Prince-Abbot forgot to announce it. The monks of Johannisberg, where the grapes had become particularly overripe, shrivelled, and mouldy, became almost frantic with worry. They sent a fast horseman to Fulda to obtain permission, but on the way back he was held up by highwaymen (though some say by a pretty girl) in the Taunus hills near Frankfurt. When the messenger eventually returned, the monks' grapes were already rotting. Fortunately this rot turned out to be *pourriture noble* and the harvest at Johannisberg resulted in a magnificent dessert hock. The abbot's dilatoriness caused the monks to produce what are now known as Beerenauslesen and Trockenbeerenauslesen; wine from carefully selected grapes which have become almost raisins on the vine, and whose vintages were called by the late Frank Schoonmaker, "The greatest and most expensive German wines of all."

There were many other Benedictine vineyards along the Rheingau, but none to rival Johannisberg, although it is worth noting that the abbey of St Pantaleon, the largest and oldest monastery in Cologne, actually had a vineyard within the city walls.

In Rheinhessen the Black Monks' best-known vineyard was at Oppenheim, which was owned by Lorsch from Charlemagne's reign until the late Middle Ages. The wine of Bodenheim is also of monastic origin. A missionary called St Alban was martyred by the vandals and, centuries later, in 805 a monastery was dedicated to him. The monks are commemorated by the excellent Bodenheimer Sankt Alban. The abbey of St Hildegard at Rupertsberg near Bingen was established in 1148 by the redoubtable Benedictine abbess of that name. A mystic who saw visions, she was publicly acknowledged by St Bernard as a prophetess of God. From the beginning her nuns cultivated vineyards. In 1732 Baron de Pollnitz said of Bingen, " 'tis thought to produce the best Rhenish wine", and certainly the nuns played an important role in developing the local vines. They still produce excellent wine even today, though they have now moved to the Rheingau (see p. 177). St Hildegard herself is known to have approved of wine since she is credited with the saying: *"Mann macht den Menschen gewund; der Wein macht den Menschen gesund"* ("Man hurts men, but wine heals them").

In Franconia Benedictine nuns were planting vines at Kitzingen and Ochsenfurt along the Mainz valley as early as the seventh century. In 777 Charlemagne presented Hammelburg on the river Saale to Fulda. Franconian wines, which were Goethe's favourites, have been described as the German wines that most resemble those of France. The round-bellied green *Bocksbeutel* holding these "stone wines" is said to owe its peculiar shape to being designed for concealment beneath the monastic habit, though the literal translation of the name is "he-goat's scrotum". The shape, which is really that of the old pilgrim's flask or costrel, has been borrowed from Franconia by the Portuguese and the Australians. Steinwein is also rather like moselle and goes wonderfully with trout. (Strictly speaking the name should only be applied to wine from some sites near Würzburg, but this is pedantic.) There is a pleasant custom in the Black Forest of drinking it with sandwiches in the late afternoon— the "Vespers". Other Benedictine abbeys which possessed vineyards in Franconia included Seligenstadt, founded in 815 by Einhard, Charlemagne's secretary and biographer. Seligenstadt owned the Abtsberg at Hörstein, a site of some 35 acres, and Kitzingen, a convent founded by St Adelheid, Charlemagne's aunt, whose vineyards no longer exist.

In Austria Celtic tribesmen made wine in pre-Roman times, as did the Roman colonists of Vindobona (Vienna) after them, but all these vineyards disappeared at the fall of the Western Empire. Vines only returned with the German settlers who poured into the "Eastern Realm" during the tenth century. Monks came too and many Austrian wines have a

Benedictine origin, especially those of Lower Austria. The stretch of the Danube known as the Wachau is the country's finest wine-growing area. It begins at Melk, where Jacob Prandtauer's *meisterwerk*, the vast Baroque Benedictine abbey, dominates the river from its great cliff. Melk's most famous vineyard, however, is a long way from the Wachau —the Gumpoldskirchner Spiegel. Farther down the Danube the former monastery of the Undhof still produces a pleasant Riesling and the abbey of Gottweig, with its glorious staircase has vineyards just opposite Krems where the Wachau ends.

The oldest monastery in Switzerland is St Maurice, near Monthey, named after a Theban legionary who was martyred in 302 for refusing to worship the Roman gods; archaeologists have discovered there the foundations of an oratory dating from about 370. In 515 King Sigismund of Burgundy established a community of Celtic monks on the site, who later adopted the Benedictine rule. They turned the town—the Roman Agaunum—into a monastery town of considerable wealth and impor- tance, constantly rebuilding the abbey church (the present edifice dates from 1611). Today the monastery is a school, but it keeps some of the monks' treasures, including a marvellous ewer sent by Haroun el- Raschid to Charlemagne. The monks of St Maurice owned many vine- yards, especially at the eastern end of Lake Geneva. Among them must have been the vineyards at Aigle, which produce the excellent white Yvorne and the Chablais Vaudois from the Fendant grape—known locally as the Dorin. Another Swiss wine with monastic associations is the red Caves du Prieuré from Neuchâtel; Cluny was bequeathed vine- yards at Neuchâtel in 978 during the reign of the great abbot Mayeul. Near the St Gotthard Pass at Giornico, at the southern end of the valley of the Leventino in the Ticino, is the exquisite Romanesque church of San Nicolo, which dates from the tenth century at the latest; once it was part of a long-vanished monastery of Black Monks who in the thir- teenth century were subjected to the reforming abbey of San Benigno of Fruttaria. Happily this jewel of a church, even if it has lost its monks, is still surrounded by vines. Alas, the wines of Ticino are not exactly among Switzerland's best and the vintage hardly matches the architecture.

In Hungary, after Tokay, the most famous wines are those of Somló. About the year 1000 the first King of Hungary, St Stephen—Szent Istvan of the crown with the crooked cross—founded a Benedictine nunnery here so that the nuns would tend the vines. With the same end in mind he also founded the abbeys of Pécsvárad and Zoboly in the Kaliz valley. In the thirteenth century the abbot of a monastery of Somlovásarhely im- ported a French monk who was "an outstanding master of vine-growing" to improve his vineyards. Today the best Somló is made from the Furmint grape and its wines include Juhfark or "lamb's tail". (Somló is credited with interesting properties; it is said that every Habsburg Arch- duke was given a glass of it on his wedding night to ensure that he would beget sons and not daughters.) The red wine of Eger, an ancient town 120 miles north-west of Budapest, is Egri Bikavér, which is believed to owe its origin to eleventh-century French monks who can only have been Benedictines. Grown on volcanic soil and sheltered by the Bükk and Mátra mountains, it is made from about 10 per cent Cabernet Sauvignon, 20 per cent Pinot Noir and 70 per cent Kadarka—a local grape. Not a truly great wine, it is undeniably agreeable and, above all, very strong. It derives its odd name—Bulls' Blood of Eger—from a legend of the Turkish wars. In 1552 infidels, who were besieging Eger, noticed that the defenders were refreshing themselves with jugs of a red liquid; a rumour spread among the Turks that the Magyars were drinking bulls' blood, whereupon they fled. Another great wine-growing Benedictine house was Pannonhalma, in the heart of the rolling Bakony country.

Many of the deserted Black Monk abbeys which one sees on lonely Spanish hilltops are surrounded by grapes which now grow wild. Najera is in the centre of the Rioja country, a picturesque little town that contains a superb Benedictine monastery of the fourteenth century, where one may drink the local vintages, preferably the red with its strange burnt taste. In the eleventh century King Sancho of Navarre founded an abbey in the Rioja whose charter lists a number of vineyards. Even as late as the seventeenth century the government encouraged monastic viticulture; in 1603 a royal edict of Philip III ordered all able-bodied peasants in the vicinity of the abbey of San Martin de Abelda in the Rioja to do two days' ploughing, two days' pruning and two days' harvesting in the monks' vineyards. In Catalonia the famous abbey of San Cugat del Vallés, near Barcelona, dates from the fourth century but was rebuilt in the last quarter of the twelfth; its huge Romanesque cloister is particularly impressive, with carvings on the columns which depict stories from the Bible—one is the Drunkenness of Noah, a favourite medieval theme. San Cugat has a place in the history of Catalan viticulture as it is known to have possessed an unusually large number of vineyards in the tenth century.

In Portugal the abbey of Lorvão near Coimbra was notable for cultivating the vine when the country was still ruled by Moors. This indicates surprising tolerance on the latter's part, even though the sinful poets of al-Andalus often sang of the joys of Andalusian wine. Ironically, there are no vineyards around Lorvão today. Northern Portugal is celebrated for *vinho verde* ("green wine"), the white and (not so good) red wines of the Minho province which are drunk young, without maturing, and often retain the bubbles of fermentation. Their alcohol content is very slight. The white, mainly made from the Axas grape, has a faintly acid quality but is delicious with shellfish. In a valley near the picturesque old town of Peñafiel, a centre of the *vinho verde* country, one may find the Romanesque church of what was once a Benedictine monastery that grew wine. Dão is another Portuguese wine-growing region, covering over a thousand square miles south of the Douro. Dão wines vary immensely; some of the reds have been compared, not implausibly, to Châteauneuf-du-Pape, while there are also some nice whites. An ancient abbey near Viseu (the capital of the Dão country) that must have contributed to the quality of the local wines was Santa Maria de Maceira-Dão.

On the "instep" of Italy, in Calabria at Squillace on the shores of the gulf of that name, are the remains of the famous abbey of the Vivarium. In past centuries its Black Monks undoubtedly had close connections with the neighbouring vintages—Ciró, Greco de Gerace and Mantonico. Ciró is well to the north and east of Squillace, on the "heel", near the ancient Greek city of Sybarus (whose original inhabitants had such a reputation for luxury and maintained a temple of Bacchus), though its vineyards extend for miles around. In classical times Ciró had such a great name that it was actually offered to winners in the Olympic games as a prize. Today red, rosé, and white wines are produced. The red, made from the Gaglioppo vine, is the best; ruby-coloured, full-bodied and well-balanced. The rosé is indifferent but the fruity, straw-coloured white, from the Greco vine, is excellent. Greco de Gerace comes from a mountain town to the south-west of Squillace, though not quite on the "toe", which was founded in the ninth century AD by Greek-speaking refugees from Locri, five miles away, which had fallen to Sicilian Saracens. Gerace has a wonderful cathedral, half-Gothic, half-Romanesque, which dates from the days of the Norman kings and is the largest basilica in Calabria. The astonishing white Greco de Gerace is produced from Greco grapes grown on the wretched, powdery soil of the mountains, where two vines are needed to make a single litre of wine. The result is a sturdy yet smooth vintage whose alcoholic content ranges from 17 per cent to an astounding 19 per cent (compared with the white Ciró's 12 per cent) and which is best drunk young. Now there is very little of it. In ancient times it was said to induce virility, both in bed and on the battlefield. At Gerace they also produce a full dry dessert wine, from the Mantonico grape, which is not so strong as the Greco wine and which is aged in the wood. Some of the red Ciró and the Greco de Gerace are among the best of all Italian wines.

The abbey of Squillace is famous on account of its great founder, Flavius Magnus Aurelius Cassiodorus (*c.* 490-585). A member of an ancient patrician family prominent for three centuries, Cassiodorus was almost the last of the Roman aristocrats and went to Ravenna to serve the Gothic kings who had deposed the last Western Emperor but who kept much of the old administrative structure. He became *Magister Officiorum* ("Head of the Civil Service"). However, when the Goths were overthrown in the Byzantine reconquest of Italy he retired to his family villa at Squillace, where he had been born. Here, amid the villa's fishponds (*vivarium*), Cassiodorus built a hermitage and a monastery, which he governed as abbot until his death in extreme old age. The original observance was probably something like that of the *Rule of the Master*, though even in Cassiodorus's time it may have become Benedictine. The most important innovation was the emphasis placed on copying manuscripts, for which a special room or *scriptorium* was set aside. Cassiodorus, who was obviously aware of the decay of literacy and who himself wrote a number of histories, urged his monks to copy pagan as well as Christian works; in his ninety-second year he compiled a treatise on Latin orthography as a guide for copyists. This heroic task, which was part of the Vivarium's daily routine, soon spread to other monasteries and, in the absence of printing presses and amid the collapse of civilized life, was to perform an invaluable service for the West. Not only was much of Latin literature saved but also a good deal of scientific knowledge—biological, botanical, medical, architectural, mathematical and astronomical. No doubt, after a hard day in the *scriptorium*, many of Cassiodorus's monks had to be refreshed by a draught of Ciró or Greco de Gerace.

Greco de Gerace must not be confused with Greco di Tufo, a less heady but most elegant white wine which is made near Avellino, mainly from Greco grapes, but with an admixture of Coda di Volpe. Above Avellino, which is some 30 miles south-east of Naples, is the 4,000-foot-high Monte Vergine. Here in the early eleventh century came a certain Guglielmo—now St William—to build a hermitage with stones taken from the mountain temple of Cybele nearby. He soon attracted followers but, like so many other great founder abbots, left them to set up similar communities elsewhere—all over southern Italy. In 1157, a few years after he had died, his monks adopted the Benedictine rule, though they retain to this day the original white habit. Their abbey remains on its old site on the mountain, but the weather is too cold and stormy for the fathers to live there all the year round. During the winter they inhabit the Badia di Loreto at the bottom of the mountain, a Baroque palace built for an eighteenth-century abbot by the Neapolitan architect Vanvitelli (creator of the great Bourbon palace of Caserta); it contains some curious portraits of "Borbone" kings and a wonderful old pharmacy with the original Capodimonte *albarelli*. The abbey up on the mountain is still a popular place of pilgrimage, just as it was at the beginning. According to a reliable early chronicler "gold and silver, lands and possessions, in Avellino and Aversa were poured out at the feet of St William". The lands must surely have included some of the vineyards which produce Greco di Tufo. It is one of the lightest, dryest and most delectable of all Italian wines; indeed Hugh Johnson considers it among the finest from the southern half of the peninsula, though not everybody will agree with him that it has a slightly bitter taste. It goes especially well with sea food and also makes an excellent aperitif.

On the whole the Benedictines have been famous for working their own vineyards. Nevertheless there have been occasions when the fathers marketed rather than produced wine. In that splendid book *Naples: a Palimpsest*, Peter Gunn tells us how during the early seventeenth century the Black Monks of Santi Severino e Sosio in Naples had cellars "where the finest wines were sold, both wholesale and retail". This monastery's beautiful Baroque church and cloisters still stand in the Vico San Severino, though monkless; the archives of Naples were once housed here, but were destroyed by the Germans in the Second World War. Even less firm evidence is available than usual, but one may guess with some certainty that the monks sold Gragnano, the favourite wine of Pulcinella and Rosanna and of every true Neapolitan. This delightful if modest red wine, which is virtually unknown outside the area round Naples, comes from the mountains above Castellammare (the birthplace of Al Capone, who no doubt knew it well in his early years) and is made from the supposedly unique Gragnano vine. Deceptively purple and fruity looking, *spumante* to the point of frothiness, it is light both in taste and alcohol content—only 10 per cent—and should be drunk young and served cold. It accompanies fish or *frutta di mare* surprisingly well.

There have been countless other Benedictine vineyards in Italy, and indeed in Yugoslavia and even in Czechoslovakia. Many of them continue to produce palatable vintages although the monks have long departed. However, some still grow next to a beautiful abbey,

> *Or tower, or high hill-convent, seen*
> *A light amid its olives green.*

But unfortunately none of their products although often pleasant enough can be classed as truly great wines.

Chapter 5
Cistercian Wines

*I have drunk my wine with my milk; eat, O friends;
drink, Yea, drink abundantly, O beloved.*

SONG OF SOLOMON

*Love is that liquor sweet and most divine,
Which my God feels as blood, but I as wine.*

GEORGE HERBERT

The Cistercians are really white Benedictines. They began as a
reform movement and still claim that they are leading the life of the
original monks of Monte Cassino. As for their work as vignerons,
Alexis Lichine has said that no other order has contributed so much to
wine-growing.

In 1098 the founders, a bare score of idealists, settled at Cîteaux
(*cistels*, "the place of bullrushes") in Burgundy, near Nuits-Saint-
Georges. The site of their wooden-built "New Monastery" was a
desolate swamp surrounded by thick forest beneath the hills of the Côte
d'Or. They have always preferred valleys with plenty of water, as the
names of their subsequent foundations bear witness; in France Noirlac,
Clairfontaine, Belleaux, Fontaines les Blanches, Aiguebelle; in Italy
Fossanova and Tre Fontane; in England Fountains and Rievaulx; to
cite only a few. These early Cistercians or White Monks interpreted the
Benedictine Rule with an almost savage extremism, emphasizing fasting
and silence in an existence that was a fiercely demanding round of labour
in the fields and of prayer both public and private. It has been calculated
that their average expectation of life was 28 years; in France their infirmaries were encouragingly named *La Salle des Morts*. Yet they also
possessed an undeniable harmony—not only with the liturgical year but
also with the rhythm of crops and seasons.

Their churches were deliberately simple, without steeples, carvings
or stained glass; their vestments of wool instead of silk; and they
eschewed gold—chalices had to be of silver, candlesticks of iron. There
was even a "bibliographic asceticism", an attempt to forbid the illumina-
tion of manuscripts, which fortunately was largely ineffective. In the
words of one outstanding interpreter of monastic architecture: "The
dark habit of the Cluniacs had been set-off by cinnabar, ultramarine-

blue and sienna-green walls and wall paintings; the Cistercians should be pictured in grey-white woollen and linen cowls, neither bleached nor coloured, in the midst of light grey walls."

At first the Cistercian life, defined in a constitution drawn up by the English monk St Stephen Harding, attracted few recruits. Their amazing expansion began with the arrival of St Bernard, last of the Fathers of the Western Church, in 1112. This extraordinary man was a brilliant publicist whose pamphlets and letters, sent out from the abbey of Clairvaux, which he founded in 1115, made him the most influential force of his day. He attacked the Black Monks, accusing them of leading a soft life; he alleged that they kept cat-skin rugs on their beds at night to keep warm and cited their delicate dishes, their innumerable receipts for cooking fish—he also claimed that too much singing of an overlong Office made them so thirsty that they drank huge quantities of wine. But Bernard undoubtedly caused thousands to embrace the Cistercian vocation. By his death there were 700 choir monks and lay brethren at Clairvaux. This was one of 338 Cistercian abbeys, which were organized in groups, with each owing allegiance to the mother house at Cîteaux, where their abbots met in chapter every year. By the middle of the following century there were nearly 2,000 Cistercian monasteries and 1,400 Cistercian nunneries. It seemed as though "all the world was turning Cistercian".

However, this phenomenal expansion was not entirely due to St Bernard. Nor is it quite true that "under the white hood all Cistercians are sons of Bernard". There were other attractive leaders like the English St Aelred of Rievaulx, who, although alarmingly austere, possessed both gentleness and humanity and who built his house in Yorkshire upon friendship. Indeed, despite his undoubted saintliness and his magnetism there is something disturbing about St Bernard—an almost Manichean puritanism, aggression and intolerance. He is famous for his ruthless destruction of the marginally, and unwittingly, heretical theologian Peter Abelard (the lover of Héloïse). Yet during St Bernard's ferocious dispute with abbot Peter the Venerable of Cluny over the relative merits of Black Monks and White, abbot Peter could write, "Candid and terrible friend, what could quench my affection for you," even though Bernard had attacked him with the most wounding irony. Beyond question, many men genuinely loved Bernard.

Such an extreme way of life as that of the early Cistercians could hardly be expected to endure for very long, and the most austere houses were the first to slacken. The decline was made worse by such afflictions as the Black Death and commendatory abbots—titular abbots who took most of the revenue. During the late Middle Ages many of the White Monks were leading lives of some comfort; there were even Cistercian colleges at the universities of Paris and Oxford. Just before the French Revolution the Cistercians of Pontigny were in the habit of inviting

ladies into the monastery for concerts and presenting each one with a bouquet of flowers.

There were many attempts at reform, like that in the sixteenth century of the Feuillants, who slept on the bare ground and drank out of skulls. A more lasting reform was that by Armand de Rancé in the seventeenth century at La Trappe in Normandy (where ragged monks had hitherto supported themselves by poaching). The "Thundering Abbot" and his Trappists led a life scarcely less extreme than the Feuillants—Thomas Merton considered the mentality of La Trappe to have been that of a "suicide squad". Nevertheless the Trappists eventually arrived at a more balanced way of life and no doubt their ideals will always survive. Today they are represented by the Cistercian brethren of the Reformed Observance.

The Cistercians' greatest monument is the architecture of their abbeys in their heyday—grimly sober yet with a demure beauty that hints at a concealed message. White Monk churches were famed for their acoustics, carefully designed to enhance the plain chant. Their windows were spaced to moderate or intensify light in such a way as to give emphasis to particular aspects of the liturgy. The very proportions of these buildings were calculated according to the now long-forgotten laws of a symbolist mathematics. It was an architecture which was brilliantly harnessed to well-defined spiritual and psychological needs. The actual style, sometimes described as "Cistercian half-Gothic", is basically functional Burgundian Romanesque, but with the pointed arch.

A second monument was the remarkable Cistercian contribution to all forms of agriculture. Their motto was said to be, "Under cross and plough." As their statutes did not allow the first White Monks to own serfs, and as they were too poor to hire labourers, they recruited lay brothers. These came from the local country people and took simple vows; they could rarely read or write so they were given less demanding offices of *paters* and *aves*; they wore brown habits instead of the white of the choir monks. Thousands of poor men flocked to the Cistercian abbeys, where they were assured of regular food and of protection from famine and slaughter. To administer outlying farms, and later the many estates with which they were increasingly endowed, the Cistercians adapted the Benedictine cell system by sending lay brethren out in twos or threes to granges for long periods. (Choir monks had to be back in the abbey by nightfall.) These granges were merely barns and cowsheds with rudimentary sleeping accommodation and an oratory. The brethren returned to their abbeys to celebrate important feasts.

Lay brethren and granges enabled the White Monks to clear swamp and woodland, and to exploit enormous tracts of lonely heath and moor that would otherwise have remained desolate. They were the drainage experts of the Middle Ages and innumerable landscapes were transformed. Gerald of Wales, no friend to the order, admitted that, "Give the

Cistercians a desert or a forest and in a few years you will find a dignified abbey in the midst of smiling plenty." The White Monks' crops, sheep and cattle-ranches gave them wealth which they had never sought; although they did prove surprisingly efficient in marketing their produce. In England the medieval Cistercians are remembered for their great sheep-runs and their contribution to the wool-trade. On the European mainland their activities had a no less impressive effect on wine-growing. At the start some White Monks seem to have disapproved of cultivating such a crop. However, very early in their history they found themselves endowed with estates possessing vineyards. Disinclined to waste, and having a more than adequate work force at their disposal, it was inevitable that the Cistercians would turn to wine-growing.

St Bernard's own monastery of Clairvaux was in Champagne in the Vale of Absinthe, so-called from its abundance of wormwood (*absinthe*). The great Benedictine scholar Dom Mabillon, who visited it in the seventeenth century, reported that "one hill is rich with vineyards and another with corn, each being a beautiful area which supplies all the food necessary for the community. On one ridge is grown the corn which the brethren eat while the opposite ridge provides the wine they drink." However, this was not true in Bernard's day. The first brethren actually lived on beech leaves, roots and nuts, though later their diet was improved. An early Cistercian wrote: "Their drink is a sort of beer; if this is not available they have ordinary water. They rarely touch wine and then only adulterated with plenty of water." But by 1143—still during Bernard's abbacy—Clairvaux had acquired a vineyard at Morveaux (where a wine-press was erected in 1153) and eventually owned 13 in all. To begin with the wine was obviously not very satisfactory; a twelfth-century monk, Nicolas of Clairvaux, wrote to the Bishop of Auxerre (whose see was then famous for its vintages) that "the wines in our region are turbid and are not made from the vines in yours, which grow in a state of blessedness". In 1667 Dom Joseph Meglinger, a visiting Cistercian from Wettingen in Switzerland, was astonished by an immense wine-cask in the Clairvaux cellars; it had no hoops but was made fast by four huge wooden beams which were tightened or loosened with wedges. Today, the eighteenth-century wing which is all that survives of

Clairvaux, is a detention centre. Among other White Monk monasteries in Champagne which owned vineyards one should not forget the pleasantly named Trois Fontaines.

However, the chief glories of Cistercian wine-growing in France were to be found not in Champagne but in Burgundy. The White Monks of Pontigny on the river Serein—a tributary of the Yonne—in upper Burgundy, a house which was founded in 1114, created no less a wine than Chablis. They bought the vineyards in 1118 from the Benedictines of Saint Martin at Tours, but had to pay an annual rent of six hogsheads of wine. Almost certainly they were the first to plant the white Chardonnay, the grape from which all fine white Burgundies are made. The pale, bone-dry vintages of Chablis are among the world's greatest white wines and it is hardly surprising that they soon acquired a popularity outside their native region. The little town of Chablis is in a valley on the banks of the Yonne, and lay brethren took the wine down the river in flat-boats, the ancestors of today's barges. (Other orders also provided bargees; in the 1660s the Carmelite friar Laurence Herman—the author of a famous little book of piety *The Practice of the Presence of God*— was sent by his brethren to buy wine in Burgundy and had to bring it back by boat; being lame he could only move about by rolling himself bodily over the casks.)

Much of the abbey of Pontigny survives, including a glorious church that dates from 1140-70, the lay brothers' dorter and the cellar. St Thomas à Becket spent two years' exile at Pontigny, which also sheltered the relics of St Edmund of Abingdon. Today it is a seminary. There is a *Premier Cru* of Chablis, Côte de Fontenay, which commemorates the nearby White Monk house of that name, founded in 1118. Its equally beautiful church, the earliest surviving White Monk church in France, and miraculously preserved conventional buildings still convey something of the Cistercian dream.

Probably the most remarkable of all achievements in the entire history of monastic viticulture was the Cistercians' creation of Clos de Vougeot in Burgundy. Land at Vougeot, a tiny village named after the little river of Vouge, was given to Cîteaux in 1110 by Guerric of Chamballe, and the White Monks continued to buy properties there until 1336, when they finally obtained complete control of all its vineyards. They then surrounded the 125 acres of vines with a clos, or high stone wall, to make the largest vineyard in Burgundy. It was divided into three; that at the top produced the best wine, which was never sold but kept for presents. By the decadent days of the late fourteenth century, Cîteaux was employing 50 freemen to work its vineyards at Clos Vougeot and Musigny; they were obviously most in demand at the Clos, where they must have laboured side by side with the lay brethren.

All that now remains of the original grange are the cellars and cuverie which date from about 1150. In 1551 the forty-eighth abbot

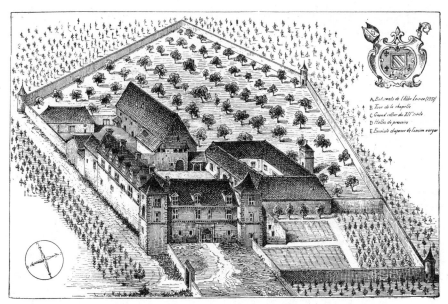

Clos Vougeot, as it was under Cistercian ownership.

of Cîteaux, Dom Jean Loysier, decided to build a combined grange and guest house. He was evidently a man of some originality, having installed a pneumatic organ in the abbey church. He employed one of his own monks, a gifted architect, to design the new building at Clos Vougeot. The monk so irritated Dom Jean by the excessive pride he took in his plans that the abbot had another architect redraw them, and then ordered the original designer to build the guest house with them by way of penance. Some say the poor monk died of chagrin. Despite its imperfections, the result is none the less imposing.

For centuries Clos Vougeot was considered the finest of all burgundies. It produced both red and white wines in equal quantities; even today the white wine produced at the tiny Vougeot vineyard yields precedence only to Chablis and Meursault. In 1361 Petrarch, when trying to persuade Urban V to return to Rome, told the Pope that the reason he was so unwilling to leave Avignon was that he had heard that it was difficult to obtain the best burgundy on the other side of the Alps. Abbot Jean de Bussière sent 30 hogsheads of Clos Vougeot, each containing 228 litres, to Pope Gregory XI on his election in 1371; and three years later he was rewarded with a Cardinal's hat. In 1667 a Trappist said that it was a waste of time attending the chapter general at Cîteaux because the abbot, "by lavishly entertaining all the abbots from Germany, Switzerland, Poland and other foreign countries and pouring out vast quantities of his excellent Clos Vougeot (which on similar occasions has worked so many miracles) will persuade them to do whatever he wants." Dom Meglinger, who attended the chapter general, reported afterwards that while the food was frugal, and so strange as to be unappetizing, it was redeemed by the delicious flavour of the wine. Indeed, there was said to be a proverb among the Burgundian Cistercians, "*qui bon vin boit, Dieu voit.*"

The White Monk vignerons evolved special methods of cultivation. For fertilizer they used nothing but marc—what is left after pressing the grapes when the juice has been drawn off. In poor years the good fathers even fortified the wine with *eau-de-vie-de-marc*. However, their real secret was the extraordinary tender care which they lavished on the vines; indeed, almost on each grape.

In 1790 Cîteaux was dissolved, all its possessions being confiscated and sold by public auction. (Today, only a few fragments of the medieval buildings survive—a fifteenth-century library and the copyists' cloister—together with a block dating from about 1760.) When the commissioners came to Clos Vougeot they were met by the last cellarer of Cîteaux, Dom Goblet, who burst into tears. Perhaps he remembered the works of Micah: "Woe is me! For I am as when they have gathered the summer fruits, as the grape gleanings of the vintage; there is no cluster to eat; my soul desired the first ripe fruit." But the commissioners were not hard-hearted men and they gave him two silver dishes as a keepsake and enough bottles of his wine to last him for the rest of his life. Until he died in 1810 Dom Goblet had more than sufficient to drink of his wonderful elixir, which has been described as the most feminine and subtle of all burgundies; he always refused to part with a single bottle.

It was during the Revolution that a Colonel Bisson established the tradition that any French troops passing Clos Vougeot must present arms. Stendhal, that inexhaustibly interesting man, was a deep admirer of its wine, and indeed until the present century it ranked first among burgundies. Saintsbury dissented. "Clos Vougeot," he wrote, "excellent as it is, seems to me often if not always, to have the excellencies of claret rather than those of burgundy; it does not 'hold to the blood of its clan' quite firmly enough." Most wine-lovers have good cause to regret the passing of the monk vigneron. Since 1889 Clos Vougeot has been progressively fragmented into no less than 60 small vineyards and its glory, if not altogether a thing of the past, is undeniably erratic.

68

The "château" at Clos Vougeot remains, with its ancient cellars and wine-press room which still contains a press dating from Cistercian times. It is now the headquarters of the Confrèrie des Chevaliers du Tastevin, who have lovingly restored it to its original appearance and who hold their colourful functions in it. Clos Vougeot is both a noble example of a White Monk grange and a fitting monument to a magnificent wine-growing achievement.

Many other fine burgundies are in debt to the Cistercians. They had a vineyard at Meursault as early as 1108, which (although it produces some unacknowledged red wine) is famous for its beautiful white vintages. Cardinal de Bernis, Mme de Pompadour's beloved little abbé, always celebrated Mass with a Meursault—he once explained that he did not wish to grimace when confronting his Lord. The manor and vineyard of Perrières, one of the most renowned growths of Meursault, belonged to Cîteaux until the Revolution and the White Monks' fourteenth-century cellars, which can hold up to 400 hogsheads, may still be seen at Meursault. Cîteaux was also making wine at Musigny at a very early date, both red and white.

At Beaune the vineyard of Cent Vignes belonged to Cîteaux, as did vineyards at Savigny-les-Beaune. At Pommard Cîteaux acquired Pézerolles in 1222 and the Clos Blanc in 1485. It was probably the White Monks who made a long-forgotten *vin-de-paille* at Pommard in the fifteenth century; this was a sweet dessert wine produced from both red and white grapes which gave it an "*oeil de perdrix*" colour—it enjoyed great popularity in its day.

The abbey of Maizières was founded in 1132 near Chalon. It owned the justly famous Beaune vineyard of Les Epenottes, which still produces fine wine. Today its fourteenth-century church remains, by the banks of the river Dheune.

Cistercian nuns, sometimes called Bernardines, have also made a contribution to the wines of Burgundy. By 1133 a convent had been established near Dijon at Jully-les-Nonnains, the abode of the Blessed Humbeline, St Bernard's sister. In 1125 a nun of Jully founded the convent of Le Tart, near Genlis and a few miles from Cîteaux. The sisterhood

69

decided to cultivate the vine to show that they were true Cistercians—at least this is the explanation of local legend. Clos de Tart has been called by H. W. Yoxall "as good a buy as you will find from the Côte d'Or". At the Revolution it was confiscated and sold for £3,000. The wines of Clos de Tart are famous for their longevity. The nuns also worked Bonnes Mares (originally Bonnes Mères), which is also one of the great red burgundies. Both vineyards are in the parish of Morey-St-Denis, though most of Bonnes Mares is in the adjoining and justly renowned parish of Chambolle-Musigny.

In 1888 an oenophil proclaimed the following hierarchy of "The Royal Family of the Wines of Burgundy":

> *The King*: Chambertin.
> *The Queen*: Romanée-Conti.
> *The Regent*: Clos de Vougeot.
> *The King's First Cousin*: Richebourg.
> *Princes of the Blood*: Romanée, Clos de Tart, Musigny,
> La Tâche, Echézeaux, Bonnes Mares.
> *Royal Standard Bearer*: Corton.
> *Dukes and Duchesses*: Volnay, Nuits, Pommard,
> Beaune, Savigny, Vergelesses, Aloxe-Corton,
> Chassagne.

As has been seen, a significant proportion of these glorious wines were once in monastic hands while some were actually created by them.

By contrast the White Monks' presence was little felt in the Bordeaux region. However, two wines of Cistercian origin are Château la Tour-Ségur and Château la Barbe-Blanche—both in Saint-Emilion. These vineyards belong to the priory of La Faise near Libourne, which was founded in 1137 and whose prior was *ex officio* baron of Lussac. In 1382 the priory loyally sent several casks of its wine to the English court as in those days Gascony was a possession of the Plantagenets. Later La Faise became a commendatory priory and in the eighteenth century one of its titular lay priors was Montesquieu's brother. The church at La Faise has vanished, but there are the ruins of some conventual buildings which date from the sixteenth century.

Sancerre is a most agreeable dry white wine from the Loire basin. Its cépage is the redoubtable white Sauvignon, introduced to the Sancerrois in the thirteenth century by Cistercians from the abbey of Beauvoir near Quincy, ten miles away. The soil of the vineyards is the same as English Kimmeridge clay and partly responsible for the wine's distinctive flavour. An outstanding growth of Sancerre is the Clos de la Poussie, a deep saucer-shaped vineyard of some 25 acres which was created by the White Monks. Like Clos Vougeot it was confiscated at the Revolution and later broken up into over 50 separate vineyards. Fortunately for the

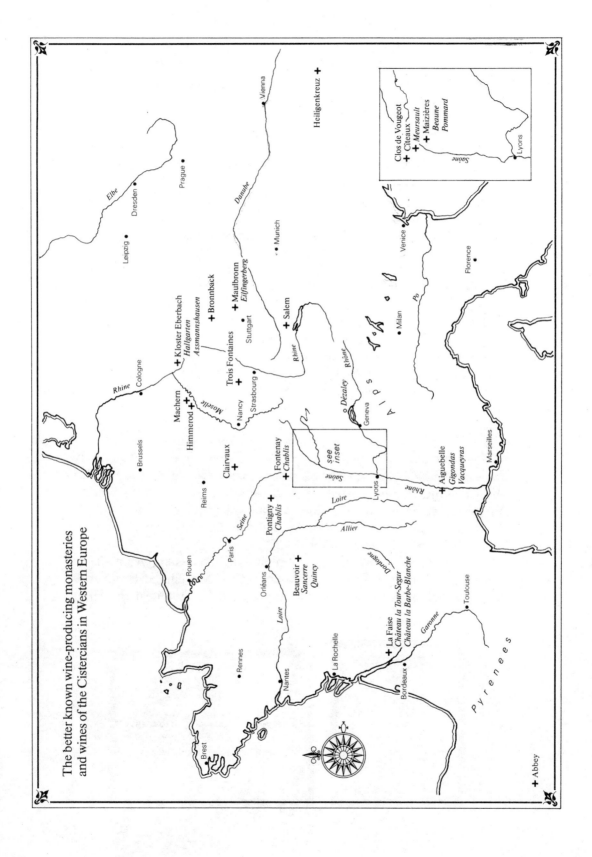

The better known wine-producing monasteries
and wines of the Cistercians in Western Europe

Elbe

Dresden •

Prague •

Leipzig •

Danube

Vienna •

+ Heiligenkreuz

Munich •

Rhine
Cologne •

+ Kloster Eberbach
Hallgarten
Assmannshausen

+ Bronnback

+ Maulbronn
Elfingerberg

+ Salem

Stuttgart •

Machern
+
Himmerod +

Moselle

Trois Fontaines
+

Strasbourg •

Nancy •

Rhine

Rhône

Brussels •

Clairvaux
+

Fontenay
Chablis +

o *Dézaley*

Geneva •

A l p s

Milan •

Po

Florence •

Venice •

Reims •

Seine

Pontigny
Chablis +

see
inset

Saône

Lyons •

Rhône

+ Aiguebelle
Gigondas
Vacqueyras

Marseilles •

Rouen •

Paris •

Loire

Allier

Orléans •

Beauvoir
+
Sancerre
Quincy

Dordogne

Rennes •

Loire

Nantes •

La Rochelle •

+ La Faise
Château la Tour-Ségur
Château la Barbe-Blanche

Garonne

Toulouse •

Bordeaux •

P y r e n e e s

Brest •

+ Abbey

Clos de Vougeot
Cîteaux +
+ Maizières
Beaune
Pommard

Meursault

Saône

Lyons •

modern wine's quality these have all been bought in by the same proprietor who has reunited the Clos. There is also a red Sancerre of less distinction, made from Pinot Noir.

As for the abbey of Beauvoir, which was founded beside the river Yèvre in 1234, a nave remains from the monastery church of about 1250 while what is left of one of the other buildings has been converted into a theatre. Incidentally, the town of Sancerre is a beautiful place, set high on a conical hill and full of old houses. With perhaps a little exaggeration it has been described as looking like a miniature Carcassonne without walls. The wine goes particularly well with the local *crottins*—round goats'-milk cheeses.

In recent years the white wine of Quincy has been "discovered". Some enthusiasts consider a good Quincy better than any Sancerre. Like Sancerre it is made from Sauvignon grapes growing on Kimmeridge soil and like Sancerre it owes its birth to the White Monks of Beauvoir. The same pale yellow colour as Sancerre but even drier, it should be drunk young—between two and five years old. (The Quincy country is not far from Bourges, whose noble cathedral merits a detour.)

The abbey of Saint Mesmin-de-Micy, on the banks of the Loire near Orléans, was founded by Clovis and endured till the Revolution. It changed its original rule to that of St Benedict, then became Cistercian and finally adopted the macabre Feuillant reform. It was famous for vineyards but the wine produced is long forgotten. An obscure Orléanais wine, Pont-aux-Moines, may commemorate these White Monks.

The Rhône has also benefited from Cistercian vignerons. The heady wine of Gigondas has already been mentioned. One of the best reds of the Côtes du Rhône villages is Vacqueyras, deep purple in colour. Vineyards at both Gigondas and Vacqueyras were cultivated by the White Monks of Aiguebelle, near Montélimar, from the abbey's foundation in 1137 until the Revolution.

The Cistercian achievement in Germany was no less important. They had vineyards on the Ruwer (a tributary of the Moselle) at Himmerod near Wittlich as early as 1134. St Bernard himself founded the Him-

merod house and is said to have banished nightingales from the surrounding woods so that their singing would not distract his brethren. About the same date White Monks also acquired vineyards at Kasel and Eitelsbach and in the Tiergarten at Trier. The Rhineland vineyard of Rauenthaler Nonnenberg commemorates a convent of Cistercian nuns. The White Monks' supreme work in Germany was the vast enclosed vineyard of Steinberg in the Rheingau, near the pretty little town of Hattenheim. Steinberg still produces delicious white wines—André Simon considered it one of the three best vineyards in Germany. A Trockenbeerenauslese Steinberger is generally acknowledged to be among the world's truly great wines.

The Steinberg, which derives its name from the wall with which the monks enclosed it, is on a hill which was given to the Cistercians of Kloster Eberbach in the first quarter of the twelfth century by the Archbishop of Mainz. After clearing dense woodland, they created a vineyard that covered 62 acres; with characteristic thoroughness, whenever they leased out a meadow they retained the use of its willows— "withies" being indispensable for binding vines. The result was the biggest and most magnificent vineyard in all Germany, though for many years the emphasis was on quantity rather than quality. In 1500 a monstrous vat was constructed at Kloster Eberbach, 28 feet long and 9 feet high, it was held together by 14 ropes and had a capacity of 82 *stück* (over 22,000 gallons). This figure was only a fraction of their production; we know that in 1506 the abbey's warehouse in Cologne contained not less than 538 *stück* (nearly 150,000 gallons) of its 1503 and 1504 vintages.

The abbey of Kloster Eberbach still survives in a little green valley not far from the Steinberg. It was plundered many times, being eventually secularized in 1800, but remains in a miraculous state of preservation with dorter, chapter-house, infirmary and refectory looking much as they must have looked in the twelfth and thirteenth centuries. The refectory is breathtakingly beautiful, a perfect example of that Cistercian style which hovers between Romanesque and Gothic. It was obviously designed to elevate the monks' minds after "orgies of fasting", while slowly eating their scanty repasts of roots with the expressionless faces demanded by the Cistercian rule. During those rare meals, which were exalted into all but sacramental banquets, a brother would read a sacred work from a pulpit high above the seated brethren.

Today Kloster Eberbach belongs to the German state wine-growing organization, which sometimes gives dinner parties there in a sensitively restored Baroque dining-room. Here no doubt the abbots, in later and more relaxed days, once "sipt wine from silver, praising God". Hugh Johnson writes: "It is hard to say which is the most fascinating part of this lovely place; the great empty church with its magical echoes, the cloisters, the vast dormitories or the old press-house, where the giant wine-presses of the Middle Ages still stand."

Many other famous vineyards in the Rheingau were first planted by the Cistercians of Kloster Eberbach—for example Hallgarten. It was the White Monks who introduced to the Rhine the *Blauburgunder*, the Pinot Noir grape from which all red hocks are made. Local tradition says that St Bernard himself brought it from Burgundy. After trying it at Kloster Eberbach, with poor results, the Cistercians had better luck at Assmannshausen. Most English wine-writers consider there is no good German red wine; Julian Jeffs says that "their redness is a disguise, worn thinly; they taste rather like a second-rate hock with a dash of burgundy", and calls Assmannshausen "a catastrophe". Saintsbury differed; he liked red hocks, especially "Assmannshausen which is certainly the best", and credited them with being "specifics for insomnia after a fashion which seems to be little known even among the faculty"; his prescription for sleep "without deferred discomfort" was a small tumbler before retiring. (The present writer once drank an entire bottle and never slept better in his life.) Those Rhinelanders who drink red hock as an ordinary everyday accompaniment to their meals would never pretend it is a great wine but they obviously have considerable regard for the *Blauburgunder*.

On the Moselle, half-way between Trier and Coblenz, is the White Monk monastery of Machern, founded in 1238 and dissolved in 1803. It is near Zell, on the lower part of the river, and its old vineyards are still producing some very pleasant wines. The abbey is now the estate office. Another reasonable red wine is made in Baden. Affentaler, from near Buhl, is darker in colour than most red hocks, being produced from a variety of the *Blauburgunder* called *Blau Arbst*. Four centuries ago the nuns of the Cistercian convent of Lichental sent to their mother house in Burgundy for the Pinot Noir in order to make a tonic wine for invalids. Today Affentaler is sold in bottles that bear a hideous red-eyed monkey. The name is a pun—*affe* is German for monkey—on the site where the wine was first produced, the Affental; in fact this originally meant *Ave-tal* or "Hail Mary Valley". One of the largest vineyards in Baden is that founded by the Cistercians of the abbey of Salem, which dates from 1137. This was rebuilt in 1697 but passed to the Margrave of Baden on its dissolution in 1803; today both abbey and vines belong to Margrave Max of Baden. It is a gigantic, well-preserved monastic complex with nearly 200 acres of vines, noted for an unusual rosé.

In Württemberg there exists a Cistercian survival quite as miraculous as Kloster Eberbach. Maulbronn, near Speyer, was founded in 1138 by the Knight Walter von Lomersheim, who entered the community himself. The building of the abbey at *Mulen Brunnen* ("mill well") began in 1147, a year after its monks had been visited at an earlier site by St Bernard, who had come to Speyer to preach the Second Crusade. The monastery prospered, acquiring over 100 estates on both sides of the Rhine. Although in a Protestant area Maulbronn was preserved from

Cistercians in a vineyard, from a German faience tile (1733).

destruction at the Reformation by being converted into a Lutheran seminary, a fate which also saved it from transformation by the Baroque movement. Within a moated wall an entire monastic complex remains as it was in the mid-sixteenth century, with buildings dating from the Romanesque to the Renaissance which include an especially fine thirteenth-century refectory and a charming *lavatorium*—a kind of "fountain chapel" where the White Monks washed. A vivid impression of the sheer size and force of such an abbey as an economic concern is given by the great range of estate offices which has also survived, among them a vineyard office. If Maulbronn could hardly be compared with Kloster Eberbach as a wine-producer, it none the less owned many vineyards and made some good wine. Eight centuries ago Count Ludwig of Württemberg bequeathed its monks his estate at Eilfingen, and their 600-year tenure amply demonstrated their skill as vignerons. The Eilfingerberg vineyard is sometimes said to derive its name—"eleven finger hill"—from a medieval cellarer: the abbot would only allow him to test the wines during Lent by putting his finger into the bungholes and then licking it; asked how the wines were developing, the cellarer replied with feeling, "one needs eleven fingers". Today Eilfingerberg, a vineyard of 40 acres of red marl planted mainly with Riesling, still produces some of the best wine in Württemberg. The Cistercians also made Steinwein. The vineyards of the abbey of Bronnbach, founded in 1151, continue to produce very dry white wines, all in *Bocksbeutel*.

Germany also owes a debt to the Cistercians for extending not merely viticulture but the wine-trade itself. Monk bargees took wine down the Rhine and into the Scheldt so that it could be sold in the rich markets of the Low Countries. From there their vintages reached England and even poverty-stricken Scotland. For this trading Kloster Eberbach maintained an entire fleet of barges.

Nothing could be more Austrian than Heiligenkreuz, with its onion-tower and half-Gothic, half-Baroque buildings in their cheerful setting in a valley deep in the Wienerwald near Mayerling. It was founded by St Leopold, a Babenberg Archduke, in 1133 and was—and happily still is—one of the greatest Cistercian monasteries in Austria. (A grisly relic of St Leopold may be seen in the treasury of Klosterneuburg, his skull crowned with a jewelled coronet—an object which should not be viewed when sober.) Its church was begun in 1187 but dates mainly from the thirteenth century, while there is also a thirteenth-century cloister. The basilica of Heiligenkreuz is famous for a number of features including a "hall-choir" and beautiful stained-glass windows from the Middle Ages, together with a Baroque sacristy with fine stucco work and a superb ceiling by Franz Anton Maulbertsch. This delightful abbey has always produced a simple and pleasant white wine of the sort which is so familiar to those who know and love the Vienna Woods.

There are two Cistercian vineyards in Switzerland which are worth mentioning, Clos des Abbayes and Clos des Moines are at Dézaley near Lausanne and produce an excellent white wine from Fendant grapes (the same as France's Chasselas). Indeed it was the White Monks who first brought the vine to this area. The abbey has long since been secularized, but the measure of its wine is that it can no longer be bought but is reserved by the municipality of Lausanne for the exclusive entertainment of official guests. André Simon thought it "one of the finest white wines of Switzerland".

In 1756 the Cistercian abbey of Desterro at Lisbon was destroyed during the terrible earthquake of that year. The monks who survived took refuge on the south side of the Tagus, doubtless because they owned vineyards there, and founded the new abbey of Nosso Senhora de Nazare de Setubal. The wine of Setubal, which is very little known in England or North America, is made from several varieties of muscatel and is fortified with brandy. It is very sweet and scented, a rich amber in colour which deepens with age to brown—the older it is the better. Old Setubal has been compared with brown sherry. There is also a red Setubal which the monks may well have enjoyed, but it has little appeal to foreign palates of the present day.

Like Benedictines, the Cistercians once possessed innumerable vineyards in Spain and Italy. But though their wines are pleasant enough they have been omitted on account of lack of space. Also it has to be admitted that surprisingly few of the better Italian wines are known to have associations with the peninsula's White Monk abbeys. A possible exception is the monastery of Sant' Andrea—a typically Cistercian church of the thirteenth century—at Vercelli, not far from Lake Maggiore, which may well have had a link with the neighbourhood's distinguished Gattinara Spanna; this is a light red to almost orange coloured wine, full-bodied and long-lived, made from the great Nebbiolo grape. But even if the beautiful Romanesque monastery of Sant' Antimo is only a few miles from Montalcino, its brethren cannot claim any credit for the legendary Brunello di Montalcino which did not attain its present perfection until after the monks had gone.

However, the Cistercians' claim to immortality as vignerons can rest upon their creation of Clos Vougeot and Kloster Eberbach. For the White Monks did not merely own them, they made them, the two largest and most successful walled vineyards in Europe.

Chapter 6
Carthusian Wines

I have trodden the winepress alone;
and of the people there was none with me

ISAIAH

Many are called to be Carthusians
but few are chosen.

CARTHUSIAN PROVERB

The Carthusians are generally considered to be the most austere of all monks. They are the custodians of the oldest and purest form of monasticism and, to a large extent, of the classical tradition of Western mysticism. The Roman Church has long regarded them as the highest form of monastic life. They have never had to be reformed because their observance has never slackened, and in England they were the only order to stand up to Henry VIII. (Sir Thomas More had many friends among them and seriously considered entering the London charterhouse.) Their solitary life has a curious fascination for even the unbeliever; there is some analogy with the lure of a desert island, while Sir Sacheverell Sitwell is attracted by their "aristocratic seclusion". The order is well known for its liqueur, which must wait for another chapter, but it may come as a surprise to learn that its brethren have produced wine.

Their founder, Bruno Hartenfaust, was born in Cologne about 1035. He was a man of attractive personality, gifted with both magnetism and erudition, but the qualities which have carried most strongly over the centuries are common sense, sympathy and serenity; there is something curiously modern about him when compared to such saints as Bernard of Clairvaux or Peter Damian. He was also a monastic genius of profound originality. However, he began as a secular priest, being a canon of Reims cathedral, where he taught theology and became Master of the Schools in about 1050.

There is a macabre legend about Bruno's conversion to the monastic life. The archdeacon of Reims was a certain Raymond Diocres who had a weakness for the more lascivious Latin poets, much frowned upon by the puritans of the day. Raymond died and Bruno attended his dirge (the soul wake which is now sung only in monasteries). As was then the custom the coffin was left open. Suddenly the dead man sat up and cried in a dreadful voice, "I am summoned before the awful judgement seat of God!" The funeral was postponed. Next day he sat up a second time crying, "I am being tried before the awful judgement seat of God!" The funeral was again postponed. Finally, on the third day Raymond sat up for a last time and, with a terrible scream, shrieked, "I am condemned before the awful judgement seat of God!" He was buried in unconsecrated ground. Bruno is said to have been so horrified that he immediately fled from the cathedral to the mountains. Modern Carthusians take this story with a pinch of salt.

The facts, so far as we know them, are that Bruno refused to become Archbishop of Reims about 1080, as he had decided to join a little band of hermits in the forest of Colan (who later became the first Cistercians). After a few years he left them and with two devoted companions settled in a rocky valley high up in the Alps, about 20 miles from Grenoble — the Grande Chartreuse. Soon the three were joined by other hermits, and built the first chartreuse (or charterhouse). It has a little stone church, a wooden refectory and chapter-house, and cells which were wooden chalets joined by a covered passageway. There was also a small wooden cloister next to the church, and a guest house. Another community, of 16 brothers, was established farther down the mountain to look after the fathers' material needs. In Bruno's time the Grande Chartreuse really was a "desert", surrounded by a trackless pine forest with an alarming population of wolves and bears; often cut off from the outside world by snow and ice for more than half the year. Bruno only spent six years there. In 1090 he was summoned to Rome by his friend the French Pope Urban II and again offered an archbishopric; he again refused and went off to found two more charterhouses in Calabria, where he died in 1101.

Bruno's inspiration survived. He had created a monastery that combined community life with that of the hermit. While an uncompromising advocate of the solitary vocation who liked to disappear into the depths of the forest, he none the less believed that total seclusion was dangerous for most men and therefore insisted that his monks should meet at fixed times. The object of their life was to attain spiritual union with God through solitary prayer and meditation. Something of Carthusian ideals may be learnt by reading *The Cloud of Unknowing*, which was long believed to be of Carthusian origin.

In 1132 an avalanche destroyed Saint Bruno's monastery, killing seven of the fathers. Prior Guigo rebuilt it a mile lower down the valley and the following year wrote down the rule which is still observed today, though with certain modifications. Carthusians are divided into choir monks and brethren, only the former being hermits. Each hermit monk lives alone in his four-roomed cell, meeting without speech in church three times a day; the silence is broken by a weekly walk during which conversation is compulsory. Apart from a communal meal in the refectory on Sundays, food is delivered to the cell through a turnstile by a brother and eaten alone. The diet, which never includes meat, is restricted to roughly one and a half meals a day. Even fish and dairy produce are omitted during Lent. There is a weekly fast on bread and water but in wine-producing countries the main meal is accompanied by a pint of wine, in others by beer or cider. Perhaps two hours a day are spent in physical exercise, pacing the long passage inside the cell, woodwork or gardening (each cell has its own patch of garden). The sole luxury in a charterhouse is a magnificent library. The habit is of thick white serge, characterized by an unusually large hood and a band that joins the front and back of the scapular at knee level. When a Carthusian dies he is laid on a board to which his habit is nailed and he is then buried without a coffin. Undoubtedly the silence and loneliness are the most difficult part of the life. Moreover a bell tolls with merciless regularity telling the hermit when to rise, when to say his Office, when to eat, when to take exercise and when to come to church; he is alone but never left alone. Still more taxing, as soon as a Carthusian has accustomed himself to solitude, he discovers that as well as meetings in chapter he has communal duties. Ideally a charterhouse consists of no more than 12 choir monks, yet the offices of prior, procurator, sacristan and novice master all have to be filled.

The brethren lead a communal yet hardly less silent and ascetic life; eating and working together in separate quarters. They too have their own cells, though these are only bedrooms. Under the procurator's direction they cope with the charterhouse's material requirements, cooking and delivering the fathers' meals and working in the fields. It is the procurator and the brothers who have always been the Carthusian vignerons. When a vineyard is at some distance from the charterhouse a group of brothers are sent to work it, arrangements being made for them to lodge nearby; usually they are accompanied by a professed monk, who both directs them and acts as their chaplain.

The shape of the classical charterhouse is dictated by the rule. The choir monks' cell-cottages are ranged along the sides of an unusually long cloister; the fathers also have their own refectory for Sundays and a chapter-house. The church is usually without a tower and divided into two by a passage from the cloister, so that the fathers can reach it with the minimum social contact; the fathers' half is separated from that of the brethren by this "passage-screen". The brethren have their own cloister as well as their refectory, while the prior's cell often stands in a third cloister.

The Carthusians spread slowly but steadily throughout western Europe, founding houses in towns as well as in wildernesses. Their growth and their survival has been largely due to a rigorous testing of vocations —a choir monk's probation lasts for five years, a brother's for 11. The order is partly indebted to the Cistercians for an overall organization

that links each charterhouse under the prior-general at the Grande Chartreuse, where all the priors assemble once a year.

Their wine-ration is increased on rare occasions, on those peculiarly holy feast days when the fathers eat together. A special wine is served, sometimes of Carthusian origin, from the chartreuse of Mougères. Their hospitality, though understandably infrequent, can be memorable. There is today a certain charterhouse which has as its neighbour a Franciscan friary. Once a year the friars walk the five miles to the charterhouse, where they are royally entertained to luncheon with excellent Mougères and a glass of green or yellow Chartreuse to finish the meal.

The Carthusians have made a number of good wines, sometimes in unexpected places. There was a time when Parisians swore by Parisian wines and even the King of France drank them. One of the best of these long-vanished vintages appears to have been that grown at Villeneuve-le-Roi by the Carthusians of Paris. Their charterhouse, founded in 1257 by St Louis, was outside the city walls, near where the Palais de Luxembourg now stands and in the modern Avenue de l'Observatoire. When Charles VIII (1482–98), the conqueror of Italy, dined in the Paris charterhouse he was so taken with its wine from Villeneuve-le-Roi that he commanded that it be served daily at his own table. (It was to this charterhouse that Marshal d'Estrées gave the formula of the liqueur now known as Chartreuse, though later the secret was passed to the Grande Chartreuse.) In 1790 the monks were expelled and their charterhouse was turned into a gunpowder factory; shortly afterwards it was demolished by order of the Convention. However, even by then the Carthusian wine of Villeneuve-le-Roi had long been forgotten.

The Carthusians owned excellent vineyards at Beaune in the 1340s. Also at Beaune they acquired Perrières in 1381 and, in the same year, the only outstanding vineyard at Brochon which, although next to Gevrey-Chambertin, is otherwise an unusually undistinguished parish of the Côte d'Or. This was Les Crais Billon (from which the eighteenth-century playwright Crébillon took his name), which still produces fine wine.

Most of these vineyards must at one time have been managed by the magnificent chartreuse of the Sainte Trinité at Champmol in the suburbs of Dijon, which was founded in 1385 by Duke Philippe le Hardi of Burgundy to pray for his dynasty and to provide a mausoleum. It was a double charterhouse with 24 monks. Designed and built by the architect Drouet de Dammartin, Champmol was also a gallery, for the Duke had a picture placed in each cell, painted by such contemporary masters as Simone Martini, Jan van Eyck and Henri Bellechose. Claus Sluter, the most renowned sculptor of the age, contributed to the church's decoration and designed the tombs of the Dukes of Burgundy with their many *pleurants* or mourners, while Melchior Broederlam painted the altarpiece for the high altar. Possibly Sluter's greatest creation was the *Puits de Moïse* or "Moses's Well"; he placed a calvary over the well in the cloister garth, a symbol of the mingling of wine and water in the Eucharist. The head of Christ is particularly impressive, with a heavy, disturbing majesty.

The charterhouse of Champmol was sacked by Calvinists in the sixteenth century, rebuilt during the eighteenth and finally gutted at the Revolution. What remains is now a lunatic asylum, though the west doorway with Sluter's statues has survived. Fortunately the tombs and part of the *Puits de Moïse* may be seen in the Dijon museum—once the palace of the Dukes. Most of the paintings survive too, though scattered in galleries throughout the world.

Another example of a great Carthusian monastery founded as a ducal mausoleum, is the famous red-brick and terracotta *certosa* at Pavia, established in 1396. This was not occupied by the monks until Duke Gian Galleazzo Visconti—"the Viper of Milan"—threatened them with expulsion from his domains if they did not accept. Indeed during the Middle Ages the Carthusians enjoyed a wide popularity, and not merely with Dukes. When the Grande Chartreuse was burnt down in 1371 large sums of money were collected in England as well as in France and Italy to help with the rebuilding. The intercessional value of Carthusian prayer, rather than admiration for their way of life, was the reason for this popularity.

In Bordeaux the Quai des Chartrons, the Bordelais wine merchants' traditional centre, commemorates a short-lived charterhouse founded in 1383 by monks from the chartreuse of Vauclair in the Dordogne, who had fled from English freebooters and who returned to their original home in 1460. A second Bordeaux charterhouse was founded in 1605 by Ambrose de Gasq, seigneur de Bleignac, who himself ended as a Carthusian in Italy. The brethren of this chartreuse seem to have cultivated the vines of Château la Louvière, best known for its white wine, in the Graves. This belonged to the Benedictine abbey of Saint Ferme, where the Gasq family were commendatory abbots in the seventeenth century. The Bordeaux charterhouse was demolished at the Revolution. However, throughout the Bordeaux region an unusual type of château, one-storeyed, built round a courtyard and only one room deep, is still known as a "chartreuse"—e.g. Château Langoa-Barton. This is almost certainly because of a resemblance to a certain form of chartreuse, of which that at Le Liget (Indre-et-Loire), rebuilt in 1690, is a good example. (There is a Sauternes called Château de Chartreuse, but I have not been able to find any connection with monks, though there may well be one.)

The strong, dark wine of Châteauneuf-du-Pape has many admirers. André Simon tells us that, "The red wines of Châteauneuf-du-Pape possess remarkable tonic properties. They diffuse a heat within and ensure a lasting glow which is a gift entirely their own and one which is not due to any greater alcoholic strength than other red wines." It is made from no less than 13 varieties of grape, the Grenache predominating, grown over a very large area. It takes its name from the ruins of the summer palace that the Popes built during their stay at Avignon in the fourteenth century and which was destroyed by the Huguenots. The vineyards of Châteauneuf-du-Pape are in the Rhône basin; there are so many of them that their wine varies considerably in quality. An excellent one is Clos de la Chartreuse from a vineyard which was once worked by Carthusian brethren from either of two charterhouses in the vicinity— at Bompas and at Villeneuve-lès-Avignon.

The chartreuse of Bompas is about nine miles from Avignon and its crenellated walls and the remains of a fortified tower still dominate the valley of the Durance. It was founded in 1318 in a former Templar commandery that had passed to the Knights Hospitallers, who gave it to the Pope, John XXII, who in turn presented it to the Carthusians. The fathers' long remembered the Hospitaller Grand Master, Fra de Ville-neuve, as one of their greatest benefactors.

The chartreuse of the Val-de-Benediction is at Villeneuve-lès-Avignon, a little town that is on the opposite bank of the Rhône to Avignon. This charterhouse was founded in 1356 by Pope Innocent VI, who built a tomb for himself in it and commissioned Matteo de Giovanni to decorate the walls with frescoes. It was sacked by Huguenots in the sixteenth century, rebuilt in the seventeenth, dissolved at the Revolution and finally demolished in 1840. However, although ruined much has survived, including the nave and side-chapels of the fourteenth-century church, a fifteenth-century cloister and a magnificent gate of 1649. In its heyday Villeneuve-lès-Avignon was one of the most splendid of all charterhouses, something of a southern Champmol, being embellished with fine paintings of the little-known school of the Avignon primitives. Among these was a *Coronation of the Virgin* by the school's greatest master, Enguerrand Charenton, which was probably commissioned by the fathers in about 1455; it may still be seen in the town's *hospice* for old people, also a museum. (Another work of Charenton commissioned by the chartreuse, a *Pietà*, is in the Louvre.)

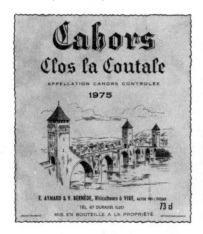

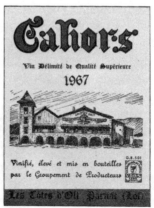

The "Black Wine of Cahors"—Morton Shand calls it "almost as black as ink"—is nowadays no longer black but only a deep red. In its old, black days its principal vine was the Malbec (or Auxerrois) and its best growths were on terraces carved out of the slopes of the valley of the river Lot between Cahors and Puy-l'Evêque. None the less it has some claims to be considered a classic French wine. It was imported into England on a large scale until the eighteenth century, the painter Ingres always drank it for his health despite living in Paris, and Alexandre Dumas respected it. The "*Fontaine des Chartreux*" in modern Cahors commemorates the charterhouse of Nôtre-Dame-de-Cahors, founded in 1328; like Bompas it had been a Templar commandery—a famous banking centre—which had passed into the hands of the Knights Hospitaller, who handed it to the Carthusians. The monks must have been well used to the black wine and almost certainly produced it for their own consumption. (The fountain itself is over the source of an ancient spring whose spirit was once worshipped by the Gauls and then by the Romans.)

The Grande Chartreuse itself seems to have made wine at one period. The poet Thomas Gray (author of the *Elegy Written in a Country Churchyard*), who visited it in 1739 and considered its situation "one of the most solemn, the most romantic, and the most astonishing scenes I ever beheld", tells us in his letters that their house "is, you must think, like a little city; for there are 100 fathers besides 300 servants [i.e. brothers], that make their clothes, grind their corn, press their wine, and do everything among themselves." The great monastery suffered a number of disastrous fires and had to be rebuilt several times, while in 1562 it was sacked by Huguenots. The Carthusians' worst trials came at the Revolution, when all French charterhouses were dissolved and many monks were martyred. (Ironically a Carthusian, Dom Gerle, is portrayed in David's *Oath of the Tennis Court*.) Some fathers managed to stay on at the Grande Chartreuse until the eviction of July 1793 and one or two remained in hiding in the neighbourhood; the last brother did not leave until 1812. The Carthusians returned to their Alpine home on the glorious day of 8 July 1816. Anti-clerical legislation drove them out again in 1904, despite furious opposition from the entire countryside—the officer in charge of the eviction broke his sword in disgust.

During the nineteenth century the Carthusians slowly re-established themselves in France, sometimes taking over former monasteries of other orders. At the Revolution the thirteenth-century Dominican priory at Mougères in Languedoc, between Pézenas and Caux, and built on the site of a Roman villa on the banks of the little river Peyne, had been auctioned as a *bien national*. The buyer was a pious lady of Pézenas, Mme de Maury, who, when she died in 1810, left it to her cousin to give to the first "White Fathers" who should return to France. He gave the derelict friary to the Carthusians, who took possession in 1825, their first prior being Dom Palamon Santy. Gradually they restored and converted the ruins amid the poplars and acacias. The church was not finally rebuilt until 1865—a pleasant, red-tiled white edifice which became again the place of pilgrimage it had been before the Revolution.

There had been vineyards at Nôtre-Dame-de-Mougères since Roman times, producing red and white wines which, if hardly distinguished, were at any rate drinkable. The procurators and the brethren did their best to improve this not very promising heritage. All their labours seemed in vain. First, the phylloxera destroyed the vines and then, in 1901, the community was banished from France. No one—at least no one save perhaps a Carthusian—could have foreseen the extraordinary development of the Mougères vineyard in modern times.

Even Carthusian cats have contributed to wine-growing in France. Where grapes are concerned rats and mice can occasionally prove no less a plague than small birds, especially if the vines grow near farm buildings. The monks bred a sturdy short-haired blue—still known as "chartreux"—which is an excellent mouser and must have earned its keep in the Order's vineyards.

During the later Middle Ages the Carthusians were much in evidence in Germany, above all in the great cities. Professor Knowles informs us that "the strict Carthusians prospered and increased when all others declined and the two centuries 1350-1550 were the epoch of their widest dispersion and influence—indeed the only period in which their mark on the external life of the church, by their writings and their reforming zeal, has been at all notable." Indirectly the Carthusians were the source of the spirituality of *The Imitation of Christ*. In many places—e.g. Cologne—their example enabled Catholicism to resist successfully the Protestant onslaught at the Reformation.

One of these German city charterhouses was the *karthaus* of St Alban, just outside Trier. It was founded in 1335 by the Archbishop-Elector Balduin von Leutzenburg, Arch-Chancellor of the Holy Roman Empire and, according to tradition, "one of the finest men that ever wore a mitre", who endowed it with a vineyard of 70 acres at Eitelsbach on the right bank of the Ruwer. The vines are on a large hill which to this day is known as the Karthäuserhofberg. For 500 years until the monks were driven out by French Revolutionary troops in 1794—it was finally secularized in 1803—the vineyard was worked by Carthusians. It produced, and still produces, what Hugh Johnson calls "the most delicate and haunting, lightest and tenderest of all German wines". A peculiarity of this justly famous moselle is its wine label, the smallest of all German labels, as its bottles are the last to use the old pallium or neck label instead of the larger waist label. It is also the German wine with the longest name—Eitelsbacher Karthäuserhofberger.

In Switzerland André Simon considered that of the little wine made in the Canton of Thurgau the only vintage "with any claim to quality is the red Karthäuser". This comes from vineyards that originally belonged to

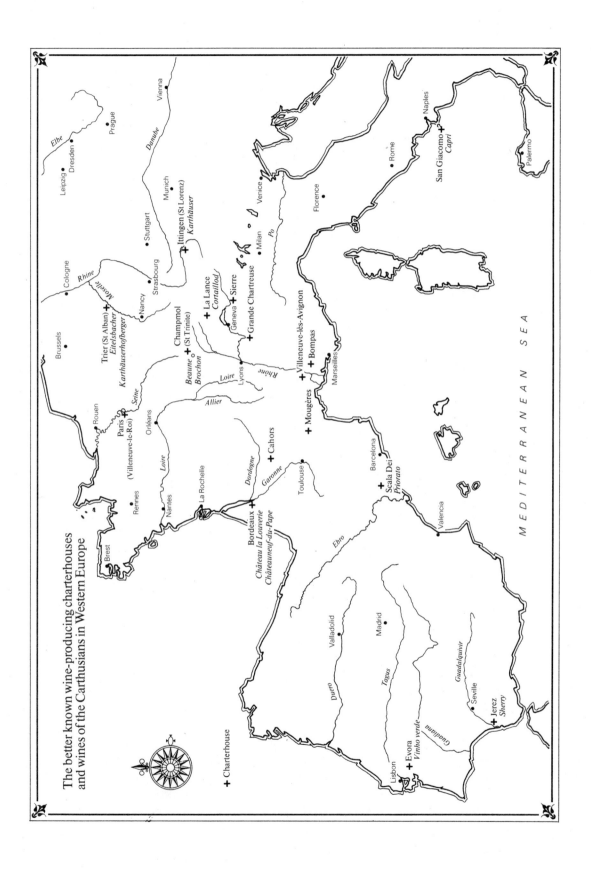

The better known wine-producing charterhouses
and wines of the Carthusians in Western Europe

+ Charterhouse

MEDITERRANEAN SEA

Brest
Rennes
Nantes
La Rochelle
Brussels
Cologne
Rhine
Moselle
Trier (St. Alban)
Eitelsbacher
Karthäuserhofberger
Nancy
Strasbourg
Rouen
Seine
Paris
(Villeneuve-le-Roi)
Orléans
Loire
Allier
Champmol
(St Trinité)
Beaune
Brochon
Lyons
Rhône
La Lance
Cortaillod
Sierre
Geneva
Grande Chartreuse
Villeneuve-lès-Avignon
Bompas
Mougères
Marseilles
Cahors
Toulouse
Garonne
Dordogne
Bordeaux
Château la Louverie
Châteauneuf-du-Pape
Barcelona
Scala Dei
Priorato
Valencia
Ebro
Madrid
Valladolid
Duero
Tagus
Guadalquivir
Guadiana
Seville
Jerez
Sherry
Evora
Vinho verde
Lisbon

Stuttgart
Munich
Ittingen (St Lorenz)
Karthäuser
Danube
Vienna
Prague
Leipzig
Dresden
Elbe
Milan
Po
Venice
Florence
Rome
San Giacomo
Capri
Naples
Palermo

the *karthaus* of St Lorenz on the banks of the river Thur at Ittingen, near Frauenfeld and not far from the shores of Lake Constance. Ittingen was founded in 1458, being established by Pope Pius II (Aeneas Sylvius Piccolomini) in a former monastery of Augustinian Canons. Sacked by Protestant troops during the Reformation, it was finally suppressed at the beginning of the nineteenth century. Although converted into a delightful private house, much of Ittingen has survived in good condition; there is a fine late-Gothic church with a splendid Baroque high altar and some choir stalls that date from 1703. The house was recently up for sale.

Another Swiss charterhouse that grew vines was at La Lance in the Neuchâtel Jura. Founded in 1318, its Gothic cloister has survived though, as at Ittingen, the monastery has been converted into a house. Almost certainly the monks of La Lance produced the Cortaillod which André Simon thought the best red Neuchâtel—"not unlike a Brouilly or Beaujolais wine". A *karthaus* was also founded at Sierre (Siders) by the Lac de Geronde. Its monks may well have originated the local wines, which must have been excellently suited to medieval palates. These are a sweet dessert wine, produced from a muscat grape, and a *vin de paille* from Furmint and Malvasia grapes; the latter is only produced in years when the weather is good, which is why it is called *Soleil de Sierre*.

In Spain one of the few red wines to be taken seriously besides Rioja is Priorato. This is grown in an enclave in the Tarragona region and made from the Garnacho Negro grape. Unlike the wine of Tarragona, Priorato is very dry, almost black in colour and extremely strong—its alcoholic content is more than 18 per cent. These distinctive qualities are largely derived from the decayed lava of the volcanic mountain slopes where the vines are grown. In fact the wine is really too dry and much of it is used for blending. George Saintsbury referred to it as "far from contemptible", though he appears to have thought that it was Portuguese. A white Priorato is also produced, very sweet and made from the Garnacho Blanco and Pedro Ximénez grapes. In addition there is a *vino rancio*; it is aged in the open air in large pear-shaped glass bottles called *bombonas* and is said to taste rather like sherry.

Priorato takes its name from the enormous ruined *cartuja* of Scala Dei (ladder of God), which was founded in 1163 on the lower slopes of the Holy Mountain of Sierra de Montsant by King Alfonso II of Aragon. It owned the six villages and their vineyards from which the wine originated (though the area has now been extended). Undoubtedly it was Carthusian patience which created these unusual wines. The *cartuja* was dissolved in 1835 by the "liberal" Spanish government, its last prior being Dom Alvaro Gomez Becerra. The *cartuja* is commemorated by the quaint label on some modern Priorato; two angels standing on bunches of grapes flank a ladder crowned by a cross—the *scala Dei*.

During its heyday Scala Dei boasted a painter of some distinction,

Don Joaquin Juncosa, who entered the house in 1660. He painted portraits of many of the order's Spanish priors and also of some of its saints, together with a number of scenes from the life of the Virgin Mary at the *cartuja* of Monte Alegre. In Juncosa's old age an unsympathetic prior insisted that he observe the rule properly, whereupon he fled to Rome and appealed to the Pope. The Pontiff dispensed him, giving instructions that he should not be tormented by the bell sounding the Hours of the Carthusian Office. Don Joaquin died at a hermitage in Rome in 1708. (Perhaps one might mention here that no less an artist than Goya painted murals in the *cartuja* of Aula Dei near Saragossa.)

The great *cartuja* outside Jerez had a small bodega in the town as early as 1504, and in 1658 was known for the excellence of its wine. It still survives, though now in other hands, in the Calle Naranjas. Ownership of a bodega implies both a large financial investment and considerable labour on the monks' part. The word bodega is best translated by the ungraceful term "winery", for it includes everything necessary for making and selling wine—presses, cooperage, cellars and sales office. Moreover sherry, a blended wine made from a variety of grapes (chiefly the Palomino) and fortified by brandy, is almost as complicated to produce as champagne; the characteristic *flor* or yeast film keeps the wine fermenting for a long period and each cask develops different qualities. Blending requires special skill, as also does the *solera* system— the constant replenishment of a blended cask with new wine.

No one knows when brandy was first used to fortify sherry. Suggestions that it was employed as early as Chaucer's time are nonsense, based on a wild supposition that the art of distillation was "inherited from the Moors"—if it had been, Spanish brandy would have been exported long before sherry. Large quantities of brandy only became available during the seventeenth century after the invention of improved distillation techniques. Even if Jerez levied a tax on *aguardiente* in the sixteenth century, it is hard to believe that a great deal of sherry was fortified before 1600. The one big monastery at Jerez was the *cartuja* and, as the Carthusians are known to have been among the first distillers when it was a laborious and time-consuming art, it is not altogether inconceivable that they were

the first to fortify sherry and to produce the wine which we have today.

This *cartuja* "of the Defence of the Blessed Virgin Mary" was founded at Jerez in 1475, but was not occupied until three years later. Besides its sherry it was also famous for breeding horses, its "Andalusian barbs". Once it contained many paintings by Zurbarán, the eccentric genius who was fascinated by the white habits of the Carthusians. The *cartuja*'s chief remaining glory is its magnificent Gothic church with a façade in the Apulian style bearing seven life-sized statues of Carthusian saints; it dates from 1571 and is the work of Andrés de Ribera. The Jerez *cartuja* was dissolved by government edict in 1835, to be used as a cavalry barracks for many years. The monks returned in 1948.

There were only two *cartuxa*s in Portugal, one at Lisbon and the other at Evora. The latter is known to have produced its own *vinho verde*.

Capri, with its dark memories of the Emperor Tiberius and luxurious villas, is not perhaps the most likely place to harbour Carthusians. Yet they were there and in the eighteenth century Montesquieu visited them, recording the visit in his journal together with his appreciation of their excellent wine. This would have been the pale dry white Capri which has since become something of a rarity—there are few vineyards on the island today and most of the wine sold as Capri comes from Ischia or near Naples. However, the *certosa* of San Giacomo, founded in 1371 by a Neapolitan courtier, is still there, not far from the Blue Grotto, and is one of the few buildings to survive from medieval Capri. The monks did not always have a tranquil life; in the sixteenth century the pirate Barbarossa invaded the island and made it his headquarters. The community was finally evicted by Joachim Murat during his short reign as King of Naples. Part of the *certosa* is now a public library, part is a school and part is an art gallery (devoted to the strange works of a Herr Dieffenbach), while nearly all the cells leading off the great cloister are in ruins. None the less the monastery remains miraculously intact amid its oleander trees. Recently the Augustinian fathers, who manage the school, have restored the beautiful Gothic church. Its choir stalls have gone, with much of the Baroque frescoes, but even so it retains an ineffable feeling of Carthusian peace and holiness.

There is no other really reputable wine in Italy associated with the Carthusians. However, some visitors to Pisa may have noticed the vines which grow next to the beautiful *certosa*.

Despite its unusually testing novitiate, the Carthusians have occasionally produced some colourful misfits. In Knowles's words, the order has always attracted "a number of aspirants of enthusiastic or neurotic temperaments, some of whom succeeded, then as now, in winning through at least the early stages of the difficult probation, to prove a source of infinite vexation to all in authority". In this context Saint-Simon tells a highly improbable story of a Carthusian driven mad by lack of meat, who shot his prior and fled to Turkey where he turned

Muslim. He was made governor of the Morea, which he then surrendered to the Venetians in return for free pardons from the Pope and Louis XIV. So bitter were the former Carthusian's recollections of a meatless life that in old age, having returned to France, he would set up a table in full view of a local charterhouse and gorge himself on a side of beef in the hope that some of his ex-brethren would see him.

Ironically, the Carthusian diet seems to make for health and old age. In 1948 the British Ministry of Health was so impressed by the longevity of the death certificates from the only modern English charterhouse that it actually sent a team to investigate the phenomenon. The team was unable to discover any explanation.

Another eccentric Carthusian was a wandering physician from Sussex, Dan Andrew Borde (1490-1549), who wrote the first English guidebook to Europe. After 20 years in the charterhouse at Hinton in Somerset he left, informing Prior Batmanson that, "I am not able to byd the rugoro-syte off your relygyon." None the less he added "my hartt ys euer to your relygyon, and loue itt". The understanding Dan Batmanson obtained a dispensation for him from the Grande Chartreuse. ("Relygyon" was the old word for a religious order.) Dr Borde, as he liked to be known henceforward, had a horror of water. In his *Breviary of Health* he tells us that he never drinks it but has ale instead, or otherwise, "I do take good Gascon wyne, but I wyl not drynke stronge wynes, as Malmesey, Romney, Romaniske wyne, wyne Qoorse, wyne Greke and Secke." Instead, "a draught or two of Muscadell or Basterde, Osey, Caprycke, Aligant, Tyre, Raspyte, I will not refuse; but white wyne of Angeou or wyne of Orleance, or Renyshe wyne, white or red, is good for al men." In his dietary, which he published in 1542, he says of wine:

> moderatly dronken, it doth actuate and doth quycken a
> man's wyttes, it doth comfort the hert, it doth scoure
> the lyuer; specyally yf it be whyte wyn, it doth reioyce
> all the powers of man and doth nowrysshe them; it doth
> ingender good blode, it doth comforte and doth
> nourysshe the brayne and all the body, and it resolueth
> fleume; it ingendereth heate, and it is good agaynst
> heuynes and pencyfulness; it is full of agylyte;
> wherefore it is medsonable, specyally whyte wyne, for it
> doth mundyfye and clense wounds & sores.
> Furthermore, the better the wyne is, the better
> humours it doth engender.

Such men are hardly typical of this, the most austere of all orders. A far more representative English Carthusian was Prior John Hoghton of the London charterhouse, who, with his fellow priors, was hanged, drawn and quartered by Henry VIII for refusing to take the oath acknowledging the King's spiritual supremacy; in all 18 Carthusians died for their conscience, a large proportion of the order in England; St John Hoghton was canonized in 1970. (There is a haunting painting of him by Zurbarán.) That fanatically Protestant historian J. A. Froude, who normally despised monks, compared the English Carthusians' stand to that of the Spartans at Thermopylae.

Nor have Carthusian labours in earthly vineyards been altogether unimpressive. It may seem a little surprising that hermits should grow wine, yet they have produced, among others, good burgundy and an excellent Châteauneuf-du-Pape, the superlative Karthäuserhofberg, the sturdy Karthäuser and the volcanic Priorato, besides plenty of good sherry. But nothing should ever surprise one about the Carthusians, who are perhaps the most unusual and most mysterious of all monks.

Chapter 7
The Monks of War and their Wines

jamais homme noble ne hait le bon vin.

RABELAIS

*The strange association of a monastic
and military life
which fanaticism might suggest,
but which policy must approve.*

GIBBON

T he military religious orders, the Templars, the Hospitallers, and many others, consisted essentially of warrior monks who were dedicated to fighting the infidel in a perpetual crusade. They took the three monastic vows of poverty, chastity and obedience; said Office in choir together; ate communally in refectories; and wore a habit; and in fact when not on campaign led a life—in commanderies which were also priories—almost exactly like that of ordinary monks. A more exact term for them might perhaps be military friars; the old English name for the Templars was "Red Friars", while even today professed Knights of Malta are styled "Fra".

The first of these military orders was the Poor Knights of Christ and of the Temple of Solomon (the Temple was situated in Jerusalem in the area where the Dome of the Rock and al-Aqsa mosques now stand), who were founded in 1119 in the newly conquered Holy Land. St Bernard drew up a rule for them largely based on that of his Cistercians, and their first task was to protect pilgrims on the road up to Jerusalem, and then to defend the Latin kingdom. The Templars' great rivals, the Knights Hospitaller of St John of Jerusalem, of Rhodes and of Malta—nowadays commonly called the Order of Malta—were founded a little earlier. Their original purpose was to provide shelter and accommodation for pilgrims and to nurse those who fell ill; later, no doubt inspired by the Templars' example, they too took up arms in defence of Crusader Palestine, probably in the early 1120s. The third great military order, the Teutonic Knights of St Mary's Hospital at Jerusalem, were founded in

1198 at Acre. As well as defending the Holy Land they discovered a new vocation in converting the pagans of Prussia, Latvia, Lithuania and Estonia, where they created an *"Ordensstaat"*, which by the end of the fourteenth century stretched from Brandenburg to the Gulf of Finland, but which was eventually destroyed by the Poles and the Russians. (The Teutonic Knights' best-known memorial is the Iron Cross, which was inspired by their own "cross of religion".) There were also the Iberian orders—in Spain Santiago, Calatrava and Alcantara, in Portugal Aviz. In addition there were a number of minor brotherhoods like the Knights Hospitaller of St Lazarus—the leper knights whose calling was the protection of lepers—and the exclusively English Knights Hospitaller of St Thomas of Acre.

The rules of nearly all military orders specify that the fighting brethren must drink sufficient wine to sustain their health and strength; as Napoleon said: *"Pas de vin, pas de soldats."* Furthermore, the Hospitaller orders also needed it for medicinal purposes. In consequence they maintained vineyards not only in Palestine and the Lebanon but all over Europe. In "Outremer"—Beyond the Sea—as they called it, the Knights Hospitaller of St John had their greatest vineyard just outside Tripoli (in the modern state of Lebanon). In 1236 the Hospitaller Commander of Tripoli gave permission for the Order's peasants at Mont Pelerin to plant vines in return for a third of the wine produced; there are many records of similar agreements. We know, from documentary evidence, that after the Arabs' partial reconquest of Palestine in 1187—when the Crusaders' territory was drastically reduced—the Hospitallers had to supplement their locally grown wine with large imports from Cyprus and Sicily. At Acre alone they had to maintain a hospital with 1,000 beds.

After the final loss of the Kingdom of Jerusalem and the final expulsion of the Crusaders in 1291, both Hospitallers and Templars moved their headquarters to Cyprus. However, the Templars' wealth excited the greed of Philip IV of France, who invited their leaders to Paris in 1307; arrested them; and then destroyed the entire brotherhood with trumped-up charges. Their Grand Master, Fra Jacques de Molay, was burnt alive over a slow fire for heresy after seven years of imprisonment, torture and forced confession. All that remains of the Templars are a few of their curious circular churches—modelled on that of the Holy Sepulchre at Jerusalem—and place names such as the Temple in London.

However, the Templars are also remembered as vignerons. In the Middle Ages "to drink like a Templar" indicated a mighty thirst. In Champagne they had many vineyards and a commandery at Reims. Unfortunately the Templars' cartulary—register of deeds and charters—has been lost, but they almost certainly owned vines at Épernay that produced a still champagne, probably like modern Bouzy and one of the most sought after of all medieval vintages. During their persecution

they hid in the caves at Chalons-sur-Marne. In Burgundy a Templar chapel with Romanesque windows may still be seen in the Saint-Jacques suburb of Dijon. In the claret country they gave their name to Clos des Templiers (Pomerol), Château les Templiers (Saint-Emilion) and Château Templiers (Pomerol). Château de l'Eglise in Pomerol owes its name to the church that they built in the thirteenth century while they owned the village of Lalande next to Pomerol. Château Gazin was yet another Templar vineyard in Pomerol. They also had Château Mont-despic at Salles-de-Castillon in Saint-Emilion. An excellent red wine from the Loire valley, Champigny, still has a vineyard called Clos des Templiers; the cépage is Cabernet-Sauvignon and Cabernet Franc, and its vintages were among the favourites of King Henry III of England. In Roussillon the vineyards of Masdeu ("God's Farm" in Catalan) near Collioure once belonged to the Templars.

In Italy, at Brindisi in Apulia, there is an ancient round church dedicated to St John but built by the Templars, not far from a graceful old fountain where, it is said, the Crusaders watered their horses before sailing to the Holy Land. Always desperate for wine, the brethren would have had recourse to the local vintage—that of Locorotondo. This is a greenish-coloured wine, dry but full, which is made from a mixture of Verdecca and Bianco d'Alessano grapes.

The Portuguese Knights of Christ have some claim to be considered the Templars' heirs as they inherited a part of their possessions. This brotherhood's monument is the headquarter's commandery of Thomar with its exotic Manoelino chapter-house. One of their Grand Masters was Prince Henry the Navigator, who devoted their energies to exploring the African coast in the hope of finding Christian kingdoms who would help in the fight against the infidel. In 1425 they colonized the Canary Islands and Madeira. In the former they exterminated a strange white race who may have been the last Cro-Magnon men. In the latter they showed themselves more benevolent, bringing the Malvasia (Malmsey) grape from Monemvasia in the Morea and from Crete; it is still known in the islands as the Malvazia Candida and, in André Simon's words "is of a rich golden colour when ripe, and yielding a luscious white wine with a peculiar bouquet". The fact that Malmsey survived the Turkish conquest of Greece at all was entirely due to the Knights of Christ and their Grand Master. Probably Madeira in its modern forms was first drunk in large quantities at Thomar by the brethren.

After the dissolution of the Templars, the Knights of St John wisely transferred their headquarters from Cyprus—where they were not welcome—to Rhodes to avoid the same fate as the Templars. However, they retained their vineyards in Cyprus, notably those around Kolossi, which in the 1290s became their Grand Commandery in the island. These grew the Mavron and Xynisteri grapes, producing a sweet brown wine called Commandaria, which was one of the most prized vintages in medieval Europe. Nowadays it is the product of countless co-operatives, and such esteem may seem a little surprising. But in the sugarless Middle Ages sweetness was valued above all else. Also there was a certain art in dilution. Commandaria was always drunk with four parts of water to one of wine—some English Knights who drank it neat died. When in Cyprus in the thirteenth century, on his way to the crusades, St Louis asked the sieur de Joinville why he did not water his wine, telling him that "if I did not learn to mix my wine with water while still young but intended to do so in my old age, gout and stomach trouble would afflict me and I should never enjoy good health. Furthermore, if I continued to drink unwatered wine when old I should be drunk every night and it really is too disgusting a thing that any honourable man should be in such a state." The old commandery of Kolossi still stands, in surprisingly good condition.

The Hospitallers stayed for over two centuries at Rhodes, building a magnificent monastery city, much of which survives—the "Street of the Knights" is particularly well preserved. Here they drank the red wine of Rhodes, one of the best from the Aegean islands and famed since classical times. A white wine is still produced from vines growing under the ruins of the brethren's commandery on the acropolis of Lindos. Naturally they imported in their galleys all the heavy muscat wines of Greece, Cyprus and Crete which were so beloved by the medieval palate —Malmsey from Monemvasia in the Peloponnese and from Candia, and the muscats of Patras and Rion, as well as their own Commandaria. From Negropont, where they had a commandery, they would have had the white Chalkis. For a brief period at the end of the fourteenth century the commander of the Morea occupied the mountain castle of Acrocorinth and no doubt he would have seen that plenty of the Corinthian red Nemea reached Rhodes.

They also owned vineyards in Burgundy—they were present at Volnay by 1207. They needed wine at home as well as at the front for the hospitals that they maintained all over Catholic Europe, dispensing both

hospitality and medical care to travellers. Sometimes such hospitals were attached to a commandery, staffed by a knight commander, a chaplain and two or three serving brethren; sometimes they were "frank" houses run by hired wardens. Frequently these hospitals administered adjoining vineyards, for wine was not only essential for entertaining and nursing but was also an important source of income for maintaining the order's fleet and military operations; "responsions" or revenues were sent to the national priory (Clerkenwell) in pre-Reformation England for dispatch to the convent. Even if the brethren never worked in the fields, as estate managers they took a keen interest in wine-growing.

However, most of their vineyards in Burgundy, apart from Volnay in 1207 and one at Pommard from 1234, were acquired at a later date than those of other orders. In 1635 they bought vineyards at Beaune, in particular Savigny, where they owned Les Marconnets. In Chassagne they possessed the Abbaye de Morgeot, where they later introduced a grape from Malta, the Pinot Maltais or Pinot Morgeot, which was grown beside the more usual Pinot Noir. Although the new grape is excellent for quantity the quality is inferior and the experiment can hardly have been a success. The Knights are commemorated by the Chassagne vineyard Clos Saint Jean.

In Bordeaux they inherited many of the Templar properties. At Saint-Emilion one may still see a Hospitaller commandery with Romanesque windows. Château la Commanderie—where there is a boundary stone with a Maltese cross—and Clos du Commandeur, both in Pomerol, also belonged to them. In Alsace they owned the best of the Bergheim vineyards. In Roussillon they acquired the Templar vineyards at Masdeu (Roussillon wines are not to be despised, especially Côtes d'Agly).

In Germany and Austria they were no less active as vignerons, as far south as Styria. Their commandery at Mailberg in northern Austria is still occupied by them and produces some excellent wine.

In Switzerland the late Gothic church at Küsnacht, on the right bank of Lake Zürich, was once the chapel of a commandery of Knights Hospitallers. Küsnacht is the beginning of a nine-mile stretch of vines along the shores of the lake and some of the vineyards seem to have been owned by the Knights. The vine is the Pinot Noir (known locally as the Klevner), which makes a rather sour red wine. One of the better vintages is produced at the village of Meilen (which is *en route* to Stäfa), where there is a skilfully restored *ritterhaus*—a commandery of the Knights that dates from about 1200 and is of the greatest interest.

In Portugal the Knights of São João were present at Leça do Balio from the twelfth century. The chapel of the great commandery was built by the bailiff Estevão Vasques Pimentel, who died in 1336, and is a mighty Gothic structure with three naves, a fine rose window and a splendid Manuelino calvary from the early sixteenth century; it is fortified, its walls being crenellated and defended by a machicolated

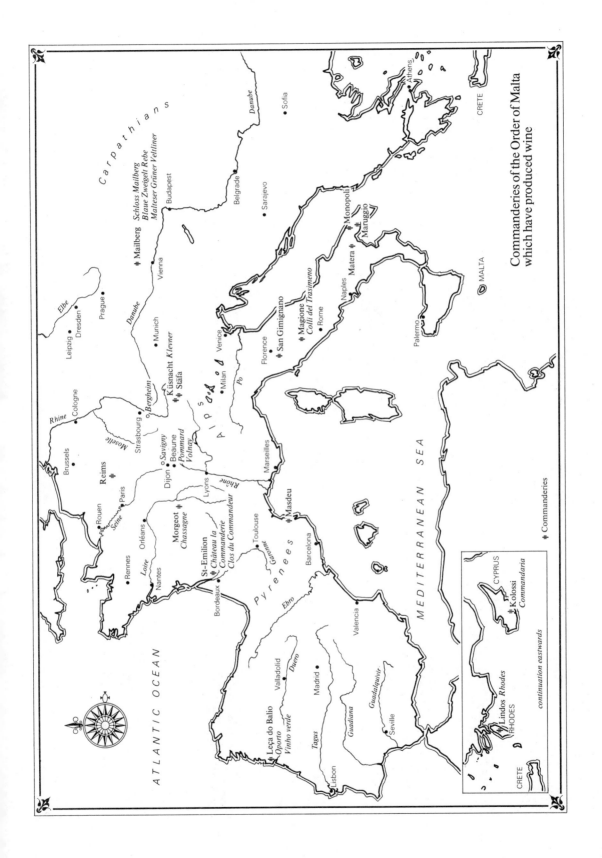

Commanderies of the Order of Malta which have produced wine

ATLANTIC OCEAN

MEDITERRANEAN SEA

Carpathians

Elbe

Rhine

Moselle

Danube

A l p s

Rhône

Seine

Loire

Garonne

Ebro

Duero

Tagus

Guadiana

Guadalquivir

Po

Pyrenees

Athens

CRETE

Sofia

Belgrade

Sarajevo

Budapest

Vienna

⚓ Mailberg *Schloss Mailberg*
Blaue Zweigelt Rebe
Malteser Grüner Veltliner

Munich

Prague

Dresden

Leipzig

Cologne

Brussels

Strasbourg

⚓ Bergheim

Küsnacht *Klevner*
⚓ Stäfa

Reims ⚓

Paris

Rouen

Rennes

Nantes

Orléans

Dijon ○ Savigny
● Beaune
● Pommard
Volnay

Lyons

Marseilles

Venice

Milan

Florence

⚓ San Gimignano

Magione ⚓
Colli del Trasimeno
● Rome

Naples

Matera ⚓ Monopoli ⚓
Maruggio ⚓

Palermo

○ MALTA

Morgeot
Chassagne

St-Emilion ⚓
⚓ *Château la
Commanderie
Clos du Commandeur*

Toulouse

Bordeaux

Barcelona

⚓ Masdeu

Valencia

Valladolid

Madrid

Seville

Lisbon

Leça do Balio ⚓
Oporto
Vinho verde

⚓ Commanderies

CYPRUS

K Kolossi *Commandaria*

CRETE

Lindos *Rhodes*
RHODES

continuation eastwards

keep, each angle flanked by a supporting watch-tower. Inside there are some fine monumental effigies on the tombs of the knightly brethren. They almost certainly owned vineyards at Oporto nearby, producing two totally different sorts of wine; the sweet red vintages which today we call port (though then unfortified) and the *vinho verde*—the light whites and not so agreeable reds of the Minho province, which ends just before Oporto.

The Knights were evicted from Rhodes by the Turks in 1523 and from 1530 to 1798 their headquarters were in Malta. There have been vineyards in Malta since Phoenician times (though these were temporarily wiped out by phylloxera in the early 1900s). However, in the Knights' time, as now, the thin Maltese vintages were probably mainly white. A good deal of wine was obviously imported from Sicily, though the order's sea "caravans" must have brought back from their raids a fair supply of the Greek wines they had known on Rhodes. Large amounts were necessary, not only for the brethren in their "auberges" but for the patients in the great hospital who, according to the custom of the order, drank it from silver. It was also needed in battle. During the terrible siege of 1565 Grand Master Fra Jean de la Valette had casks ferried over to the doomed garrison on St Elmo, the quickest and most sustaining food in combat being bread soaked in wine. Wine-soaked bread was occasionally given to the wretched galley slaves to stop them fainting at their oars.

The Order of Malta possessed numerous vineyards in Italy. One at Magione in Umbria is still producing wine for the Knights (see p. 181). Others are almost forgotten, such as that near the ancient town of Matera in Basilicata, on the edge of the Murge mountains. The Knights are known to have been here since at least 1268, the first mention of a commandery being in 1392, and in the seventeenth century a Fra Zurla rebuilt the commandery church, decorating the campanile with the eight-pointed cross. The vineyards were some miles away and probably produced strong, harsh red wines, almost black in colour, which the brethren must have drunk watered; today such "black wines" are mostly sent

Overleaf: *the 16th-century "château" of Clos de Vougeot in Burgundy, a Cistercian grange built by the monks of Cîteaux.* Above: *the ancient wine-press at Clos de Vougeot. "Clos Vougeot" was the best Cistercian wine in France.* Opposite: *white-habited Benedictine monks of the Olivetan congregation at dinner in their refectory. From a fresco (c. 1498) by Luca Signorelli in the abbey at Monte Oliveto near Sienna.* Below: *the Cistercian abbey of Kloster Eberbach, near Hattenheim, where the monks made their best German wines.*

Above: *Christ in the wine-press,*
from a German miniature of about 1500.
Facing page, top: *Benedictine nuns*
of the abbey of St Hildegard, near
Rüdesheim, in their wine cellar.

Bottom: *the abbey of St Hildegard*
and its vineyards which produce
a broad range of excellent
wines including an eiswein,
a wine made from winter grapes.

Above: *Carthusian monks of the Grande Chartreuse gathering herbs essential for the making of their liqueurs.* Right: *the Cistercian abbey of Poblet which was producing wine in 1316 and has recently started to do so again.* Far right: *the commandery and vineyards at Mailberg in Austria which have belonged to the Knights of Malta since 1128.*

Overleaf, top: *the mission church of the Christian Brothers among its vineyards in Napa Valley, California.* Bottom: *Christian Brothers harvesting grapes in their vineyards which produce some famous wines including Château la Salle.*

108

north for blending. (Even though the wine is poor, Matera is a fascinating place, with whole streets of cave-like dwellings built into the rock face, overhanging one another.) Not far away a commandery at Monopoli, on the Adriatic coast between Brindisi and Bari, possessed a vineyard at the little hill town of Cisternino which, one may guess, produced a heavy, dry, greenish white wine like the nearby Martina Franca, most of which is nowadays used in the manufacture of vermouth. It is probable that this commandery also owned vines at the neighbouring towns of Fasano and Putignano, where one sees the Maltese cross on several buildings; both towns belonged to the Knights for centuries—Putignano from 1358 to 1808. Maruggio, the seat of another commandery, lies on the inner side of the "heel" of Italy, not far from the coast south-west of Taranto. In the seventeenth century Fra Giovanni Battista Nari (the titular Grand Prior of England) increased its income by endowing it with a house and "cantina" in the piazza in front of the commandery church, which became known by the townspeople as the "*cantina dello signore*". The Maruggio wine is also likely to have been "black"— perhaps resembling the Primitivo of Manduria close by, which is said to age until it becomes surprisingly acceptable. All these little vineyards were within easy reach of ports and no doubt their vintages, however modest, were regularly shipped to Malta on small sailing vessels.

The Teutonic Knights cultivated the vine in East Prussia—and probably in Latvia too—producing a vintage that was so thin and sour that it had to be sweetened with honey and drunk spiced and mulled. However, they were able to supplement it with more palatable wines from *komtureien* in the Rhineland and Austria and even from a few in France, Italy and Greece. Some famous modern vineyards on the Rhine have an indirect connection with this redoubtable order. They are those which produce the deservedly renowned wines of Reichsgraf von Plettenberg, for the Count belongs to the same ancient family as the great *Landtmeister* Wolther von Plettenberg, who from 1493 to 1533 ruled at Riga over the Teutonic Knights of Latvia, Lithuania and Estonia—the last heirs of the Brethren of the Sword. In Württemberg the vineyard of Gundelsheimer Himmelreich, by the river Neckar and lying beneath the great Schloss Horneck, once belonged to this order as did the castle. No doubt Gundelsheimer Himmelreich was served at the Grand Commandery at Mergentheim, a tiny independent state within Württemberg, where, after his expulsion from Prussia in the 1520s, the *Hoch-und-Deutschmeister* held his little court, with white-cloaked knights-in-waiting and lifeguards; although Napoleon ejected the "High and German Master" from Mergentheim, from 1695 until the end of the Habsburg army the latter financed a crack Imperial (later Austrian) infantry regiment, the *Hoch-und-Deutschmeister*, whose band survives even today. In Austria, south of the road from Baden to Vienna and amid the woods of the last Alpine slopes, is the delightful village of

Gumpoldskirchen. It is the centre of a large wine-growing area that produces mainly sweet white wine from Riesling and Rotgipfler grapes. Here too there is another mighty castle of the Teutonic Knights, still in good repair and guarding one of the region's four best vineyards—Gumpoldskirchner Wiege, the "cradle" vineyard.

Most of the Spanish military orders' huge estates lay on the arid *meseta*, which they conquered from the Moors, though they must have possessed vineyards at Tarragona and undoubtedly had them at Jerez. The Knights of Santiago owned vines in the Rioja country. The headquarters of this order's Portuguese branch were at Palmela, south of the Tagus and easily reached from Lisbon, in a castle commandery on the slopes of the Sierra da Arrábida. A fourteenth-century keep survives, together with a fine Gothic church of the next century which is dedicated to "São Thiago" (St James of Compostella, the order's patron); the commandery's other buildings have been converted into a hotel. Palmela vineyards, once the Knights' property, produce a good strong red wine and also a dessert muscatel.

A military order that was purely Portuguese was that of Evora, or Aviz as it was later known. It was founded in 1160 at Evora, 100 miles south of Lisbon, but the Knights changed their name when they received the town of Aviz as a royal gift in 1211. The habit was white with a green cross. In 1384 their Grand Master, Dom João, who was a bastard of the royal house, seized the vacant throne of Portugal and founded a new dynasty—that of Aviz. The order was dissolved by King Pedro in 1834. It had many rich estates, especially at Evora (which is still a beautiful town), but the only wine it produced there was *vinho verde*.

The Knights of St Lazarus are an ancient if less famous military order whose origins are somewhat obscure. Perhaps understandably they claimed to have been founded by Lazarus himself, but their first known appearance was in Palestine about 1120. They were pledged to nurse and defend lepers and some of their early knights were themselves lepers. To begin with their rule was "Basilian", which possibly indicates a south-Italian origin. Later they administered a whole network of leper hospitals in England, Scotland, France and Naples as well as in the Holy Land. One "Lazar House" which may have belonged to them is Château la Gaffelière—a *Premier Grand Cru Classé* of Saint-Emilion.

Chapter 8
The Wines
of Other Orders

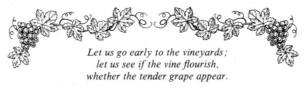

Let us go early to the vineyards;
let us see if the vine flourish,
whether the tender grape appear.

SONG OF SOLOMON

and the mountains shall drop sweet wine,
and all the hills shall melt.

AMOS

Strictly speaking the Benedictines and Cistercians are the only religious orders who have made a really significant contribution to viticulture. Perhaps some credit may be claimed for the Carthusians, who created a number of wines, and even for the Knights of Malta. However, if piecemeal and often restricted to a single vineyard, the contribution of other brotherhoods was amazingly widespread and deserves recognition.

Among older orders are the Camaldolese, whose hermit monks lead an even more solitary life than Carthusians. One of their monasteries is the Sacro Eremo Tuscolano, where the hermits are supported by a house of cenobite Camaldolese (i.e. living in community). This abbey is near Frascati and for close on 1,000 years its monks have made a delicious dry white Frascati. The Camaldolese boast one of the most interesting saints in the entire calendar. Tommaso di Castacciaro, who is still venerated in Umbria, was born at Castacciaro in the thirteenth century, the son of poor parents. Soon after entering the order he became a hermit, so solitary that his brethren almost forgot him. But in extreme old age San Tommaso (the canonization is purely local) emerged from his hermitage to perform a miracle that was based on the most respectable precedent—he changed water into wine. He died in 1337 and his feast is on 25 March.

Another early order are the monks of Grottaferrata in the Alban hills, a survival from Byzantine Italy. Founded by St Nilus of Calabria before the year 1000, they still follow the Basilian rule and celebrate the

Mass according to the Greek rite. The wine of their village obviously owes its origin to them and is another excellent Frascati. It is marketed with neighbouring vintages under the collective name of Castella Romani.

Although they follow the Benedictine rule, the monks and nuns of the order of Fontevrault constitute an order of their own. The strangely shaped kitchen of their great mother house at Fontevrault, near Saumur, is a French counterpart of the famous Abbot's Kitchen at Glastonbury. It was once one of the most distinguished monasteries in France and still contains the tombs of King Henry II of England, his Queen, Eleanor of Aquitaine, and their son, Richard Coeur de Lion. A double abbey for both men and women, it was founded with the order by Robert of Arbrissel in 1099. During the eighteenth century it held more than 60 monks and 200 nuns ruled by an abbess who was invariably a lady of high degree, sometimes even of royal blood. The nuns too were usually ladies of rank and were noted for their needlework; Louis XV sent his daughters to Fontevrault to be educated. The fine church with its cupolas has survived, though like the wonderful kitchen it is heavily restored. No doubt the latter saw many bottles of Saumur from the abbey's own vineyard, Fontevrault l'Abbaye; in the early years it would have been worked by the lay brethren, who were probably the first to make this pleasant, honey-coloured wine.

During the twelfth century the poet Guyot de Provins commented— in his *Bible Guyot,* a social satire—on the fine wines to be found in Augustinian refectories. Yet the "Black Canons" seem to have had comparatively few vineyards. However, as one of the must numerous of all medieval orders and one which has left so many ruined monasteries, the Augustinians deserve to be mentioned. Following the rule of St Augustine (or at any rate a rule he was supposed to have compiled), its canons led a partly monastic, partly pastoral life in small priories; or ran schools and hospitals and even leper houses and cemeteries. Although regarded as the most relaxed of all orders, they none the less produced

such mystics as Thomas à Kempis and Walter Hilton. But while they were good farmers and owned wide estates, surprisingly few vineyards are definitely known to have belonged to them. A French priory that probably did possess vines is Belleville on the edge of the Beaujolais country. In Germany, on the middle Moselle, the Augustinian abbey of Stuben—whose aristocratic nuns had to prove 16 quarterings of nobility—owned the Frauenberg vineyard from 1136 to 1788; today it produces splendid Rieslings. There is also the convent of Kloster Marienthal, founded in 1136 and dissolved in 1802, whose interesting ruins are situated in the beautiful Ahr valley near Linz, among vineyards which still produce a fine red hock. The grape was undoubtedly tended by the Augustinians of the beautiful Baroque abbey on the Wachau at Durnstein, which Sir Sacheverell Sitwell describes as "perhaps the most delightful town in Austria". In Portugal, at Torres Vedras—where Wellington built his "Lines"—there is an interesting sixteenth-century Augustinian priory which, although converted into a police barracks, has largely survived. Its brethren probably grew and relished the neighbourhood's excellent red Estremadura.

The Premonstratensian—or "White"—Canons are also known as Norbertines, after St Norbert, who founded them at Prémontré near Laon in the early twelfth century. They were an order of strict Canons Regular who followed the Augustinian rule and combined a contemplative life with pastoral work, supporting themselves by manual labour. Their expansion in the twelfth and thirteenth centuries was second only to that of the Cistercians. They had several houses in England, including Welbeck. Some Premonstratensian abbeys were among the most magnificent in northern Europe, especially those in the Low Countries and in Hungary and Bohemia. They were—and still are—perhaps the most picturesquely habited of all religions, with a white cassock and cape, a white biretta and a white lace rochet (a kind of surplice); abbots and priors also wear a white fur cape. In the exotic Latin kingdom of medieval Cyprus their house of Belpais was both the most celebrated and loveliest monastery in the realm. The wines of Belpais were second only to those of Commandaria. Today the abbey's Gothic ruins stand amid the vineyards of one of the most important co-operatives in Cyprus.

The non-Catholic is rarely able to distinguish between monks and friars. Basically a monk is a man who has taken the three monastic vows of poverty, chastity and obedience and also the vow of stability—of staying in his monastery for the rest of his life, where his chief duty is to sing the praises of God in choir with his brethren at the appointed Hours. A friar, on the other hand, although he takes the three monastic vows, does not take that of stability. Nor is it his chief duty to sing Office in choir—it is to spread the Word of God by preaching.

In the thirteenth century there was a movement within the Church that sought a return to the simple life of the Gospel. Many groups, such as the Poor Men of Lyons, were banned by the Pope. Francis of Assisi and his followers were a group of this sort, but they survived because he was both a saint and a religious genius. The Franciscans who followed were, however, always prone to division and the first Grey Friars have split into many groups; even today there are at least three different sorts of Franciscan.

A contemporary of St Francis, the Spaniard Dominic Guzman organized an "order of preachers" to combat the Cathar heretics of southern France. The Dominicans, the *Domini Canes* or "Hounds of the Lord", spread the Gospel through the universities by such talented theologians as Albertus Magnus and Thomas Aquinas. Later the Dominicans staffed and operated the Inquisition. One famous Dominican was Savonarola, the scourge of Florence, who was eventually burnt by his brethren by order of the Pope.

The Franciscans also had their intellectuals—brilliant university dons like Roger Bacon, Duns Scotus and William of Ockham. What Franciscans and Dominicans had in common was the ideal of bringing the faith to heretics and the living reality of Christ to men everywhere—especially on the highways and byways.

There were other orders of friars on the same model. The Carmelites originated in the Holy Land as hermits on Mount Carmel, but were reorganized as friars by the English St Simon Stock in the mid-thirteenth century; in 1949 they returned to their miraculously preserved medieval priory in Kent. They have divided into two separate orders, the Calced and Discalced Carmelites, the latter's greatest son being St John of the Cross. The Augustine Hermits also began as scattered solitaries who were forced by the Church to organize themselves into an order; their best-known member is Martin Luther. In addition, there were the Servites, the Minims (basically Franciscans), the Crutched Friars, and the Friars of the Sack; the last were dissolved very early on.

The Dominicans were known as Black Friars, from the mantles which they wore over their white habits. Similarly, the Carmelites were called White Friars, on account of a white mantle over a brown habit. The Franciscans took their name of Grey Friars from the fact that until the fourteenth century they wore grey; later they adopted black or brown.

Although friars ate together in refectories and slept in communal dormitories, their friaries were never as important to them as an abbey to a monk. Their rule dictated that they must be constantly moving, always sleeping under a different roof. Their sole revenues were, in theory, derived from alms and never from estates. Architecturally few friaries could rival an abbey. There were exceptions, especially in Italy, where the refectory with its eucharistic symbolism was often deliberately elaborate; sometimes there was a fresco of the Last Supper—as at Santa Maria delle Grazie of the Dominicans at Milan, the supreme example, where the artist was Leonardo da Vinci.

The early Franciscans were specifically forbidden to make wine. The thirteenth-century prelate, preacher and chronicler Jacques de Vitry applied to the friars words from Jeremiah—"Neither shall ye build houses; nor sow, not plant vineyards, nor have any." Yet by the end of that century their orchards and vineyards in the suburbs of great towns, and even inside them, were a source of offence to those brethren who wished to practise true poverty. The decline that would produce such Franciscans as Chaucer's unsavoury friar had begun.

In the thirteenth century the Franciscans produced a writer who, if not exactly a "wine writer" in the popular, modern sense, tells some extremely illuminating anecdotes about wine in his time. This was Fra Salimbene of Parma, born in 1221, whose chronicle is a kind of picaresque autobiography. He wandered not merely through Italy but through France as well. "Note that in the [Franciscan] Province of France are eight custodies of our Order whereof four drink beer and four drink wine," he informs us:

> Note also that there are three parts of France which
> give great plenty of wine—namely La Rochelle,
> Beaune and Auxerre. Note that the red wines are held
> in small esteem for they are not equal to the red wines
> of Italy. [One wonders if this was a purely personal
> judgement.] Note likewise that the wines of Auxerre
> are white and sometimes golden and fragrant, and
> comforting and of strong and excellent taste, and that
> they turn all who drink them to cheerfulness and
> merriment; wherefore of this wine we may rightly say
> with Solomon 'Give strong wine to them that are sad,
> and wine to them that are grieved in mind: Let them
> drink and forget their want, and remember their
> sorrow no more.' And know that the wines of Auxerre
> are so strong that, when they have stood awhile, tears
> gather on the outer surface of the jar. Note also that
> the French are wont to tell how the best wine should
> have three B's and seven F's. For they themselves say in
> sport

> *Et bon et bel et blanc*
> *Fort et fier, fin et franc,*
> *Froid et frais et frétillant.*

He concludes that "the French delight in good wine, nor need we wonder, for wine 'cheereth God and men', as it is written in the ninth chapter of Judges."

Fra Salimbene obviously liked to drink himself. He quotes with relish the song of "Master Morando, who taught grammar at Padua" and "who commended wine according to his own taste in this fashion":

Drink'st thou glorious, honey'd wine?
Stout thy frame, thy face shall shine,
Freely shalt thou spit:

Old in cask, in savour full?
Cheerful then shall be thy soul,
Bright and keen shall be thy wit.

Is it strong and pure and clear?
Quickly shall it banish care,
Chills it shall extrude:

Scorn not red, though thin it be:
Ruddy wine shall redden thee,
So thou do but soak:

Juice of gold and citron dye
Doth our vitals fortify,
Sicknesses doth choke:

But the cursed water white
Honest folk will interdict,
Lest it spleen provoke.

He lovingly records other verses in the same bibulous vein.

The inquisitive friar is particularly interested in the drinking habits of other nations:

It may be said literally that French and English make it
their business to drink full goblets; wherefore the
French have bloodshot eyes, for from their ever-free
potations of wine their eyes become red-rimmed and

bleared and bloodshot. And in the early morning after
they have slept off their wine they go with such eyes to
the priest who has celebrated Mass, and pray him to
drop into their eyes the water wherein he has washed
his hands. [He is kinder about the vast thirst of the
English.] We must forgive the English if they are glad
to drink good wine when they can, for they have but
little wine in their own country.

Fra Salimbene speaks with high approval of Philip, Archbishop of
Ravenna:

This Lord Philip, when he was in his villa called
Argenta on the banks of the Po and when he went to
and fro through his palace, was wont to go singing
some responsory or antiphon in praise of the glorious
Virgin from one corner to another of that palace. And
in summer time he would drink at each corner; for at
each corner of the palace he had a pitcher of excellent
and noble wine in the coldest water. For he was a
mighty drinker and loved not water with his wine.

Among Franciscan vineyards is Château le Prieuré in Saint-Emilion
which belonged to the Cordeliers, a reformed group. There is also said to
have been a Clos des Cordeliers. In the Deux Mers one finds the Clos des
Capucines (the Capuchins being another reformed group), a white
Bordeaux made from Sauvignon grapes. In Germany the Franciscan
Cardinal Nicolas Caroli founded a friary and a vineyard at Baden in
1426; the latter still produces an excellent light Franconian wine while
what is left of the friary has become the headquarters of a leading
Swiss wine merchant, Domaines Schenk. In Austria the pretty church
of the Franciscans at Stein in the Wachau, the "Minoritenkirche",
stands amid vineyards that once supplied the brethren with pleasant if
undistinguished wine. One might also mention that a much esteemed
Hungarian grape that grows near Lake Balaton is called the Szurkebarat
or Grey Friar (it is in fact the French Auvergnat Gris). In Portugal there
is a particularly beautiful Franciscan church at Oporto dedicated to "São
Francisco"; enlarged in the sixteenth century, its elegant interior dates
mainly from the next two centuries. In the same town there is a Franciscan convent of Santa Clara, begun in 1416 but rebuilt in the sixteenth
century. Almost certainly these houses once owned vineyards producing
port or *vinho verde* or both.

In France Dominican friars used to be known as Jacobins—"Hooded
Crows"—because of their black and white habits. The Jacobins' convent
in the centre of Saint-Emilion is a delightfully romantic ruin, with a

square old tower and a Renaissance doorway covered in creepers and climbing shrubs; its cellars are still used for storing wine. Founded in the thirteenth century and abandoned during the eighteenth, it once owned Clos de Jacobins. In Portugal the great cathedral of Vila Real was formerly the church of a Dominican friary. Vila Real is where Mateus is produced; red, white and rosé—of which it has been written: "they form an intermediate stage between childish fizzy drinks and the adult taste for wine."

The brown and white Carmelites are the friars who seem to have owned most vineyards. In the Middle Ages they shared Savigny-les-Beaune with the Cistercians; no doubt they administered it from the exquisite Carmelite friary at Beaune which still survives. Another vineyard that belonged to the Carmelites of Beaune was the best one at Les Grèves, *"La vigne de l'enfant Jésus"*—named after the arms of Beaune, which bear Our Lady carrying Our Lord. As for claret, in the Graves they owned Les Carmes-Haut-Brion and in the Premières Côtes de Bordeaux the Clos de la Monastère de Broussey. In addition there is a white wine of Saumur, Clos des Carmes. In Germany the castle of Vogelsburg in Franconia was for centuries a Carmelite friary whose brethren owned the famous Eschendorfer Lump, which continues to produce some of the best and most expensive Franconian wines. The Carmelites of Frankfurt owned a distinguished vineyard that still functions at Hochheim in the Rheingau, from which the English word hock is said to derive.

The Society of Jesus was founded in the sixteenth century by the Basque soldier Iñigo de Loyola, to become the spearhead of the Counter-Reformation. As schoolmasters, the Jesuits shaped the entire ruling class of Catholic Europe; as confessors they directed Kings and Emperors; as missionaries they ranged from Ireland to Russia and from India to Texas; in China they converted the last Ming Emperor and became astronomers, clock-makers, mathematicians and gardeners to his Manchu successors. Technically known as "clerks regular", the Jesuits do not sing Office in choir and strictly speaking, there is no such thing as a Jesuit monastery, though there are some famous Jesuit churches. However, they have made wine. In Germany they are commemorated by Förster Jesuitengarten and Winkeler Jesuitengarten. The Friedrich-Wilhelm school at Trier was founded by Jesuits in 1563; although the order left in 1773 the school still continues, drawing some of its income from vineyards which once belonged to the Jesuits.

At Naples during the seventeenth century the Jesuits were active—apparently almost dominant—in the city's wine trade, both retail and wholesale. They were so envied for their profits that a wily Spanish Viceroy, the capricious Duke of Ossuna, asked them how much their best wine cost a barrel; when they replied disarmingly that it was a mere four ducats he at once insisted on buying the lot for the navy, and then sold it privately at 20 ducats a barrel. The Neapolitan Jesuits also owned vineyards on the slopes of Vesuvius, which produced the wine known as Lacrima Christi. The white, which is dry, pale yellow and (sometimes) flowery, is made from three grapes—Biancolella, Coda di Volpe and Greco di Torre—and has both admirers and critics. Red Lacrima Christi has no real claim to its title, as it is comprised of a variety of inferior neighbouring vintages grown on the lava. The white, let alone the red, has not yet succeeded in obtaining the DOC label *(Denominazione di Origine Controllata)*. The Baroque sounding name derives from the legend that Christ once ascended Monte Vesuvio and, looking down on Naples, shed tears when he beheld the depravity of its inhabitants; a blasphemous modern version of this legend says that he did indeed ascend Vesuvius and shed tears, but it was the poor quality of the wine which made him weep.

In Italy the Jesuits long produced an excellent Frascati—and (as will be seen) do again today. During the seventeenth and eighteenth centuries they grew wine for sacramental purposes in America; in Paraguay, in Baja California, and in Louisiana where there is some evidence that they were the first vignerons to attempt to exploit native American vines.

Another order of "clerks regular" are the Vincentians or Lazarists, the order founded in the seventeenth century by St Vincent de Paul to bring religion to the poor in isolated country districts as well as in urban slums. (Some may remember that fine old film of the 1940s, *Monsieur Vincent,* in which the late Pierre Fresnay—an agnostic—gave such a moving performance.) In the Graves the Vincentians are commemorated by a peculiarly illustrious vineyard, that of Château La Mission-Haut-Brion. Cocks et Féret, the magisterial directory of Bordeaux wines, pays them a considerable tribute: "These priests with their shrewd intelligence possessed in the very highest degree the ability to select a vineyard and then to cherish its vines. Their thorough knowledge of the science enabled them to develop the very finest cépage possible." Ironically, though this glorious claret was originally intended by its creators for the delectation of Princes of the Church, it became the favourite wine of the most dissipated French rake of the entire eighteenth century—the Duc de Richelieu. At the Revolution the fathers were evicted, their vineyard being sold in November 1792 for 302,000 livres (£12,000 in English money of the time). But their little chapel, next to the château, is beautifully maintained even today.

Local legend says that St Vincent—not St Vincent de Paul, but a St Vincent from fourth-century Spain who is the patron saint of all winelovers—grew so deeply depressed by the lack of good wine in Heaven that God gave him permission to revisit Burgundy and Bordeaux. Vincent overstayed his leave and the angels sent to fetch him home eventually found the saint in the cellars of the Mission-Haut-Brion, horribly drunk. The *bon Dieu* was so annoyed that he promptly turned poor

Vincent into stone. The petrified saint may still be seen at the Mission, at least (in Morton Shand's words) "a curiously primitive statuette of a bearded, mitred figure with a vacant, wine-sodden expression, frantically clutching at a bunch of grapes".

The Vincentians seem to have had another vineyard in Gascony, but of less distinction. This was Château la Croix-David at Bourgeais (Lansac) on the right bank of the Dordogne.

Even hermits have cultivated the grape. Unfortunately no connection can be proved between wine-growing and the hermit Aemilianus from whom Saint-Emilion takes its name—although one finds a Château l'Hermitage in the Saint-Emilion. The outstanding hermit's wine is of course to be found on the Rhône. There is a legend that the Hermitage vineyards, on the left bank of the river, were first planted in 1224, by the hermit Gaspard de Sterimberg, once a knight who had fought in the Albigensian Crusade. What may be the ruins of his chapel stands on a hill above the vineyards. It is said that both chapel and vines were bestowed upon him by Queen Blanche, the mother of St Louis.

Some connoisseurs think that a really good Hermitage ranks with a great burgundy or claret. Saintsbury described a red Hermitage as "the *manliest* French wine I ever drank". The wine has the merit of living to a vast age, some having been known to endure for a century. As Dr Middleton said in *The Egoist,* "Ancient Hermitage has the light of the Antique, the merit that it can grow to an extreme old age." Unfortunately its virtues seldom appear before 20 years and, as nowadays few people have the time or the money to spare, they have in consequence become almost forgotten. A classical red Hermitage is therefore rarely to be found. Modern growers are using new methods to produce a quick-maturing wine, which can best be described as a passable alternative to the lesser burgundies.

Many orders of nuns besides Benedictines and Cistercians have owned vineyards and have frequently worked in them. In Beaune the cellars of the Visitandines—an order founded by St François de Sales in the seventeenth century for widows and ladies of poor health—are a splendid witness. Another Beaune vineyard that once belonged to nuns is Clos des Ursules, commemorating the teaching Ursulines. Convent vineyards in Saint-Emilion include the Château les Demoiselles, the Clos des Religieuses and the Château des Religieuses.

One may end this chapter by describing what Hugh Johnson has called "the most remarkable and beautiful building in the whole world of wine". This is the Hospice de Beaune. In fact the nurses in picturesque habits who staff it are not nuns at all, but their work, their appearance and their associations justify the inclusion of the Hospice in this book. It was founded in 1443 by Nicolas Rolin, Garde des Sceaux (Lord Chancellor) of the Duchy of Burgundy, as a hospital for the poor and aged. The portraits of the founder and his wife, Guigone de Salins, painted by no less an artist than Roger van der Weyden, still survive. The Grande Hôtel Dieu, to give it its proper name, is an extraordinary example of fifteenth-century domestic architecture, crocketed and pinnacled with high Gothic roofs and narrow galleries, multicoloured tiles, and a cobbled courtyard. The 65 patients are still nursed in four-poster beds hung with red velvet curtains, and their medicines are dispensed from medieval albarellos by the Dames Hospitalières. The Hospice is maintained by the proceeds from certain vineyards left for this purpose by Rolin and his wife; down the centuries other benefactors have bequeathed further vineyards. Once a year their wines are auctioned at the Hôtel Dieu. These wines—more than 30—include some of the finest in Burgundy. Two are named after the nurses; one, a Beaune, Dames Hospitalières, the other a Pommard, Dames de la Charité.

Chapter 9
English Monks
and English Wine

Old summers when the monk was fat.

TENNYSON

I cannot eat but little meat,
My stomach is not good:
But sure I think, that I could drink
With him that weareth an hood.

BISHOP JOHN STILL

The Romans established the vine in Britain. It is likely that they did so in the late third century, as in AD 280 the Emperor Probus permitted the planting of vines in Gaul, Spain and Britain, where it was hitherto forbidden. The more important Roman vineyards were probably at the great villas of Somerset and Gloucestershire, though the remains of one have been found at Boxmoor in Hertfordshire. Monks may also have arrived during the later Roman period from Gaul, but there is no evidence; the legend of a Romano-British community with a wattle and daub oratory at Glastonbury could well have a basis in fact. The earliest known British monasteries were those established in Wales and Cornwall during the fifth and sixth centuries. These were not wine-producing areas yet the first Celtic monks undoubtedly had wine. Modern archaeology has shown that it continued to be imported long after the departure of the Roman troops in 407; amphorae from the eastern Mediterranean, which must have contained wine—from Rhodes or Chios, it has been suggested—have been found on the awesome cliff-site of the small fifth-century Cornish community at Tintagel (of Arthurian fame), and elsewhere. Coptic chalices of green glass have been discovered in Ireland, chalices which can only have come from Byzantine Egypt by way of Britain.

For all their imported wine these early British monks, whose monasteries were established in Iron Age hill forts or abandoned Roman fortresses, were desperately remote from the rest of Christendom. With weirdly tonsured heads (shaven in a band from ear to ear but leaving

122

long, flowing hair) and tattooed green eyelids, they were noticeably different from the monks of the European mainland, and evolved strange customs such as sacrificial bull-slayings. No Welsh or Cornish monk would join in converting the English pagans who had stolen Britain from them—and who, incidentally, had brought about the destruction of the Romano-British vineyards.

The conversion of England was begun by a Benedictine from Rome, St Augustine, the first Archbishop of Canterbury, who had been sent by another Benedictine, Pope Gregory the Great. Augustine (who may well have planted vines) founded a Church whose first glory was its monks—Cuthbert of Lindisfarne, the Venerable Bede, Alcuin of York, and Willibrod and Boniface, who converted northern Germany. It had nuns too, though comparatively few, whose abbesses were sometimes of royal blood like St Ethelburga of Barking. An Anglo-Saxon abbey was very different from the great monasteries of the high Middle Ages, consisting of a cluster of thatched wooden halls round a church that was sometimes, though not always, of stone. There were never any of the huge abbey towns of the Carolingian lands, nor any great network of monastic estates. Early English viticulture had therefore little chance of taking root in the basic economy of the island, even though the monks may have been determined vignerons.

These monks' cultural inspiration came from the Continent. Abbot Benet Biscop made several pilgrimages to Rome in the seventh century, bringing back books, pictures and stained glass on pack-mules over the Alps and along what remained of the Roman roads of Gaul. Almost certainly when the abbot took ship for the final lap of his dangerous journey he had some fine wine with him. In time such personal consignments became rarer.

In the eighth century Islamic conquests disrupted Mediterranean shipping while the internal trade of Gaul broke down. In consequence little wine came to England from the Continent until the end of the eleventh century. Yet the monks had to find wine to fill their tiny chalices of gold, silver, pewter, crystal, glass or plain earthenware from which they, and at that date their laity too, drank the Precious Blood through a silver reed (a method used by Popes until recently). If the occasional ship did reach England with a cargo of wine or raisins, such supplies were hopelessly inadequate. It has been surmised that at Jarrow cider was sometimes used for the Mass, while Alcuin actually complained of "this foreign wine made from grapes". Later, however, when he was the friend and tutor of the Emperor Charlemagne, Alcuin learnt to love real wine and no doubt that of Touraine in particular, for he spent much time at the abbey of Saint Martin at Tours. During his return to England, which lasted for two years, he wrote pathetically to a friend at court of how "the wine is gone from our wine skins and bitter beer rageth in our bellies"; fortunately he had ordered "two crates of wine, excellent and clear" from Uinter the Physician. Such shipments must have been difficult to arrange and enormously expensive.

The English monks therefore had to produce their own wine, and Bede tells us in his *History of the English Church and People* (completed in 731) that "vines are cultivated in various localities". These vines must have been planted by the monks. They used their wine not only for the Mass but also as a luxury for feast days, drinking from two-handled wassail cups. (According to a thirteenth-century *customary* of Westminster, whenever the monks there drank in the refectory they held the cup in both hands "because this was the fashion of the English people before the Normans came into the lands".) The Anglo-Saxon monks pruned their vines in February and gathered the grapes in October, which they called *Wyn Moneth;* there was even an Anglo-Saxon word for vendage —the *wîngeardnaem* or wine-garnering.

In 793 "the heathen miserably destroyed God's church in Lindisfarne by rapine and slaughter", says *The Anglo-Saxon Chronicle.* The following year Bede's old monastery at Jarrow was looted, and for a century England was ravaged by Vikings. The abbeys with their treasures were an obvious target for the pirates who bore away all the beautiful chalices and wassail cups. By 900 King Alfred—who approved a law ordering anyone who damaged a vineyard to pay compensation—found that monasticism no longer existed in England. A revival began in the tenth century under St Dunstan, abbot of Glastonbury and later Archbishop of Canterbury. It developed a peculiarly British phenomenon that survived until the Reformation, that of the cathedral-priory staffed by monks instead of canons, with a prior instead of a dean. Unfortunately the new monasticism had a very restricted revival confined to southern England. Northumbria was occupied by pagan Norse settlers and the abbeys of Bede and Benet Biscop had vanished beyond recall.

Undoubtedly viticulture benefited. A grant by King Edwy in 955 of vines at Pamborough near Wedmore to the monks of Glastonbury still survives. However, of the 38 vineyards that were listed in the Domesday Book in 1084 only a dozen were monastic; but one should remember that at the time of the Norman Conquest there were probably no more than 850 monks in the whole of England.

The Normans introduced both another monastic revival and the most flourishing period of English wine-production. Just as Frenchmen ousted English lords of the manor, French abbots were installed in all the English abbeys, while Cluny founded many dependent priories. All these new abbots and priors, and the monks who came with them, were wine-drinkers and there was an immediate increase in the number of vineyards. The last entry in the copy of *The Anglo-Saxon Chronicle* once kept at Peterborough Abbey says of the Norman abbot Martin of Peterborough ("a good monk and a good man") that he "admitted many monks and planted vineyards".

The accession of Henry II in the mid-twelfth century, with all his great possessions in western France, resulted in a considerable rise in the amount of imported wine. To begin with the bulk came from Anjou, via the port of La Rochelle. It was the otherwise deplorable King John who first brought the wines of Gascony to England in large quantities. Eventually special wine-fleets plied between Southampton and Bordeaux, as many as 1,000 vessels being engaged in the trade. Understandably magnates preferred fine French vintages to their own thin wines, and this preference was not restricted to the rich; in the late fourteenth century, England, with a population of under two million, was drinking far more claret than it does today. The result was to make English viticulture an almost entirely monastic preserve, even if a few lay vineyards persisted until about 1400, as at Windsor. Many of the latter were taken over by the monks, often as legacies. There was a sound economic reason for their doing so.

Until about 1100 English monks were all Benedictines—the "Old English Black Monks". But then new orders arrived, Cistercians, Premonstratensian and Augustinian Canons and Carthusians. In the thirteenth century came the friars. In that golden age of English monasticism every order attracted vast numbers of recruits; in 1160 the Cistercian community at Rievaulx in Yorkshire was 740 strong, and some other houses grew nearly as big. The Black Monks also increased their membership. On the eve of the Black Death in the mid-fourteenth century there were 1,000 English religious houses containing perhaps 14,000 monks, friars and canons regular and 3,000 nuns. By then every important abbey had become a vast complex with church, refectory, dormitory, chapterhouse, infirmary, guest house, courtyards and cloisters, enclosed by a high battlemented wall; outside were barns, fishponds, gardens and vineyards—though the latter were often within the abbey precinct.

With their choir monks, lay brethren and serfs, monasteries possessed a work force whose produce could undercut the cheapest foreign imports. And besides making economic sense there were other reasons why English monks should turn to viticulture. First, Benedictine and Cistercian monasteries are, ideally, self-supporting. Second, vineyards provide an opportunity for the manual labour, which is an essential part of the Benedictine rule, in a form well suited for the novitiate of aspirant choir monks; they could work within the monastery precincts, under the eye of the novice master (even today there are Benedictine, Cistercian and Jesuit vineyards worked by novices, though not in England). It was therefore well worth the monks' while to cultivate the vine.

Eventually there may have been as many as 300 monastic vineyards in medieval England, though the majority have almost certainly not been identified—there was rarely any reason to mention them in documents. The monks may even have introduced European techniques. The remains of what may well have been terrace cultivation exist at Fladbury in the Vale of Evesham (an independent abbey in the seventh century but later absorbed by the Black Monks of Worcester), at Great and Little Hampton in Worcestershire, and at Claverton in Somerset. Although the terraces at St Catherine's Chapel next to the Benedictine Abbotsbury in Dorset are "lynchets" constructed during the Iron Age for growing grain, there is a tradition that the monks used them to catch sun for their grapes. The same method is employed all along the Rhine in areas that enjoy no better weather—some German wines actually do better in rainy years. William of Malmesbury, describing the fenland abbey of Thorney in the twelfth century, tells his readers that there vines grow along the ground or raised on low stakes *(bajulos palos)*—as in the Médoc today. This method seems also to have been in use in the vineyard at Christchurch, Canterbury—its site was probably near St Gregory's Church—in 1152 and in the vineyard at Abingdon in 1388, while both Gerald of Wales and Alexander Neckhem (writing in the twelfth and thirteenth centuries respectively) speak of vines being grown on stakes or trellises.

The monastic vineyards of England were mainly confined to ten counties. Those in the Severn Valley and the Vale of Evesham and in the South East—Kent, Sussex and Hampshire—were the most reputable, especially in the areas where the best hops are grown today (a few farmers are now replanting hopfields with vines). About 1125 William of Malmesbury claimed that in Gloucestershire, "The country is more thickly planted with vineyards than any other part of England and they are more productive and far more pleasant in flavour. For the wines do not offend the mouth with sharpness, being no less sweet than those of France." Michael Drayton, who was born in 1563, wrote:

> *For Gloster in times past her selfe did highly prize*
> *When in her pride she nourisht goodly Vines*
> *And oft her cares represt with her delicious Wines.*

The Black Monks of Gloucester Abbey no doubt grew their grapes at Viney Hill outside Gloucester. Benedictine Gloucester is for some the most beautiful of all English abbeys, especially notable for its exquisite cloister and a monumental trough in which the monks washed their hands and faces. Of other abbeys in the county, Tewkesbury also had its own vineyards, while at Deerhurst there was a vineyard that belonged to far-off Westminster.

Yet even Gloucestershire took second place to Worcestershire, of which the late Edward Hyams claimed "until about 1300 the region was a sort of English Bordeaux". Here over 20 monastic vineyards have been identified and doubtless there were others. The Benedictines of the cathedral-priory of Worcester owned vineyards at Fladbury, Hallow, Grimley, Brushley, St Martins, Cotheridge and Broadwas; at the latter the villeins of Doddenham Priory—a dependency of the cathedral—were bound to work two days a year in the monks' vineyard. Pershore, another great Benedictine house, had its own vines, as well as those growing within sight of it at Hunger Hill and Allesborough Hill, besides others at Severn Stoke, Leigh and Abberton. Evesham, the third of the county's great monasteries, possessed vineyards at Great and Little Hampton and at South Littleham. Tewkesbury, although in Gloucestershire, owned no less than four vineyards at Chaddesley in 1290. Nor were the Black Monks the only monastic vignerons in Worcestershire—the Augustinian Canons of Droitwich Priory also produced wine. Yet most of these Worcestershire vineyards seem to have been converted into parkland at some time during the thirteenth century—hardly any are mentioned after 1300. The exception is Abberton, which, in lay hands, appears to have survived even the Dissolution and may have been making wine as late as 1554. But though the *Victoria County History* states "the Vineyard is a field name of fairly common occurrence in Worcestershire", there is no evidence that any of the county's other monastery vineyards continued into the sixteenth century.

Worcester Cathedral still retains some of its monastic buildings, overlooking the Severn. King John's will is kept in the chapter-house—his tomb is in the cathedral. At Pershore, founded in 689 and the oldest of the three monasteries, half of the former abbey church is still in use; it looks down on another noble river, the Avon, and has been called the loveliest parish church in England. Of the once mighty abbey of Evesham, which dates from 702, only an entrance arch, Norman gate-house and a magnificent Perpendicular bell-tower remain on its green hill above the Avon; Simon de Montfort is buried here. Until the Dissolution the abbot ruled the town of Evesham as though it were his personal property. Either directly or through their tenants, these three mighty Benedictine houses initiated perhaps the most important viticultural expansion in English history—though one must not exaggerate its scale.

Among many other Benedictine abbeys and priories which owned vineyards were Westminster, St Albans, Canterbury, Glastonbury,

Abingdon, Bury St Edmunds, Norwich, Rochester, St Mary's York, Ely and Winchester (reputedly the producer of the best wine in England). Vine Street Police Station is on the site of the old Westminster vineyard. At St Albans part of the main street was formerly known as the "Vinetry". The remains of a gate which led into the monk's vineyard still exist at Bury St Edmunds. At Norwich the vineyard appears to have been in a cloister, the monks paying to have it replanted in 1297, 1300 and 1323. Readers of Charles Dickens's *Edwin Drood* will remember the lawn called "The Vines", next to Rochester Cathedral. This too is a former monastic vineyard, granted expressly for the purpose by William the Conqueror's brother, Odo of Bayeux; its produce was supplemented from a vineyard at Halling outside the city—in 1325 Bishop Hamo of Rochester sent a gift of his wine to Edward II.

Vine Hill, near the ancient London church of St Etheldreda, was once a vineyard belonging to Ely; in 1299 the monks of Ely paid the large sum of 35s. 3½d. for the erection of a thornwood hedge 121 perches long around this Holborn vineyard, an area of about four acres, capable of producing 1,600 gallons of wine a year. Both men and women were employed to weed and dig it over, being paid 69s. 1½d. in 1299. At Ely itself, known as *l'Isle des Vignes* to the Normans, the vignerons toiling amid the fens must have seen the building of the great octagonal lanthorn over the cathedral priory in the fourteenth century—perhaps the men who built it slaked their thirst with Ely wine. The Ely monks had other vineyards as well, near Cambridge and at Somersham Manor in Huntingdonshire.

Essex was another important centre of medieval English viticulture. Most of its vines seem to have been in lay hands, though clearly some passed to the monasteries by bequest or purchase. A vineyard near Little Maplestead was acquired by the local commandery of Hospitallers (Knights of Malta), whose characteristic round church (originally a Templar style) is still standing. It is possible—though disputed— that the Knights had another vineyard in one of the Farringdon wards of the City of London, near their Grand Priory at Clerkenwell.

A tonic wine seems to have been made in Wiltshire. We know from the Liberate Rolls of Henry III that in 1241 the Cluniac Prior of Ogbourne St George presented him with three tuns of iron-flavoured *(ferratum)* wine. This monastic tradition of medicinal wine has been revived in modern times by the Benedictines of Buckfast.

The vine was even cultivated in Wales. The twelfth-century historian Gerald of Wales writes of excellent vines grown at the monastery of Caerleon-upon-Usk when he was a boy, while the Cistercians of Margam in West Glamorgan certainly had a vineyard in 1186. (In the nineteenth century the Marquess of Bute tried to produce wine at Castell Coch, with disappointing results.) But there was no shortage of foreign vintages in medieval Wales. A wealthy fifteenth-century nobleman like the renowned

Rhys ap Maradudd of Tywyn could, according to his bard Dafydd Nanmor, import large quantities direct "from the rich vineyards over the south waters".

As elsewhere in Europe, English monks made their tenants plant vineyards, exacting tithes of grapes and wine. A few abbeys would have produced a surprisingly large vintage in good years, especially in Worcestershire. Some vineyards were quite big—the Domesday Book mentions two of 12 acres—though even a small area under vines can yield a considerable quantity of wine. No one knows where the monks pressed their grapes, but it is not too much to suppose that it often took place in the great abbey tithe barns. These were sometimes old Saxon halls adapted to a new use, and from which the barns derived their distinctive construction. As for machinery it is possible, though this again is only surmise, that cider-presses were employed. Obviously the English vendage was a fairly simple business, small consignments of grapes being brought in from a number of small, widely scattered vineyards. The wine would have been matured in the wood and then put into leather bottles, of the sort which held farm labourers' cider until the last century.

What did old English wine taste like? We do not know what types of grape were grown—with the probable exception of the Pinot Meunier— so only the wildest guesswork is possible. The few reds may have been a bit like the German Spätburgunder; others were coloured with fruit juice—from mulberries or, as at Rochester, blackberries (from Halling and Snodland) and would have been distinctly curious. The whites, to judge from modern English wine, may have resembled the rougher vintages of Germany and Austria—rather like coarse Schluck. Although in bad years it is very thin and sour, this was not always so, as William of Malmesbury makes plain in his praise of Gloucestershire wine. However, those acquainted with modern English viticulture will admit that while some English wine is palatable enough, a good deal suffers from being made from grapes that have not had sufficient sun. Indeed some writers allege, entirely without evidence, that the later English vineyards' sole function was to make verjuice—unfermented grape juice. Possibly some of their produce was sold in this way, but even then it is more than likely that it was purchased by vintners to turn into wine. And there is ample evidence that up to the end of the fourteenth century the abbey vineyards made their own wine. When in 1336 the abbot of the Cistercians at Beaulieu in Hampshire was formally rebuked by his fellow abbots "for drinking with knights", he may well have been drinking his produce. All monasteries consumed a great deal, and home-grown wine must have been a useful supplement to the expensive imported vintages.

As Dom Knowles admits, "the monastic good cheer was to continue as a commonplace until the Reformation and beyond". He considers that the Black Monks may have drunk a little more than their rule intended, for the medieval Englishman was famed throughout Christen-

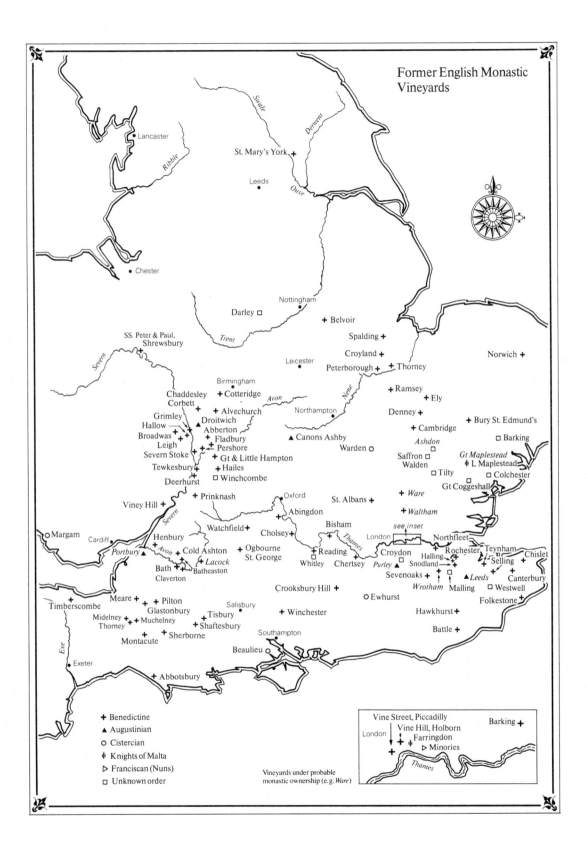

Former English Monastic Vineyards

Lancaster

Ribble

Swale

Derwent

St. Mary's York

Leeds

Ouse

Chester

Nottingham

Darley □

Belvoir +

Trent

Spalding +

Croyland +

Leicester

Peterborough + + Thorney

Norwich +

SS. Peter & Paul,
Shrewsbury

Severn

Chaddesley
Corbett

Birmingham
+ Cotteridge

Avon

Ramsey +

Ely +

Grimley
Hallow — +
Broadwas +
Leigh +
Severn Stoke +
Tewkesbury +
Deerhurst +

+ Alvechurch
+ Droitwich
Abberton +
+ Fladbury
+ Pershore
+ Gt & Little Hampton
+ Hailes
□ Winchcombe

Northampton

Nene

Denney +

Cambridge +

+ Bury St. Edmund's

□ Barking

Warden ○

Canons Ashby ▲

Ashdon

Saffron □
Walden

□ Tilty

Gt Maplestead
⚕ *L Maplestead*
□ Colchester

Gt Coggeshall

Viney Hill + +

+ Prinknash

Severn

Oxford

Abingdon +

St. Albans +

Bisham +

Ware +

+ *Waltham*

see inset

London

Northfleet +

○ Margam

Cardiff

Henbury +
Portbury ▲

Avon
+ Cold Ashton
+ *Lacock*

Watchfield +

Cholsey +

Thames

Reading +
Whitley +

Chertsey +

Croydon +
Purley ▲

Halling +
Snodland

Sevenoaks

Wrotham

Rochester +
+
+ +
Malling ▲ *Leeds*

Teynham
+
+ Selling

Chislet +

Canterbury +

□ Westwell

Bath +
Claverton
+ Batheaston

Timbercombe +
Meare +
Midelney +
Thorney +
+ Pilton
Glastonbury +
+ Muchelney

Crooksbury Hill +

○ Ewhurst

Folkestone +

Salisbury

+ Tisbury
+ Shaftesbury

+ Winchester

Hawkhurst +

Montacute +
+ Sherborne

Southampton

Battle +

Exe

Exeter •

+ Abbotsbury

Beaulieu ○

+ Benedictine

▲ Augustinian

○ Cistercian

⚕ Knights of Malta

▷ Franciscan (Nuns)

□ Unknown order

Vineyards under probable
monastic ownership (e.g. *Ware*)

Vine Street, Piccadilly
Vine Hill, Holborn
Farringdon
▷ Minories

London

Barking +

Thames

dom for heavy drinking. The spiteful Gerald of Wales informs us that the twelfth-century Benedictines of Christchurch, Canterbury, served at their table excessively large quantities of mulled wine, ordinary wine, "unfermented wine" and mulberry wine (perhaps a coloured white). Even if Gerald was exaggerating, it appears to be beyond dispute that the Black Monks of Battle Abbey in Sussex were each allowed a gallon of wine a day, an allowance which was increased for brethren who fell ill.

While some monks—and nuns too—may have been thankful for such consolations, it is only just to stress that in all orders there were men and women who drank wine sparingly if at all. The early Cistercians, and the Carthusians of any period, led lives of the utmost self-denial. The opulent Benedictine abbeys could produce such noble ascetics as Thomas de la Mare of St Albans, who died in 1396 aged 87 after having been a monk for 70 years and an abbot for nearly 50. He rarely ate or drank more than once a day and "with a charming smile" made brethren who came late to dinner forfeit their wine.

In fairness, too, it must be said that wine had to take the place of tea and coffee, and even in certain seasons of green vegetables, while what was undrunk may have gone for alms. Water being unhealthy, beer was the basic drink of English monks, though it was very different from the modern English bitter made with hops; it was either very strong, like barley wine or the audit ale still to be found at Trinity College, Cambridge, or else like the weak small beer which is dispensed even now at the medieval Hospital of St Cross at Winchester. On feast days there was often mead *(hydromella)*, especially in Anglo-Saxon times when wine was a precious luxury. Extra allowances of food known as pittances supplemented the two meals of the Benedictine rule and these frequently included wine. On great feast days there were always special *caritates* of wine at dinner and at supper.

As in Prussia and Poland, English wine was frequently improved by additives. The posset cup was valued as a hot beverage with the wine drunk mulled, heated with honey and spices. There was also *hypocras,* a wine cup flavoured with cinnamon, sunflower seeds, ginger and pepper, and sweetened with sugar, which was much in vogue in medieval England. Chaucer wrote of one of his characters in the *Canterbury Tales*:

> *He drinketh ipocras, claree, and vernage*
> *Of spyces hote, t'encresen his corage.*

("Vernage" was the Tuscan *vernaccia* which Dante respected so much that he placed Pope Martin IV in Purgatory for *"digiuno l'anguille di Bolsena e la vernaccia"*—"eating the famous eels of Bolzano boiled in vernaccia".)

Beyond question lack of sun discouraged the monks. In 1230 vines were planted on a hillside at Pilton Manor near Shepton Mallet in

Somerset, the summer palace of the abbots of Glastonbury, and in 1235 William the Goldsmith was appointed to manage the vineyard and see that its grapes were made into wine. Yet after only 30 years the vines were uprooted and the hillside was converted into a game-park. It would seem that a series of bad summers from about 1220 to 1260 dealt a heavy blow to medieval English viticulture, and not just to Pilton. In Worcestershire Grimley and Droitwich ceased about 1240 and many of the county's other vineyards came to an abrupt end in the mid-thirteenth century. It is probably significant that the abbot of Bath sold his monastery's vineyard at Timberscombe in 1240. In Kent, Christchurch was given up by 1230 at the latest. The monks did not possess such modern techniques as *chaptalisation* (adding honey or sugar to aid fermentation), which can make sunless vintages more palatable. None the less, a few monastic vineyards persisted, a fact that should encourage modern growers.

It is pleasant to record that today the very same site at Pilton has been replanted and is producing agreeable white wine, possibly the best in England. Nothing remains of the palace of the abbots. "Palace" is perhaps a misnomer. In 1240 abbot Michael of Amesbury built a comparatively modest house among the vines; it consisted of a great hall, a solar, two chambers, a kitchen and, significantly, a cellar—in addition there was a tithe barn, the predecessor of the mighty fourteenth-century barn which still stands. Alas, the only building to survive from abbot Michael's day is the dovecote. However, although the monks' buildings have gone, they were replaced in the eighteenth century by a charming Gothick house which even now gives Pilton something of a monastic air. Other modern English vignerons have planted vines on or near former abbey vineyards. At Wilberton in the Isle of Ely a wine is produced from grapes which grow not far from the Benedictine cathedral priory; fittingly it is called "St Etheldreda". Another present-day vineyard with a monastic ancestry is Beaulieu, from which comes rosé as well as white. The modern vineyard at Brede in Sussex also has monkish associations, though admittedly somewhat tenuous; here the parish church belonged to the Benedictines of Fécamp. (The nearby manor house in part inspired Rumer Godden's novel *This House of Brede*.)

English wine, doctored or not, constituted only a small proportion of what was drunk by the monks. Like everyone else they drank imported vintages. Cistercian Quarr in the Isle of Wight frequently chartered a ship from Southampton to bring back a cargo of claret from Gascony; the vessel would be part of the large wine-fleet which gathered in the Solent late every summer. Chartering in this way must have been expensive because the sailors had to face the perils of Biscay storms and Basque pirates. One wonders whether the Cluniac priories in England were sent burgundy by their mother house—it is more than likely.

Probably the wines most enjoyed by medieval English monks were the heavy, sweet products of Cyprus and Greece such as Malmsey (i.e. from

Monemvasia), which were particularly sought after in a sugar-starved age but which have less appeal for modern palates. The last prior of Worcester, Dan William More, who resigned at the Dissolution in 1536, has left accounts in his own hand which include such items as "a potell of secke & a potell of red wyne"; "on Cristmas day 1 quarte of mawmesey"; and "a potell of osey & a potell of rumney". Osey was "Aussay" or sweet Alsatian wine, while rumney was Romany—i.e. wine from Romany or Romania, the land of the Greek "Keysers" (Byzantine Emperors).

One may well ask why the English monks persevered with their own erratic vintages when so much good foreign wine was available. There were probably two reasons in particular. First, the English climate was —and is—no less suited to wine-growing than that of Germany or Czechoslovakia or, in exceptionally bad summers, even from that of Champagne (the still white champagne of a sunless year is undrinkable). Second, much imported wine was of very poor quality—sour, insufficiently racked and fined, and full of lees, or what is now called corked. The quality which the medieval wine-drinker sought above all else was clearness. The best red *clairet* was often a blend of red and white wine, while the worst was sometimes white mixed with fruit juice. The English monks did at least know what they were drinking when they drank their own wines.

What killed English viticulture was not so much bad weather as the collapse of the monastic work force. The great pandemic known as the Black Death, the recurrent outbreaks of which lasted from 1348 to 1370, had a catastrophic effect on all orders. The plague came to St Albans at Easter 1349, taking the abbot and 48 other monks. At Westminster the same year the abbot and 26 brethren perished. At Cistercian Newenham in Devon only the abbot and two monks survived from a community that had been 25 strong. Some houses were entirely wiped out. By 1370 the number of English monks, friars and canons had dropped to about 8,000 compared with 14,000 a hundred years previously. Lay brothers virtually disappeared and their place could not be filled by servants and hired farm workers who had to be paid. In consequence cells and granges were less efficient and it was impossible to run even the abbeys themselves in the old way; in 1538 Rievaulx had only 22 monks compared with 740 —the population of a minor medieval town—in the twelfth century.

Even before the Black Death all orders had been moving away from working the land themselves towards an economy of rents and leases, and this process now accelerated. Viticulture had no attraction for the new tenant farmers, who had to pay labourers increasingly high wages. The last Canterbury vineyard was given up in 1350, a significant date. Henceforward evidence for viticulture of any sort in England becomes rarer and rarer. Abingdon was still making wine in 1388, but obviously on a very small scale; in that year the abbey vineyard sold 13s. 4d. worth of wine, 20s. ½d. worth of grapes, 2s. worth of verjuice and 4d. worth of vines. Probably most monastic vineyards ceased production in the fifteenth century when there was a flood of imported wine; in 1448-49 three million gallons came from Bordeaux alone.

About 1540 the ex-Carthusian Dr Andrew Borde wrote: "But this I do say, that all the kyngdomes of the worlde haue not so many sondry kyndes of wynes as be in Englande and yet there is nothynge to make wyne of." Nevertheless, there were undoubtedly grapes in Tudor England and it is safe to assume that some English monasteries continued to produce a little wine until the very end. There was certainly a vineyard at Cistercian Warden in Bedfordshire in 1535, when the subprior was caught in it with a whore; at least, according to that liar Dr Layton. (This is where the Warden pear comes from, introduced by the White Monks; it is commemorated in the abbey arms—azure, with a crozier between three gold pears.) Moreover Claverton in Somerset was a lay vineyard—though belonging briefly to Bath abbey—with a history of wine-production which endured from the early Middle Ages until the eighteenth century; its terraces could still be discerned in the 1950s.

The monastic inspiration had been waning since the thirteenth century. After the Black Death there was a very rapid decline. Some religious remained exemplary, like the Carthusians and the new Franciscans at Greenwich (Queen Catherine of Aragon's favourite community); others caused scandal—fox-hunting abbots, wenching friars, nuns who kept hordes of lapdogs. Most, however, lived a comfortable second-rate life, fulfilling the basic requirements of their rule while taking advantage of any possible mitigation. A typical example was eating meat; the rule forbade it, so the brethren dined in the infirmary where it was allowed. They began to be paid wages and to have their own rooms.

The abbeys themselves remained as splendid as ever. The impression they gave at first sight must have been rather like a combination of cathedral and Oxford college—particularly striking in a small town or in the depths of the countryside. Some of the cathedral priories have survived, but they have lost their outbuildings, their farms and their walls; together with their old opulence, the jewelled shrines, gold plate and wonderful libraries. Until the end the monks continued to beautify the abbeys, as at Fountains in Yorkshire, where in the 1520s the Cistercian abbot Marmaduke Huby built a mighty bell-tower—glorious but none the less a symptom of decay.

By the sixteenth century an abbot was more of a county magnate than a father of souls. A monk would speak of "my master", not of "Fr. Abbot". Such a superior lived apart from his brethren in a palatial abbot's lodging, where he was waited on by gentlemen and maintained considerable state. Often he entertained nobles and even royalty, who frequently kept the great feasts at an abbey and sometimes stayed for long periods. Many abbots possessed a lodging in London as well, for

25 of them sat in the House of Lords until the Dissolution, like the abbots of Glastonbury and Westminster. (The Prior of the Knights of Malta at Clerkenwell ranked as premier baron of England.) In his own county an abbot was as great a man as any Duke and often dominated the local town. An "abbot ambling on his pad" in his black fur cape and surrounded by his gentlemen-in-waiting must have been a much more imposing figure than Chaucer's "abbot able", who was probably only the prior of some small house.

One of these princely abbots provided a hint as to how English monks actually drank their own wine. In June 1538, Dr Layton, the most infamous of the commissioners charged with finding evidence for the Dissolution, alleged that Dan John Cordrey, abbot of Bisham in Berkshire, sat in his chamber over a mixture of white wine, sugar, borage leaves and sack "whereof he doth sip mightly until midnight" (possibly *the* Pimms No. 1!). The abbot may well have been drinking his own white wine; Bisham certainly had vineyards at one time.

The Reformation was not the only cause of the Dissolution of the Monasteries. Historians discern a radical change in the mental and social climate of the early sixteenth century. Anti-clericalism, or at least a hostile attitude towards clerics, joined forces with a new breed of ruthless, ambitious men. Moreover many Catholics could see little use in the abbeys. Some of the monks themselves agreed. In 1537 Dan Richard Beely of Pershore alleged that in his monastery "Monkes drynk an bowll after collacyon tell ten or xii of the clock, and cum to mattens as dronck as myss [mice]." First the smaller houses went down in 1536, then the greater in 1538. It is debatable how much society was affected—all one can say is that on the whole rich men profited and poor men suffered. Aesthetically the Dissolution was a tragedy. Not only were the monks' beautiful buildings wrecked or demolished but their wonderful libraries were scattered—manuscripts went in bulk to be wrapping paper or serve the privy. From the vignerons' point of view the fall of the abbeys was the end of a tradition that had endured since Roman times. John Parkinson, author of the seventeenth-century *Theatre of Plants,* unhesitatingly attributed the decline of English wine-growing to the passing of the English monks with whom "the knowledge of how to order a vineyard is entirely perished".

The monks were long remembered. Poor men lamented the sheep runs which replaced the abbey farms and cost them their living, while rich men feared a Catholic restoration which might make them disgorge monastic property. The seventeenth-century historian Sir Henry Spelman believed that the Dissolution had been sacrilege, that a curse had fallen upon those families who had purchased abbey lands. In the eighteenth and nineteenth centuries what remained of the abbeys inspired romantic awe. As late as 1849 Charlotte Brontë (in *Shirley*) could speak of "a phantom abbess or mist-pale nun among the wet and weedy relics of that ruined sanctuary of theirs mouldering in the core of the wood". Since then the scouring and restoring activities of the Department of the Environment have dispelled much of the magic.

The picture of English viticulture which has emerged in this account is somewhat different from that usually given, so a summary may be useful. When the monks first arrived in Saxon England they planted wine for the Mass. But although wine-growing became a recognized part of early English life, it never achieved economic importance. Then the Viking invasions and the virtual extinction of English monasticism, followed by a very slow and restricted recovery, made it impossible for the monks to make another significant contribution to viticulture until after the Norman Conquest. From 1100 to about 1220 the area of land under vines rose dramatically; this was the most important period of English wine-growing and for most of it vineyards were all but entirely in the hands of the monks—their vast labour force made it practical for them alone to cultivate the vine on a large scale when so much imported wine was available. Unfortunately a seemingly interminable series of bad summers caused a large number of monastic growers to lose heart and to abandon their vineyards. An even worse blow was the diminution of the monastic work force and the switch to a tenant farmer economy, accelerated by the Black Death. Certain abbey vineyards carried on into the fifteenth and even sixteenth centuries despite the flood of imported wine; probably a little abbey wine was produced until the end. But the Dissolution of the Monasteries was not, as has so often been stated, the reason for the death of English wine-growing; it had been dying for many years, even at the abbeys.

One may well ask why did the monks fail to establish English viticulture on a permanent basis, when they succeeded in Germany where the climate is scarely more suitable. For it is an historical rather than a geographical accident that England is not yet truly a wine-growing country. There were two fundamental reasons for the English monks' failure. First, the German monasteries, bigger, better organized and more numerous—England never possessed anything like the great Carolingian abbeys with their vast estates—began growing vines much earlier and on a far larger scale. In consequence viticulture soon became a vital element in the German monastic economy, as it never was in England, while the monks of Germany were able to recover far more quickly from the devastation of the ninth and tenth centuries. Second, during the breakdown of trade in the Dark Ages there was always a market in Germany for home-grown wines; there were great Imperial and noble villas whose lords were eager to buy the local vintages, which were easily shipped along the Rhine and the Moselle and their tributaries. When long-distance trade revived, German wines were sufficiently established to compete with imported wines. In contrast English vineyards were still few and struggling at a time when vast quantities of cheap but excellent foreign wine began to flood the land. Indeed the wonder is that there were as many English vines as there were. The little abbey vineyards of Worcestershire and Gloucestershire, of Ely, Abingdon and Canterbury and all the rest were a remarkable achievement in such adverse circumstances.

It is surprising that English medieval viticulture, let alone English monastic viticulture, has never been the object of a genuinely scientific and scholarly investigation. The late Miss M. K. James produced a number of brilliant papers on the import of wine (published posthumously in 1971 as *The Medieval English Wine Trade*), but until a scholar of equal distinction turns his—or her—attention to English viticulture in the Middle Ages, we must remain largely in the dark.

The monk vignerons of medieval England may have bequeathed a humble memorial. In 1835 Messrs Winkles stated that "in parts of the weald of Kent the vine still grows wild in the hedges". In 1951 a flourishing vine was discovered at Wrotham in Kent. Now known as the Wrotham Pinot, it has been identified as the Pinot Meunier. At Wrotham there was a summer palace of the Archbishop of Canterbury, the ruins of which may still be seen, and the Benedictines of his cathedral priory could well have planted vines. It is not too much to suppose that the Wrotham Pinot is a survivor from an English monastery vineyard.

Chapter 10
Dom Pérignon
and Champagne

Dom Pérignon loved the poor and he made good wine.

CHAMPENOIS PROVERB

un bénédictin ignorant est un être indéfinissable.

DOM DIDIER DE LA COUR (1550–1623)

The most famous of all monk vignerons is undoubtedly Dom Pérignon. The achievement of the blind old Benedictine of Hautvillers is well nigh incredible. The first wine-grower in Champagne to find a method of making white wine from black grapes, he then discovered a method of keeping the bubbles in by inventing the bottle-cork and was the creator of sparkling champagne as we know it today.

Pierre Pérignon was born at Sainte-Ménehould in eastern Champagne in 1638, the same year as Louis XIV. He belonged to a well-established family of the haute bourgeoisie, his father being a legal official. Nothing is known of his childhood. In 1658, when he was 19, he entered the famous Benedictine abbey of Saint Vanne at Verdun, where he was professed. This tells us a little about him. Saint Vanne was a strict community, the centre of a whole congregation of like-minded houses. As with the very similar Maurists, there was an unusually strong emphasis on learning. The founder of the congregation, Dom Didier de la Cour, was insistent that "an ignorant Benedictine is a nondescript". Although history was their preferred study, the brethren did not neglect science. The "Vannist" tradition seems to have made a marked impression upon Dom Pérignon; we know that he was regarded by his contemporaries as being extremely learned. His successor as cellarer of Hautvillers, Frère Pierre, tells us of his concern with detail. It is evident that Dom Pérignon had a trained and methodical mind and a genuine spirit of scientific inquiry, both of which must have been acquired during his formative years at Saint Vanne.

We also know that this excellent monk suffered from weak sight. In later life he went blind. His affliction may well have had its compensations—the deprivation of one sense often develops others and it is more than probable that Dom Pérignon had the most wonderful nose and palate.

Either in 1668 or 1670 he became cellarer at Hautvillers near Épernay, on a vine-covered slope over the river Marne. It is not known when he left Saint Vanne. Hautvillers was one of the most famous monasteries in northern France. Founded in the year 650 it enjoyed great prestige, producing no less than nine Archbishop-Dukes of Reims, the Cathedral where the Kings of France were crowned, and also possessing a peculiarly sacred relic. This was the reputed body of St Helena, mother of the Emperor Constantine the Great and discoverer of the True Cross. Her body was stolen from its shrine at Rome in 841 by a priest of Reims, and performed so many wonders in Champagne—which included rain-making for vignerons—that the Pope forgave the theft and allowed Hautvillers to keep St Helena. She continued to work a gratifying number of miracles and Hautvillers became something of a local Lourdes. Understandably the abbey benefited, acquiring considerable wealth. Among its properties were some peculiarly desirable vineyards. By 1636 Hautvillers possessed 100 acres of vines, besides a vast amount of wine in tithes. It therefore owned a larger acreage than any modern champagne firm, save Moët, and enjoyed a larger selection of grapes.

However, the wine which the abbey produced when Dom Pérignon first came there bore little resemblance to today's sparkling champagne. Not only was it still but it varied in colour, being neither red nor white but reddish or grey—*vin gris*. Admittedly, this variety of colour, *"clairet, rosé-gris, fauvelets, flives, entre blanc et rouge, de couleur oeil de perdrix"*, was not unattractive—and such wine was held in high esteem, being a favourite of both Henri IV and Louis XIV. Indeed a grey champagne was drunk by the French Kings at their coronations; for centuries they were the only Catholic laymen who were allowed to communicate in both kinds like a priest, which gives some indication of the wine's high repute. A good deal was taken down the Marne by barge to Paris, where it enjoyed a considerable vogue; many a Parisian who had never tasted claret was familiar with grey champagne.

As cellarer (or procurator) of Hautvillers, Dom Pérignon was the monastery's man of business, in charge of all matters of finance and administration. He was responsible for catering, clothing, building and maintenance; for managing the abbey estates and providing for the local charities—he appears to have been especially efficient at the latter, being long remembered for his benevolence to the local poor. In addition, he ran the monastery's woodlands and vineyards. A cellarer was judged by his ability to increase the revenues of his house and a well-known means was to improve the quality and sale of its wines. Dom Pérignon seemed determined to do this from the moment that he took office.

His first step was to dig deep cellars beneath the abbey, far more extensive than any it had had hitherto, and also *celliers* or above-ground stores. Work began in 1673. He then set out to make red champagne instead of *vin gris*. The black grape of Champagne is the Pinot Noir, but because of the northerly climate the cépage seldom ripens sufficiently to produce enough redness; hence the grey, partridge-eye, or faintly reddish colour of the ancient vintages. Through careful observation, Dom Pérignon evolved a method of producing red champagne by systematic selection and by using grapes from old vines, which have tenderer skins more responsive to the sun than those grown on young vines. He was only able to do so in years when the sun was unusually good. (I have followed Mr Patrick Forbes here; André Simon and others seem to have thought that before Dom Pérignon most champagne was a still red wine, and that *vin gris* was a novelty in the seventeenth century.)

In addition to the traditional *vin gris* a small quantity of still, white champagne had always been made from white grapes. At its best it was much valued. Dom Pérignon's successor Frère Pierre recommended it for its health-giving properties. It is still made in small quantities and is a deep yellow and dry but fruity. Unfortunately, it is only good in unusually sunny years. Dom Pérignon sought a means of making white wine from black grapes. This he did by developing a special technique of pressing—with carefully chosen unbruised grapes and using only the first part of the must.

The cellarer also improved his vines steadily, by careful planting and replanting. In harvesting he abandoned the traditional hit-or-miss process, evolving rational methods of judging the ripeness of the grapes and then blending different strains. His successor and pupil, Frère Pierre, tells us in a pamphlet written in 1730 that "Père Pérignon" had samples of the grapes brought to him as they were ripening, and having left them for a night on his window-sill, would taste them before breakfast: "He made up his blends not only according to the juice's flavour, but also according to what the year's weather had been like, whether there was an early or a late ripening caused by the degree of cold or rain, and according to whether the vines had grown thick or sparse leaves". Dom Grossard, who wrote in 1821 and had been the last cellarer of Hautvillers, says in a letter that, "When the *vendange* grew near, Dom Pérignon would tell Frère Philippe 'Go and bring me grapes from Prières, Côtes-à-bras, Barillets, Quartiers or Clos Sainte-Hélène.' He could tell at once, without having to be told what grapes came from which vineyard, and would say 'The wine of that vineyard must be married with the wine of this one' and he never made a mistake."

By 1690 the red and white wines of Hautvillers were famous. In 1694 they sold for such a high price that the amount was inscribed on the abbey wine-press. Notables from all over France were ordering them.

Yet even now the old man was not content. A second fermentation producing a *petillant* or slightly bubbling effect takes place in many wines, especially in the spring—the Italian Barbera is one example, champagne is another. The process must have been particularly noticeable when glass bottles were introduced, which happened while Dom Pérignon was at Hautvillers. He sought with inexhaustible patience how to capture wine at a certain moment of aeration and to preserve the delicious process. But it was impossible with the bottle stoppers then in use, wooden plugs wrapped in hemp soaked in olive oil which effectively prevented gases from leaving the bottle and stopped the second fermentation. It is likely that he experimented with various types of stopper before the legendary visit of two Spanish monks to his abbey—it is said that he suddenly noticed their water bottles were plugged with cork bark. In whatever way Dom Pérignon may have made the discovery, it seems beyond question that he was the first to realize the possibilities of the cork. Eventually, after years of patient trial, he produced the first truly great sparkling champagne as we know it, probably about the year 1698.

By 1700 his wine was fetching double the price of the best of the old champagnes. It became the favourite beverage of the Duc d'Orléans, who was appointed Regent of France in 1715; an inveterate drunkard, he was tipsy on sparkling champagne almost every night and had it served in vast quantities at his orgies in the Palais Royal. Later it became the preferred wine of Mme de Pompadour, who once said, "Champagne is the only wine which leaves a woman beautiful after drinking it."

It reached England in small quantities, being restricted by heavy duties, but was none the less drunk with enthusiasm by the boorish George II. Once the tariff barriers were down it conquered the English. Byron wrote of it in *Don Juan*:

> *Champagne with foaming whirls*
> *As white as Cleopatra's melted pearls.*

The poet agreed with Mme de Pompadour in considering it the only truly feminine wine. One should point out that Byron's champagne, like all pre-Victorian champagne, was sweet and more like the common French taste of today. Even in the 1860s it was sweet, the drink of George Leybourne's "Champagne Charlie"—that immortally vulgar and delightful song.

Many people have found it impossible to give champagne sufficient praise. Yet Balzac, a dedicated sybarite, referred in *Les Illusions Perdues* to "that most vulgar of all meals—oysters, Châteaubriand steak and Brie, washed down with Champagne". George Saintsbury also had his reservations: "Nothing, perhaps, does you so much good if you do not drink it too often; but, for my own part, '*toujours Champagne*' would nauseate me in a week or less." André Simon disagreed; he always drank a bottle a day and lived to the age of 93.

Dom Pérignon died in 1715, lamented not only by his brethren but also by the poor and all the vignerons of Champagne. He was buried in the church of Hautvillers, where the black marble slab which commemorates him may still be seen. There is also a carved relief that depicts the monk looking appreciatively at a bottle, though this is of fairly recent origin. The church, together with one side of the cloister, is all that remains of the abbey, most of which was destroyed after the Revolution. The good old cellarer has never received any ecclesiastical honours, and one may look in vain for his name in the *Catholic Encyclopaedia*. However, he has been given what amounts to local canonization by the Champenois, who will never forget how much they owe him as the creator of their prosperity.

Fêtes in his honour are still held in what was once the gardens of Hautvillers. The Champagne traders have also shown their gratitude. In recent years Moët et Chandon have been marketing a special marque from their very finest cuvée. They call it "Dom Pérignon" and, with its pretty label and elegantly distinctive bottle, this sometimes glorious wine has become famous.

Pierre Pérignon is indeed the outstanding example of a monk vigneron. Yet there must have been many like him in other quiet monasteries, old monks with equal skill and patience, handicapped only by the accident of inferior soil and of less glorious vines.

Chapter 11
Californian
Mission Wines

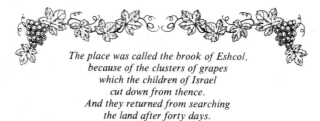

The place was called the brook of Eshcol,
because of the clusters of grapes
which the children of Israel
cut down from thence.
And they returned from searching
the land after forty days.

NUMBERS

We have planted [vines], in the hope
that this land of California
will produce wine for the Mass.

PADRE EUSEBIUS KINO (1683)

It was the Jesuits and the Franciscans who pioneered wine-growing in California, and their experience was an exact repetition of what had happened in the Old World during the Dark Ages. They came to a wilderness where they first made wine for their sacramental needs and then for their tables. Finally they were followed by secular growers who built a thriving industry.

When we speak of California, we tend to think of one of the United States. However, this area, formerly known as Alta or Upper California, did not cease to be Mexican until after the war of 1846; the long promontory which stretches from its southern border down into the Pacific Ocean is Baja or Lower California, an arid and barren land which is still part of Mexico. Upper California was not colonized until only 35 years before the revolt of the Spanish colonies and only 80 before it was taken over by the "Gringos". To modern Californians the Franciscan mission stations are the oldest non-Indian buildings in their land, displaced relics of the Old World washed up on the Pacific littoral.

The Jesuits had begun to establish missions in the wilder areas of Mexico in 1590. Although wine had been grown at Mexico City and elsewhere since the 1520s, the vineyards were too far away from the more distant missions. The Jesuits' requirements were a little different from those of the monks who had colonized the European wilderness; since the thirteenth century the Catholic laity had not taken Communion in both

144

kinds, so considerably less wine was needed. Moreover, since the sixteenth century altar wine had had to be exclusively white (this was because of the introduction of the "purificator", a white cloth with which the chalice is wiped after Communion—red stains were considered undesirable for symbolic reasons). Even so, to ensure a modest amount of white wine the missionaries planted vines.

The grape used by the Jesuits was one of European origin. The native vines were unsuitable, though the very fact that they grew there showed that viticulture was possible. The Mission grape is not a particularly good cépage and lacks acidity. However, it bears large clusters of fair-sized reddish-brown grapes and is able to resist most of the parasites that destroy many other varieties of European vine—indeed it is probably a Spanish vine grafted on to a native American vine by the first settlers, being already well established when the Jesuits adopted it. Moreover, it did not need a vineyard but could easily be grown on the mission walls themselves.

The first Jesuit mission in Baja California was established among the docile Pima Indians. It was a failure, but it is worthy of notice that a Tyrolese Jesuit, Padre Eusebius Kino, planted vine cuttings at Nuestra Señora de los Dolores as soon as he arrived. In 1697 a second mission by Padre Juan Ugarte was more successful and he grew wine for the Mass at his settlement of San Francisco Xavier. From Baja California Jesuit explorers pushed on into Arizona.

But before they could build mission stations in these more northerly lands, the Jesuits were dealt a terrible blow which put an end to their work. Their gentle and altruistic ways had earned them so much success with the Indians that the resulting prosperity of their missions aroused fierce jealousy throughout the Spanish Indies. They had set up a kind of Utopia in Paraguay, rigorously excluding slave raiders and merchants and even raising an army to protect the Indians, which caused particular resentment. In the Age of the Enlightenment the order was already unpopular in Europe and in 1759 it was banished from Portugal, in 1767 from Spain and the colonies of both. In 1773 the Jesuits were formally

suppressed by Pope Clement XIV. They did not re-establish themselves until Pius VII's bull of 1814.

Fortunately the Jesuit missions in Baja California were handed over to Franciscans, and when the Spanish government announced its intention of settling Upper California the friars were ready. In July 1769 a party of soldiers and brown-habited Franciscans landed at San Diego where, despite attacks by hostile Indians, they founded a mission station in the brushwood.

The friars' leader was a Spaniard of peasant origin from Mallorca, Fra Junipéro Serra, who although nearly 60 and crippled by a painful limp, was a man of extraordinary vigour and tenacity as well as saintliness. He belonged to a branch of the Franciscan Friars Minor and though "discalced"—i.e. wearing sandals but never socks—did not sport a beard like a Capuchin. Within three years he had established four more mission stations—San Carlos Borromeo, San Antonio, San Gabriel and San Luis Obispo. In October 1776 he founded San Francisco de Asis (or Mission Dolores as it was usually called) on the outer shore of a great inland bay, the beginning of today's wonderful city where his little church can still be found. When Fra Junipéro died in 1784 there were nine mission stations in Upper California. Eventually there were 21 in all, the last and most northerly being San Francisco de Solano, which in 1823 was established in the Sonoma Valley, a saucer-shaped valley in the hills. They were linked by the *Camino Real* or King's Highway, a rough but serviceable road running northwards along the coast, sometimes called the Mission Trail. The stations were each about 14 leagues apart— i.e. about a day's hard riding for the friars.

Californian Indians were very different from the magnificent tribesmen of the Plains. Small and un-prepossessing, they had hitherto lived a brutish existence supporting themselves by primitive fishing, or scavenging for roots and berries and even carrion. Most were lazy and timid and hardly warlike, even if they occasionally attacked the missions with wooden clubs and stone-tipped arrows. There were exceptions, such as the Yuma, who were highly intelligent and dangerous, but they were a small minority. However, the friars were quite undeterred by the unattractive nature of their flock.

The Franciscans' strategy was to lure the Indians out of the wilderness and then settle them in *pueblos* or villages around the mission stations where they could be more easily converted. The bait was a far better standard of living, with regular food, protection from Yuma tribesmen on the war path (the governor at Monterey detailed half a dozen soldiers to guard each station), and music concerts. The fathers even taught the Indians Spanish dancing—an elderly friar with castanets demonstrating a bolero or a fandango must have been an unforgettable sight.

A typical mission station was a four-sided compound around a patio with a fountain, built of massive white-washed adobe (mud brick) and

thick redwood timber, with low-pitched red-tiled roofs, each side being about 600 feet long. Its buildings included a church (sometimes of stone), a friary, barracks, warehouses, a school-room and training shops. In the words of Fra Junipéro himself, the Indians worked "at all kinds of mission labour, as farmhands, herdsmen, cowboys, shepherds, millers, diggers, gardeners, carpenters, farmers, irrigators, reapers, blacksmiths, sacristans". At their height the mission *pueblos* held over 30,000 Indians. In 1834 they owned 140,000 head of cattle, 130,000 sheep, 12,000 horses and mules and a huge herd of pigs. Yet there were rarely more than two friars at each station.

Alta California could only be reached from Mexico by a dangerous sea voyage along a rocky coast; the land route through desert country being too long and arduous. In consequence there were few colonists— 1,200 at most by the early 1800s, later rising to a mere 4,000—mainly gathered in ranches and haciendas round the port (and the administrative capital) of Monterey, and around Los Angeles. The latter was settled in 1781 from Mission San Gabriel and by 1830 had 1,500 settlers. The mission stations dominated the idyllic pioneer life, just as the abbeys had done in the Old World during the Dark Ages—there is a striking resemblance between Californian missions and Carolingian monastery towns of a thousand years before.

At Mission San Gabriel one may still see the winery which Fra Junipéro built in 1771, though the famous old "Trinity Vine" dates from after the friars' time. San Gabriel and San Fernando were the centres of Franciscan wine-making. Indians pressed the grapes on a stone floor, the must draining off into an adobe pool, where it was collected in leather bags and taken to the fermenting tanks. The friars made a dry white altar wine and also a sweet dessert wine which they called Angelica.

Angelica can still be found in California. (It has won the approval of Mr Harry Waugh in *Bacchus on the Wing*.) An amber-coloured wine, which has been compared to tawny port, it is a great favourite with local connoisseurs, but unfortunately is produced in such small quantities as to be virtually unknown outside the State of California. It is made by a curious process that is probably unique. Mission grapes—nowadays often replaced by the Chardonnay—after all traces of stem have been removed, are crushed; the juice is run off when it has fermented only slightly and *aguardiente* is added, introducing at least 20 per cent alcohol, which immediately checks further fermentation (the friars' brandy was supposed to be "as strong as their faith"). The name Angelica is sometimes said to derive from the wine being first made near Los Angeles; another explanation is that the friars considered such nectar deserved a heavenly name, while a third alternative is that it was christened to impress the Indians, who no doubt received an occasional glass or two as a reward. (Wisely, the Franciscans never taught their flock the secrets of wine-making or distilling.)

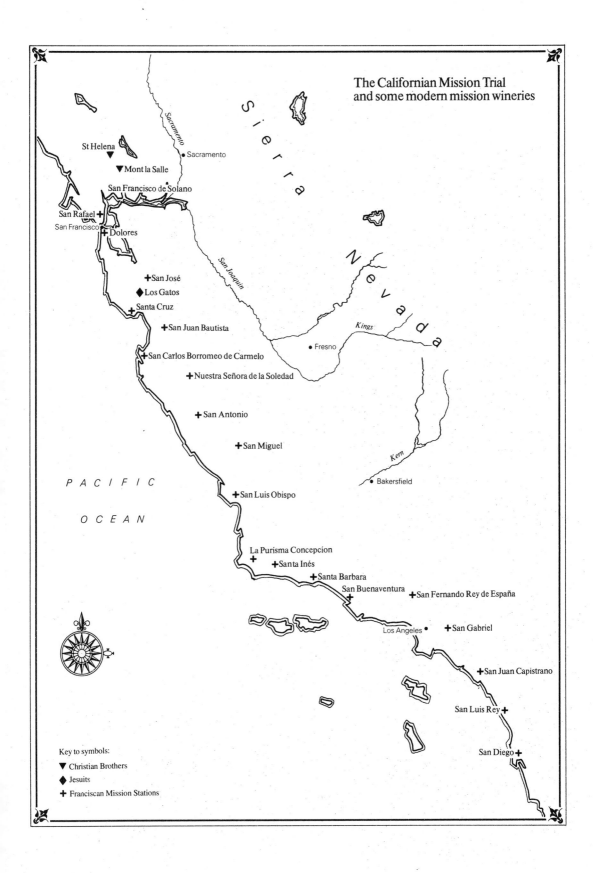

The Californian Mission Trial
and some modern mission wineries

Sierra

Nevada

Sacramento

• Sacramento

St Helena
▼

▼ Mont la Salle

San Francisco de Solano

San Rafael ✚
San Francisco • ✚ Dolores

San Joaquin

✚ San José

◆ Los Gatos

✚ Santa Cruz

✚ San Juan Bautista

✚ San Carlos Borromeo de Carmelo

✚ Nuestra Señora de la Soledad

Kings

• Fresno

✚ San Antonio

✚ San Miguel

Kern

• Bakersfield

PACIFIC

OCEAN

✚ San Luis Obispo

La Purísma Concepcíon
✚
✚ Santa Inés

✚ Santa Barbara
San Buenaventura
✚   ✚ San Fernando Rey de España

Los Angeles •   ✚ San Gabriel

✚ San Juan Capistrano

San Luis Rey ✚

San Diego ✚

Key to symbols:

▼ Christian Brothers

◆ Jesuits

✚ Franciscan Mission Stations

The last mission vineyards were those planted at San Francisco de Solano. In 1825 one was started near the mission itself, purely for sacramental purposes; it is still being cultivated, though with a different cépage. A second was established at Buena Vista in 1832, amid the eucalyptus trees; today this vineyard is the most famous traditional winery in California. Buena Vista was planted for commercial purposes; with the arrival of more settlers the friars had begun to sell their surplus produce. It was an exact repetition of the experience of the monk vignerons in early medieval Europe. By 1831 there was a thriving wine industry run almost entirely by Franciscans. (Though by then there were also a few lay growers.)

In 1833 the Mexican government decided to secularize all religious houses and in 1834-35 the Californian missions were dissolved. "Secularization" was complete by 1837. The friars had wanted to transfer the stations to the Indians, whom they regarded as the rightful owners, but they were seized by politicians and officials. Brutally exploited as cheap labour and paid almost entirely in *aguardiente,* the Indians were quickly reduced to a state of near slavery and soon dwindled to a few thousand; even this pitiful remnant was exterminated by the worse elements among the Yankee settlers who arrived in the 1840s. For a time it seemed that the Californian wine industry would collapse. But by 1837 a lay vigneron was following in the friars' footsteps, a Bordelais *ranchero* born Jean Louis Vignes who changed his name to Don Luis del Aliso. He introduced new vines and in his vineyards near Los Angeles eventually produced much more, and much better, wine than the Franciscans. In the Sonoma valley, where the friars had established their northernmost mission, the same role was played by General Vallejo and later by Count Agoston Haraszthy, a Hungarian refugee who has been called "The Father of Californian Viticulture".

Yet that title surely belongs to Fra Junipéro. Even if the friars' wines can hardly compare with the delicious vintages of today, and although their Mission grape has long been superseded, the Franciscans were unquestionably the founders of the great Californian tradition of wine-growing. Their beautiful mission stations played the same role as the abbeys of Cluny and Cîteaux. Finally, it is pleasant to record that the friars are still being worthily followed in California by the Christian Brothers and by the Jesuits. But that story must wait for another chapter.

Chapter 12
"Waters of Life"

J'avais l'estomac tout ensoleillé.

ALPHONSE DAUDET

*It is a most gallant tree of the Sun,
very sympathetic to the body of man;
and this is the reason
spirit of wine is the greatest
cordial among all vegetables.*

NICHOLAS CULPEPER

The religious orders have played a considerable part in the development of distilling. The art is sometimes said to have reached western Europe from the East or Moorish Spain between 1050 and 1100, but there is no evidence of this. However, wine was definitely being distilled in northern Italy by 1100, when the Camaldolese hermits were using a mixture of aqua-vitae and overripe plum juice as a remedy for malaria. *Acqua-di-vita* was imported to France as *eau-de-vie* and then spread north as *brentwein* or *brandwein* ("burnt wine"), from which the English word brandy is derived.

In their early days spirits were regarded as essentially medicinal—hence the name "waters of life". They were also extremely difficult and expensive to produce and in consequence were not widely available until the mid-seventeeth century. Before that time monks were best equipped for such an uncommercial enterprise. They continued distilling after new methods were introduced, and from about 1650 a remarkable number of monasteries developed their own liqueurs. In addition, it seems that certain abbeys in Normandy and Brittany distilled Calvados and Apple-jack from cider and "apple marc". (The manufacture of Calvados from English cider could provide a much needed income for some of today's English monasteries.)

Most liqueurs consist of a brandy base with an infusion of fruit or herbs. Religious orders nearly always preferred to make a liqueur rather than pure spirits. Sometimes they did so with a little too much enthusiasm. In 1668 the Gesuati (not to be confused with the Jesuits), who should have been devoting their time to nursing the plague-stricken, were supressed by Rome because the order's "entire labour" was taken up by the distillation of liqueurs and scent. (They are commemorated by two fine churches, still to be seen at Venice, and some wonderful Baroque music.)

In 1534 François I, the *roi chevalier,* visited the Black Monks' abbey of Fécamp on the Norman coast, where he was much taken with a delicious amber-coloured cordial which they served him. He gave it the name it still bears today, Benedictine. It had been made at Fécamp since 1510 by a Venetian father, Dom Bernardo Vincelli. It has the customary cognac base, sweetened with honey and an infusion of some 27 herbs including balm (melisse), hyssop and angelica—and later China tea. In the seventeenth century Fécamp joined the austere congregation of Saint Maur, whose chief labour was history and·who produced such mighty historians as Mabillon and Martène. None the less, the monks of Fécamp still found time to make the elixir *Fiscanensis* (to give it its Latin title). During the Revolution the abbey was burnt to the ground and, though the monks eventually returned, their secret seemed lost for ever. Then, 70 years after the destruction of Fécamp, Alexandre le Grand, a relative of the commissioner who had administered the ruined abbey during the Revolution, discovered the formula among some old papers. Today the liqueur is known throughout the world; it contains 43 per cent alcohol and all the old herbs (though China tea is no longer among them). The famous letters DOM do not refer to the monk's title, but stand for the Benedictine motto *Deo optimo maximo*—"to God the greatest good." In 1876 the firm which now makes and markets the liqueur built a fantastic Renaissance-cum-Gothic distillery and museum on part of the site of the old abbey of Fécamp. The same firm also makes Benedictine in Spain.

There are other Benedictine liqueurs. Kloster Ettal, a copper-domed Rococo ziggurat in Bavaria, is probably the most northerly. Ettal is near Oberammergau on the Austrian border, and was founded by the Wittelsbachs in 1330 amid the wild Bavarian mountains. It was dissolved in 1803, but the monks returned at the beginning of the present century. The chief glory is the church, begun in 1744 by Enrico Zuccali, with its exuberant stucco—half-Italian, half-Austrian. The abbey makes a jade-green liqueur, of 77 per cent proof, and also a yellow variety of 73 per cent; some is put into chocolates which are sold by the monks.

The Benedictines of Samos in Galicia in Spain make palatable liqueurs. So too do the monks of the abbey of Abu Ghosh, near Jerusalem, who produce one from oranges which is similar to Cointreau. (The name Abu Ghosh means "Father of Lies".)

Somehow one does not associate Cistercians with liqueurs. Yet they have produced some extremely pleasant varieties. During Dom Meglinger's never-to-be-forgotten visit to Cîteaux in 1667 he received a delightful surprise. He and his brethren were given by the abbot of Clairveaux six bottles of the *"liquor Bernardinus",* which was *"pro medicinali jentacule et deliciis"* ("both reviving and delicious"). Alas, this is no longer made but it must have been very like the Trappistine still produced at the abbey of La Grâce Dieu near Doubs in Franche Comté; unusual in having a purely Armagnac base, its herbs are picked by the monks on the local mountains; it tastes rather like a rustic Benedictine but is much less sweet besides being paler in colour and gentler. In the 1890s the virtues of Trappistine were advertised in a peculiarly decadent and incongruous poster by Alphonse Mucha, though the lady on it at least wears white.

Another White Monk liqueur is Aiguebelle. At the end of the last century a Fr. Hughes, who was writing a history of the Cistercian Order, found in the abbey library of Aiguebelle (near Valence) the *"Formule de la liqueur de Frère Jean"*. The green, which has a powerful bouquet with a hint of mint, now contains 35 plants—flowers, herbs, cloves and roots —which are picked and distilled in neutral alcohol by the monks themselves in copper stills, and then matured in glass-lined vats. They also make a yellow liqueur, which is a sweeter version of the green, together with various other *eaux-de-vie* including a *mirabelle* (plum), a *framboise* (raspberry) and an *abricot* (apricot); the latter is reliably reported as being "outstanding". Aiguebelle (already mentioned in the chapter on Cistercian wines) is a Romanesque monastery in a remarkable state of preservation. Swiss Trappists reoccupied it in 1815 and set about restoration work. They eventually established 14 other houses. Today its White Monks still sing the Office in a magnificent twelfth-century church, while a chapter-house, refectory and copyists' cloister have also survived from the same century.

The Cistercian liqueur that has the greatest name is La Senancole, a purely yellow fluid which resembles Chartreuse. It takes its title from the wonderfully preserved abbey of Senanque on the slopes of the savage valley of the river Senancole, in the wild and lonely mountain country near Gordes in Provence. By some miracle, Senanque, founded in 1148, has survived almost completely intact since the twelfth century, a White Monk monastery looking exactly as it must have done at the height of the Cistercian age, with a small but noble church built between 1160 and 1180. The monks returned in 1851, to be exiled once more in 1880 and return again in 1927. It is said that one day the prior, a certain Dom Marie-Augustin, was wandering through the wild scrub on the mountainside when he smelt so many delightful aromas that he had the idea of making a liqueur. As with Aiguebelle, the monks pick the herbs but the distillation is done by laymen. Yet another French Cistercian liqueur comes from the ancient abbey of Lérins, on an island opposite Marseille; "Lerina" is both green and yellow and said to "resemble Chartreuse"— without doubt it is extremely strong.

Elixir de Spa in Belgium is the creation of the Capuchin Friars—a branch of the Franciscans—who settled there in 1643. Their priory was dissolved by the Revolutionary armies in 1797, but the formula of the liqueur was discovered accidentally in an old manuscript in their library.

At the beautiful Cistercian monastery of Tre Fontane, just outside Rome, liqueurs both yellow and green are flavoured with eucalyptus leaves from trees planted by the monks. Tre Fontane has a long history, having been founded by Greek monks of the Byzantine rite and Basilican rule in 625, becoming Benedictine in 795 and finally White Monk in 1140. Other Cistercian houses in Italy which make liqueurs are Fossanova and Casamari.

The somewhat obscure Servite Friars, founded by "The Seven Founders" in 1235, produce a liqueur from pine-needles at their friary high above Florence, on the summit of Monte Senario; it is called Gemma d'Abeto ("Jewel of the Pine"). Another friars' liqueur that comes from Italy is Mentuccia ("little piece of mint"), sometimes known as *Centerbe* as it is made from 100 herbs, which are gathered in the Abruzzi mountains; the invention of a Fra San Silvestro, it is now made at the Aurum distillery near Pescara.

Six different liqueurs are made by the former Hermits—now white-habited Benedictines—of San Guglielmo at Monte Vergine near Naples. These liqueurs, one of which has an aniseed base, are made at the Loreto (see p. 59).

The Camaldolese order has already been mentioned in this book. It is the most ancient of eremitical orders, and perhaps an even rarer and more solitary vocation than that of the Carthusian. The Camaldolese have produced a number of saints besides the glorious Tommaso who changed water into wine; notably their founder St Romuald (Blessed Rudolph), St Peter Damian, Blessed Paolo Giustiniani, and also a peculiarly reactionary nineteenth-century Pope, Dom Mauro Capellari (Gregory XVI, 1831-46). The monks wear voluminous white habits and Sir Sacheverell Sitwell describes them as having an almost druidical appearance: "These Tuscan hermits, each dwelling in his little hermitage, are priests of the oak trees and of the Vallombrosan shades." The order once had branches in France, Poland and Brazil but they have long been

dissolved, though a New Camaldoli has recently been founded in (of all places) Big Sur in California. In Italy its monasteries, every one of which is named Sacro Eremo, enjoy some of the most beautiful and majestic sites of all abbeys. At the original Camaldoli, in a glade high up in the mountain woods of the Castentino, they make a liqueur flavoured with pine-needles, rather like that of the Servites, called *Lacrima d'Abeto* ("Tears of the Pine"), and also the Elixir dell' Eremita which has been compared to Chartreuse.

George Saintsbury considered Chartreuse to be one of the two kings (the other was Curaçao) of "the recognized seductions that accompany coffee after dinner" and said that none of its rivals or imitations approached it "for instruction in complexity and delight in appeal of flavour". Curiously enough, the first Carthusian who is known to have used a still is an Englishman. When in 1519 Dan Thomas Goulding was sent from the London charterhouse to that of Mount Grace in Yorkshire (whose haunting ruins are still recognizable as a charterhouse) he took with him "a doubyll styll to make with aqua-vite". The story of the greatest of all monkish cordials deserves to be told in detail.

At some time in the sixteenth century an unknown alchemist invented an elixir that was produced by infusing no less than 130 herbs in cognac and then distilling the mixture. The herbs included wormwood, carnations and pinetree buds, but the full list has never been revealed. Somehow the recipe passed into the hands of François-Hannibal d'Estrées, Marshal of the Artillery of France (and the brother of Henri IV's notorious mistress), who obviously never realized what a treasure he possessed. In 1605 he presented the formula and its complicated list of plant names to the Paris charterhouse, where it remained until the eighteenth century. There is no evidence that the fathers made any use of it during this time, and tales of Louis XIV greeting the Doge of Venice with a goblet of Chartreuse should be treated with more than a little scepticism. Then in 1737 the Prior of Paris presented the Prior-General at the Grande Chartreuse with the recipe for "The Elixir of the Marshal d'Estrées, which is a sovereign remedy of universal esteem".

It is probable that some sort of liqueur was already being distilled at the Grande Chartreuse, perhaps resembling Trappistine, while the community were fortunate to possess an experienced chemist in the person of Frère Jérôme Maubec, *"habile apotiquaire"*. After many experiments this gifted brother added three further stages of refinement to the formula, but suddenly died in his laboratory when he was on the point of perfecting it; he just had time to dictate the formula before he expired. Finally, in 1764, a Frère Antoine at last discovered how to produce commercially both an Elixir de Santé and an Elixir de Table. Brothers began to take flasks into Chambéry and Grenoble on muleback, and soon every house in the district kept a flask for use in case of sickness—the Elixir de Table appears to have been today's Green

Chartreuse, 150 per cent proof (in England it is sold at a lower strength). However, probably due to difficulties of transport, it was little known outside Dauphoné. Jean-Jacques Rousseau, who visited the Grande Chartreuse, seems to have been referring to the elixirs when he wrote in the fathers' guest-book, "I have found here rare plants and virtues rarer still."

As has been seen, the monks were evicted from the Grande Chartreuse at the Revolution. One monk, Dom Sebastien Palluis, was entrusted with the secret, but died in 1795 after terrible suffering aboard ship while being transported to Guyana. Fortunately, when in prison at Bordeaux, he had managed to pass the secret to a friend, who brought it to Dom Basil Nantais. Another copy of the precious manuscript was also entrusted to Dom Ambrose Burdet, who took refuge in England with his kinsman Sir Francis Burdett, MP, and brought it back when he returned to the Grande Chartreuse in 1817. The original manuscript was eventually acquired by a chemist who tried to sell it to the government of Napoleon; luckily they were unimpressed by the dog-eared papers, suspecting a fraud, and the manuscript was finally recovered by the monks in 1835.

It was about this time that the Carthusians recommended distilling and perfecting their liqueur. In 1838 the distillery manager, Frère Bruno Jacquet, evolved a gentler and less powerful liqueur than the Green "Mélisse" (balm-mint) or White Chartreuse. (This has not been made since 1900, although in the 1960s a dozen bottles were discovered at the English charterhouse of Parkminster and auctioned at Christie's.) In 1840 Frère Bruno perfected Yellow Chartreuse. He was now producing Green, Yellow and White Chartreuse and also the original "Herbal Elixir of the Grande Chartreuse"; but none of them were in much demand commercially. Then, in 1848, 30 French officers from a local garrison visited the monastery and were regaled with the Yellow; they thought it so delicious that they promised to ask for it wherever they were stationed; they kept their word and soon the monks were selling several million litres a year. It became, as it is now, their chief source of income, besides benefiting many other religious foundations and charities. In 1860 a bigger distillery was built at Fourvoirie eight miles away, but was destroyed by a landslide in 1935.

There have been several attempts to steal the secret. One, in 1850, was very nearly successful. The Sub-Procurator, Dom Théodore Mure, employed a clerk to assist in his administrative duties. One day Dom Théodore, who was in overall charge of the distillery, asked the Prior-General to left him have the manuscript as he wished to check a detail. He left it in his cell while he went to Vespers. The clerk broke in, took the manuscript, rushed back to his own room, packed and then fled in the belief that he would make his fortune. However, in his haste he had left the manuscript on the bed.

A far graver threat came in 1903 with the community's expulsion from France. The French government brazenly declared that it would continue to produce the liqueur at the Grande Chartreuse, in the naïve belief that modern science would easily discover the secret. In the event government production continued until 1929, the bottles actually bearing the Carthusian monogram, but both the new green and yellow liqueurs were greatly inferior to the original. Meanwhile the exiled monks continued to produce their old liqueurs and elixir at Tarragona in Spain, the results being as delicious as ever. When they returned to the Grande Chartreuse in 1940 they began to make them once more in their old home, though they still kept the distillery at Tarragona.

Today a vast modern distillery is operating at Voiron, near a convenient railway station and equipped with magnificent cellars. The distillery at Tarragona is still operating, for the benefit of the Spanish market; the brethren who manage Voiron spend three months a year there, while there is a permanent staff of secular employees at both distilleries. However, only the monks know what herbs to pick, how to mix them and in what proportions. There are still only two copies of the recipe in existence, the original and a transcript; one is in the possession of the Prior-General, and the other in a sealed bank deposit. Few will dispute that Chartreuse is the most mysterious and romantic of liqueurs. That elegant Edwardian "Saki" (H. H. Munro) once observed: "You can say what you like about Christianity; a religion which can produce Green Chartreuse can never really die."

Drinkers of Chartreuse and of the Carthusian wines of Mougères will have noticed both the order's monogram and emblem. The latter consists of an orb crowned by a cross in a circle beneath seven stars; the motto, which is not always printed, is *stat crux, dum volvitur orbis*— ("the cross stands firm while the world turns upside down").

The fathers are practical in choosing skilled businessmen, who in recent years have greatly increased the sales of their produce, especially in England and the USA. A fashionable modern beverage is "Chartreuse on the Rocks"—Green Chartreuse and ice. The Carthusians themselves only taste their glorious cordial on three feast days a year, and then only a small glass, though the elixir is sometimes administered to invalid monks. They also give a *vin d'honneur* to a few privileged guests, consisting of the Green and the Yellow mixed in equal proportions.

An Italian variety of Chartreuse, both green and yellow, and much milder, is called Certosa and used to be made at the fortified charterhouse of Galluzzo outside Florence on its cyprus-crowned hill. George Saintsbury writes of a red Certosa, which he found "far from bad". I have been unable to trace this, and suspect that the old man had confused Certosa with Cerasella, an Italian cherry liqueur (which was a favourite of the poet d'Annunzio). Another Certosa seems to have been made at the *certosa* of Trisulti. In Capri one can buy a "*liquore Car-*

thusia". This obviously commemorates the local *certosa* of San Giacomo (see p. 90), whose fathers may have distilled an elixir long ago. The modern liqueur could just possibly have some sort of monastic origin, but it does not appear to be distilled by Carthusians.

The nuns of Maiori on the Amalfi riviera make a liqueur in which the 20 herbs are so cunningly blended that they call it a Concierto. In Italy one may also purchase a Prugna (from plums) and a Sambucca (coffee-based) made by the Carmelite Friars of Gethsemane. Alas, many of these exotic cordials are ceasing to be produced, e.g. Carmeline. This almost forgotten liqueur, of a greenish-yellow colour, was once made at Bordeaux and I have always assumed that it was the invention of the Carmelites of that city. The agreeable Vieille Cure, which has a base of both Armagnac and Cognac and an infusion of 52 macerated tonic roots, is still produced at the abbey of Cenon, though commercially.

Finally, one may make the stupendous claim that whisky was invented by monks in Ireland, probably in the fifteenth century. However the first man who is actually known to have distilled it was a Scottish friar. The household accounts of James IV, King of the Scots, contain an item for 1494 which refers to an allowance of malt to distill *aqua-vitae* to one Friar John Cor.

Chapter 13
Bibulous Monks

I drink for the thirst to come.

RABELAIS

To drink like a Capuchin is to drink poorly;
To drink like a Benedictine is to drink deeply;
To drink like a Dominican is pot after pot;
But to drink like a Franciscan is to drink the cellar dry.

OLD FRENCH DRINKING SONG

It is strange how long the image of the guzzling, tippling monk has persisted as a stereotype in the literary tradition of western Europe. As will be seen, writer after writer has shown invincible prejudice and ignorance. For most of them the typical monk was a kind of gelded Falstaff. Few literary conventions have resulted in more injustice than that of the bibulous monk.

Ironically, the first reference to monastic tipplers is by St Benedict himself. In the rule he tells his monks not to be "wine bibbers" and refers to those monks who are "called Gyrovagues". These brethren "spend their whole lives wandering from province to province, staying three days in one monastery and four in another, ever-roaming and never stable, given up to their wills and the allurements of gluttony". Throughout the Middle Ages there were complaints about the Gyrovagues with their mighty hunger and, above all, their raging thirst.

Some of the medieval jokes about monastic boozers were quite affectionate. Mention has already been made of a ninth-century song about a wonderfully hard-drinking abbot of Angers. There is a famous medieval story called *The Hole in the Wall,* which dates from a slightly later period. Once upon a time there were two monasteries which stood side by side, but which were so strictly enclosed that neither had any communication with the other. One of them had a permanently drunken cellarer whose vagaries were so exasperating that finally his brethren walled him up in his own cellar. Hearing the noise, the community on the other side dug him out and made him their cellarer. But eventually they too were irritated beyond endurance and after some years walled him up. This time his original community heard him sneezing in his tomb and dug him out, acclaiming him as a saint and miracle-worker.

Most medieval jokes about the monks' weakness for good wine are less gentle. Nothing could be more savage than that strange poem *The Vision of Abbot Golias,* by Walter Map, a twelfth-century canon who fell out with the Cistercians over some disputed property. In his day Map was famous for witty conversation and amusing verse, and his satire was intended to discredit the White Monks. He tells how Golias, an archetype of loose-living prelates, visits a certain abbey where:

> *With restless hands and belly they drink up,*
> *Empty a full, and fill an empty cup.*
> *Of monk a monkey monstrous each becomes . . .*

Map himself liked a drink and he has even been credited—erroneously—with one of the greatest of all medieval drinking songs:

> *Mihi est propositum in taberna mori,*
> *Deus sit propitius huic potatori!*

Medieval literature is full of boozy monks and friars, of whom Robin Hood's Friar Tuck was a far from untypical figure. Chaucer and Boccaccio laughed at such brethren while others raged at them. Chaucer's friar in *The Canterbury Tales* is "a wantowne and a merye" who "knew the tavernes wel in every town".

At the English Dissolution of the Monasteries, tippling was a charge frequently made by the Commissioners. There had been much popular resentment of the pampered life of abbey servants—"idle abbey lubbers apt to do nothing but only to eat and drink." Dr Layton was always alleging that the brethren whom he met drank too much—the Premonstratensian abbot of Langdon near Dover was "the drunkenest knave living". During a dispute with the Trinitarians of Hounslow in Middlesex he claimed that the friars "drink weekly all the town dry" and had to be led home each night by the townsmen; he added that they would be "not a little missed of the ale tipplers".

As for the rest of sixteenth-century Europe, Erasmus—who had spent a miserable time as an Augustinian Canon—accuses the poor monks, in *In Praise of Folly,* of "gorging to the point of bursting", while Luther writes of "idle-bellied monks". There was sometimes more than a little substance in such allegations. In France many intelligent people who were Catholic reformers rather than Protestants had little time for the brethren. Clement Marot (*c.* 1495-1544) addressed verses to the dissolute Friar Lubin, to the lecherous Friar Thibault—"*gros et gras*"—and to a "*gros Prieur*" with his "*broc de vin blanc*". (*Broc* is best translated as "little brown jug".) The French Franciscans had a particularly bad press. In her *Heptameron* Marguerite of Navarre (1491-1549) has an embarrassing number of stories about Grey Friars who drink too much.

The Gargantuan King Henri IV's favourite oath at anything extra-ordinary was *"Ventre Saint-Gris!"*—"Belly of a Grey Friar!"

In the course of his odd career François Rabelais was both Grey Friar and monk. He was born about 1494 at the farm of La Devinière near Chinon, where his hero Pantagruel knew of a painted cellar, "having myself drunk there many a glass of cool wine". Clos la Devinière, his father's vineyard, still produces a white Chinon of some distinction. In 1511 Rabelais joined the Cordeliers at the Franciscan priory at Puy-Saint-Martin near Fontenay-le-Comte in Poitou. His superiors eventually took exception to his studying Greek and further-more accused him of "trailing his habit over the hedges"—by which they meant drinking and debauchery. He left, retaining a savage hatred of his former brethren, and entered the Benedictine house of Saint Pierre-de-Maillezais, also in Poitou and where there was an excellent library. In addition, he seems to have spent some time with the Black Monks of Ligugé nearby. However, by 1527 he had left the Benedictines as well, though remaining a priest, and went to study medicine at Mont-pellier. He spent the rest of his life as a doctor or a parish priest.

Rabelais' strange books tell of the extraordinary feats, wars and journeys of two giant heroes, Gargantua and his son Pantagruel, which culminate in a pilgrimage to the Oracle of the Holy Bottle. Their mighty friend, "Friar John of the funnels and gobbets", one of the great boozers of European literature, was in fact a monk and not a friar:

> [He is] young, gallant, frisk, lusty, nimble, quick, active,
> bold, adventurous, resolute, tall, lean, wide-mouthed,
> long-nosed, a fair despatcher of morning prayers,
> unbridler of Masses, and runner over of vigils; and,
> to conclude summarily in a word, a right monk, if
> ever there was any, since the monking world monked
> a monkery: for the rest, a clerk even to the teeth in
> matter of breviary.

We first meet him exhorting his brethren to defend the abbey vineyard against plundering troops.

> Never yet did a man of worth dislike good wine, it is a
> monastical apophthegm [he tells them]. Wherefore is
> it, that our devotions were instituted to be short in the
> time of harvest and vintage, and long in the advent and
> all the winter? . . . Hark you, my masters, you that
> love the wine, Cop's body, follow me; for Sanct
> Anthony burn me as freely as a faggot, if they get
> leave to taste one drop of the liquor, that will not now
> come and fight for relief of the vine. Hog's belly, the
> goods of the Church!

Using a processional cross like a quarter-staff he then fights a tremendous battle in the vineyard—and drives out an entire army.

When feasted by Gargantua this monk shows himself to be indeed an heroic drinker. So well does he fight that Gargantua rewards him by building the abbey of Thélème where, "If any of the gallants or ladies should say 'Let us drink' they all drink." Of the onset of old age the monk tells Panurge "I find wine much sweeter now," yet "I have a more dreadful apprehension than I ever heretofore have had, of lighting on bad wine." When finally the Oracle's lady-of-honour, Princess Bacbuc, gives them a drink, he cries out, "it is gallant, sparkling Greek wine; now for God's sake, sweetheart, do but teach me how the devil you make it."

Indeed Rabelais often mentions Greek wine, probably Malmsey. He also praises another sweet wine, Frontignan. No doubt he was brought up on plenty of Chinon and red Bourgueil. The fifth chapter of *Gargantua* entitled "How they chirped over their cups", is one of the greatest paeans in praise of drinking that has ever been written:

> White wine here, wine, boys! . . . Ha, la, la, that was
> drunk to some purpose and bravely gulped over. O
> lachryma Christi, it is of the best grape? I' faith, pure
> Greek, Greek! O the fine white wine! upon my
> conscience, it is a kind of taffatas wine.

One wonders if he was drinking his father's white Chinon. He was also partial to Arbois. In 1560, seven years after he had died, his old drinking companion, Ronsard, wrote an epitaph on Rabelais to the effect that a vine would surely grow out of his grave:

> *Une vigne prendra naissance*
> *Du bon Rabelais qui boivoit*
> *Toujours ce pendant qu'il vivoit.*

The concept of jolly, gluttonous, hard-drinking monks and friars persisted in the eighteenth century, as in Hogarth's *Calais Gate*. A forgotten

French poet and playwright of the early eighteenth century, Alexis Piron, wrote a cheerful little song about a friary of tipplers whose supplies run out:

Prends ton froc,
Ton sac et ton broc;
Sus! Frère Roch!
Dans le dortoir
Tout est ce soir
Au désespoir.
Tout le salé
S'en est allé
Est avalé.

The poet ends on a grim note:

Le vin de Condrieu
Nous dit adieu.

Frère Roch would have been justified in mourning. The white wine of Condrieu on the Rhône is as rare as it is magnificent, coming from only 17 acres of vineyards, which grow the rare Viognier grape. It is particularly good with the delicious cheese *rigotte*. No doubt the friar had drunk the best Condrieu, which is the legendary Château Grillet, from a vineyard of no more than four acres. Hugh Johnson says of Château Grillet, "sooner or later every wine collector has to try it".

Voltaire and the intellectuals of the Englightenment all made fun of monasticism. One of the minor characters in *Candide* is Frère Giroflée ("Wallflower"), who is a Theatine clerk regular and not a friar as English translators make him. Candide meets Bro Giroflée in Venice, in St Mark's Square, accompanied by the pox-ridden servant girl Paquette, whose downfall began with her seduction by a Franciscan confessor. The three go off together to dine at an inn "on macaroni, Lombardy partridge and caviare, with Montepulciano, Lachryma Christi and Cyprian and Samian wines". Giroflée is not a religious by choice, his parents having forced him to take the habit: "When I return at night to my monastery, I want to dash my head against the dormitory walls." (Voltaire knew his wine—the Vino Nobile of Montepulcians, grown in the hills near the Tuscan spa town of Chianciano Terme, is Italy's greatest red wine.)

The Enlightenment was quite sure that all monks ate and drank much too much. In Montesquieu's *Lettres Persanes* one of the heroes is speaking to an abbot in a monastery library when the refectory bell rings; the monk "vanished from my sight as though he had wings". In Vienna in 1780 the Transylvanian mineralogist Count Ignaz von Born

A cellarer, from an 11th-century illuminated manuscript.

published a little book in Latin called *Monchologia,* which purported to be a natural history of monks. The Count claims that they are an entirely separate species, half-way between man and monkey, and classifies them "according to the Linnaean method". They are first defined as anthropo-morphic animals which are hooded and howl by night, and are then divided into three groups—omniverous, fish-eating and herbiverous. The omniverous Benedictine is said to fast rarely and grow thirsty about four o'clock every morning, which is why Black Monks assemble at that time. The Augustinian friar, "whose face is crapulous and whose gait is staggering", suffers from an insatiable thirst for wine and has hydro-phobia; whenever he tries to slake his raging thirst with wine he becomes still more thirsty, and even when drowning in wine he dreams of more wine. His nightly howling is at its most joyful when the vine is in blos-som. *Monchologia* became very popular is translation in mid-Victorian England, accompanied by delightful caricatures. Nevertheless for all its fun, there is a note of real hatred in the book—"monks do not marry but expose their children".

The French Revolution was prolific in cartoons of monks, frequently hilarious but always savage. One portrays a monk before and after 1789 —first enormously fat and jolly and then wretchedly thin and miserable. Another shows two abbots being pressed in a wine-press and spewing out gold coins.

William Beckford's *Letters from Portugal* convey the attitude to monks of a cultivated English gentleman of the Enlightenment. In 1787-88, furnished with introductions from the Portuguese court and accompanied by a superlative French chef, he visited the beautiful Cistercian abbey of Alcobaça—the West's largest monastery. Beckford's impressions, couched in graceful Augustan prose, are invariably cynically amused. He describes a Gargantuan cuisine that included dishes prepared according to the latest fashion in Macao, but though he refers to wine being drunk in large quantities he does not give details. His account of Alcobaça ends with the wonderfully funny scene at his departure, when the entire community are in tears at losing the services of his by now revered chef. One should supplement Beckford here by an extract from Hugh Johnson's *Wine:*

> I remember at a little inn at Alcobaça (under the shade
> of the most superb of monasteries, a palace whose
> kitchen was designed for titanic feasts—a trout-stream
> bubbles in at one end, and the chimney is like a blast
> furnace) the white wine with a savoury dish of minute
> clams had a distinct and delicious scent of wild
> strawberries. It was the local ordinary wine. It would
> have been welcome anywhere, but it did not even have
> a name."

The author of the *Physiologie du Goût,* Anthêlme Brillat-Savarin, contributed as much as anyone to the legend of monkish gourmandizing. In 1817 he took his amateur orchestra to play at a Cistercian monastery near Belley on St Bernard's day. This was the greatest feast of the White Monks' year and they certainly seem to have done it justice. Brillat-Savarin mentions a pâté as big as a church, great hams, joints of veal, and a mountain of artichokes. At one end of the refectory a fountain played over 100 bottles. After a wonderful meal in which one service consisted of 14 roasts the brethren drank marvellous coffee from great bowls, "with a noise of whales blowing in the storm". Supper was no less delicious, ending with a vat of burning, sugared brandy. What the writer omits to explain is that such banquets were exceptional even on feast days—from the date this one may well have been given to celebrate the Cistercian order's return to France.

The English of the eighteenth and nineteenth centuries divided monks into two sorts—the lean and dangerous fanatic of "Monk" Lewis's Gothick novel, and the fat and jolly toper of *The Ingoldsby Legends.* Both the thin and the fat varieties are found in the works of Sir Walter Scott. Another Romantic novelist with a taste for hard-drinking monks was Thomas Love Peacock. In *Maid Marian,* Brother Michael of Rubygill Abbey has more than a little in common with Rabelais' Friar John: "My strong points are canary and venison," he boasts, continuing to say that he considers canary (i.e. sherry) to be "the only life preserver, the true *aurum potabile,* the universal panacea for all diseases, thirst and short life". His patron saint is St Botolph (pronounced "Bottle"), a "singing friar, laughing friar, roaring friar, fighting friar, hacking friar, thwacking friar; cracking friar; joke-cracking, bottle-cracking, skull-cracking friar".

The Victorians continued to see monks in this way. In *The Talking Oak* Tennyson wrote of "Old summers, when the monk was fat." Sometimes they were censorious. That mighty Protestant historian J. A. Froude, writing of the Dissolution, says that the monks "were saturated with profligacy, with simony, with drunkeness". In *Wild Wales* George Borrow, passing the ruins of an old convent of nuns at Pengwern, reflected that it had once been "a place devoted to gorgeous idolatry and obscene lust". Even into our own day many country people have the idea that each old abbey was connected to a nunnery by a secret tunnel of enormous length.

Alphonse Daudet was the humorist who made the most elegant fun of a hard-drinking cleric. In *L'élixir du Révérend Père Gaucher* he tells the story of how a poverty-stricken Provençal monastery of Premonstratensians (or White Canons) was saved from dissolution. The cowherd, Brother Gaucher, hearing that the community has no money, comes to the Prior and tells him that his aunt had taught him how to make an incomparable liqueur from the distillation of half a dozen local herbs. The liqueur, sold in "a little flask of brown earthenware sealed with the arms of Provence and bearing a monk in ecstasy on a silver label", is a triumphant success—the narrator after drinking it says "my stomach seemed as though filled with sunshine". It is *"une liquide verte, dorée, chaude, étincelante, exquise"*. The monastery finances are restored and the monks scour the mountains for herbs, or become packers, labellers, invoicers or carriers, while Brother Gaucher is promoted to "The Reverend Father Gaucher". But the work which he alone can do has unfortunate consequences, as the community realize when he comes reeling into choir and sings a music-hall song instead of the psalm. "Hélas," sighs the Prior, "this is the second evening running when I have found him to have a certain bouquet, a certain aroma." Wisely he compromises, leaving Père Gaucher with his still but telling the brethren: *"Prions pour nôtre pauvre Père Gaucher qui sacrifie son âme aux intérêts de la communité. Oremus Domine."* None the less, even in the church they can always hear Père Gaucher singing his little song in the distillery.

Amusing though some of these stories are, they sowed a bitter harvest for the monks. Even today the ordinary man often thinks of a monk as a fat layabout, guzzling and swilli, at other people's expense; an image which down the centuries has undoubtedly contributed to much senseless persecution. Indeed, for all their joviality and good fellowship Friar Tuck and Friar John have to some degree been to monks and friars what Shylock and Jud Süss have been to Jews.

Chapter 14
Dissolution

Monks are the fleas on God Almighty's fur coat.

MARTIN LUTHER

And the vineyard which thy right hand hath planted,
and the branch that thou madest strong for thyself.
It is burned with fire, it is cut down.

PSALM 80

Monks have always aroused distaste. It is hard to say exactly why. The jokes and slanders recounted in the previous chapter depict at worst the weaknesses of cheerful drones. Undoubtedly many people are repelled by celibacy; as the ex-friar Martin Luther put it:

> *Who loves not women, wine and song,*
> *Remains a fool his whole life long.*

Yet many good Catholics who like their parish priests have been only too ready to see the abbeys go down.

Admittedly the monks have often slackened in their observance. Writing in the *Paradiso* in the early thirteenth century, Dante makes St Benedict himself say:

> *La Regola mia*
> *rimasa è per danno delle carte.*
> *(My rule*
> *is left a profitless stain upon the leaves.)*

An English Catholic of Queen Elizabeth's time, William Watson, lamented:

> The rise and fall of Monastical Orders in the Worlds
> Theater represent a mournfull tragedie of mens
> miseries; how like to flowers they have now and then
> another Order, companie or societie burgeoned,
> blossomed and flourished and yet subjecte to the fates
> of freewill in all human wights and so loose their
> primitive spirit and decaie.

Not even the most bigoted Catholic can deny that there were once far too many monks and monasteries; far too many girls placed in nunneries simply because they had no chance of husbands; far too many friars who were thieving vagabonds. Possibly the majority of abbeys became no more than comfortable country houses for communities of bachelor-gentlemen or spinster-ladies who led moderately pious but scarcely monastic lives. On the other hand all Carthusian houses remained true to their ideals, while there were reforms in many other orders, like that of the Trappists. But one cannot blame educated opinion for thinking that a drastic reduction in numbers and tightening of observance were necessary. Unfortunately, on several occasions this reaction has turned into almost total hostility and in the eighteenth century it all but destroyed Western monasticism.

Even during the Catholic Middle Ages soldiers found abbeys irresistible; sacking them with no less gusto than the Vikings or Saracens before them. The English had a particularly bad record in France in the Hundred Years War. Another threat were the Jacqueries or peasant revolts. In Bohemia the monks suffered fearfully during the first half of the fifteenth century from Czech heretics, Hussites and Taborites. Wine-growing abbeys were always especially tempting targets and untold damage was done to the vineyards.

The Reformation was a mighty blow to both monasticism and wine-growing. The Reformers considered that a monk's life, with its emphasis (to them) on good works rather than faith, was a waste of time and an insult to God; a view expressed in Luther's virulent pamphlet *On Monastic Vows,* which he wrote in 1521 for an avid readership. Probably at least half the monasteries of Catholic Europe came to an end, though by a lucky accident of history they were mainly in the vineless north. Nevertheless in 1525, during the Peasants' Revolt of that year, Kloster Eberbach had to pay a ransom of 18,000 gallons of wine; the peasants drank over half the abbey's famous vat, which was never replenished and eventually disintegrated. By 1563 Johannisberg had suffered so much from Protestant raids that the community dispersed. In 1568, no doubt attracted by its Chablis, the Huguenots sacked Pontigny and held an orgy in its cellars, wearing the White Monks' copes and chasubles. They also sacked and burnt the Cistercian manor of Perrières at Meursault. Many French abbeys experienced much worse attacks during the Wars of Religion (1562-98).

The monks' next great trial was the Thirty Years War. The Rhineland and Bavaria were the scene of countless campaigns during which army after army—Protestant and Catholic, Imperial, Swedish, Spanish and French, pillaged and plundered. Abbeys were a natural prey. At Kloster Eberbach the community was evicted by the Swedish King Gustavus Adolphus in 1631 and fled to Cologne, abandoning 198,000 gallons of wine. Three years later the Swedish Chancellor, Axel Oxenstjerna, converted the abbey into a temporary residence; no doubt he and his Lutheran soldiery made good use of the cellars. In 1637 Catholic French troops joined with the Protestant Swedes in burning to the ground the entire Cistercian monastery of Orval in Belgium, having first stolen the plate and used its church as a stable. Many other religious houses suffered the same fate as Orval. If caught their monks were tortured to make them reveal hidden treasure. Wine was a magnet—the Benedictines of Maximin Grünhaus lost 375 casks at one fell swoop.

Even in peacetime and in Catholic countries the abbeys were threatened with dissolution. In 1666 Colbert, Controller-General of France, sent a letter to King Louis XIV in which he attacked monasticism. He wrote: "Nuns and other female religious, besides failing to work for the common good, deprive the country of the children they might have borne." The King, while no enemy to the religious profession, was in some measure of agreement and ordered that no new houses should be founded without his express permission.

South Germany suffered more from Louis XIV than it had during the Thirty Years War. In 1689 his armies deliberately laid waste the beautiful Palatinate. Wine-growing towns such as Oppenheim and Worms went up in flames, as did châteaux and entire villages and, of course, abbeys. Moreover crops, fruit trees and vines were singled out for destruction, and along the Rheingau many of the greatest monastery vineyards were ruined. The French repeated their atrocities in a second invasion, while during Marlborough's and Prince Eugene's campaigns of the early 1700s Bavaria was similarly devastated and pillaged; as always the abbeys and their wine cellars attracted the "brutal and licentious" soldiery. The consequences of all these wars were what might be expected; in 1600 there had been probably 300,000 acres of land under vines in Germany—by 1713 there were only about 70,000. As the principal owners of vineyards, the brethren suffered proportionately.

Yet the abbey vignerons made a spectacular recovery. At Maximin Grünhaus they planted 102,000 new vines, so that in 1783 they were able to produce 900 *fuder* of wine—9,000 litres. An earlier chapter has told of the revival of Johannisberg which began in 1716, and of how its Benedictines pioneered a revolution in German viticulture. The Cistercians of

Kloster Eberbach did not lag behind. Planting new vineyards and experimenting with Riesling and Traminer grapes, they became sufficiently prosperous to build a stone wall seven feet high and a mile and a half long round the Steinberg in 1761-63. At Eitelsbach the Carthusians from Trier steadily improved their own beautiful wine. So long as their right to live as monks remained unquestioned, such vignerons were always able to survive the worst catastrophes.

This right was just what was questioned by eighteenth-century intellectuals. The Enlightenment was a far more terrible threat than any war. Voltaire (according to Montalembert) described a monk as one "who binds himself by an irrevocable oath to oppose Reason and be a slave, while living at the expense of others". In the *Lettres Persanes* Montesquieu says of monasticism: "this career of chastity has annihilated more men than plagues or the most savage wars." He attributes to it not only depopulation and the abandonment of agriculture but also the destruction of the will to work—"in a monastery a man can lead an easy life for which in the world outside he would have to toil and sweat." Diderot made a subtler, more envenomed, attack on monastic celibacy in his novel *La Réligieuse,* which is the story of a girl forced to become a nun against her will: some sisters are moderately good women but many are superstitious fiends or lesbians, and finally the heroine elopes with her Benedictine confessor, to end as a laundress in Paris. The author asks contemptuously, "Were monks and nuns instituted by Jesus Christ? What need has the bridegroom of so many foolish virgins?"

Britain provided some especially verbose critics of monks. Thus David Hume, writing of Henry VIII's Dissolution:

> The supine idleness . . . and its attendant, profound
> ignorance with which the convents were reproached,
> admit of no question, and though monks were the true
> preservers, as well as inventors, of the dreaming and
> captious philosophy of the schools, no manly or
> elegant knowledge could be expected among men
> whose lives, condemned to a tedious uniformity, and
> deprived of all emulation, afforded nothing to raise the
> mind or cultivate the genius.

Edward Gibbon delivered a still more magniloquent broadside in his history (the idea of which had come to him in Rome "as I sat musing amid the ruins of the Capitol, while the barefooted friars were singing vespers in the Temple of Jupiter"). He alleges, among other grave charges, that in their early days monks had "adjured the use of wine". Since then, however, "every age of the church has accused the licentiousness of the degenerate monks", though this "natural descent, from such painful and dangerous virtue, to the common vices of humanity, will not perhaps excite much grief or indignation in the mind of a philosopher". Moreover "The Lord of Irony"—still "sapping a solemn creed with solemn sneer"—had "somewhere heard or read the frank confession of a Benedictine abbot: 'My vow of poverty has given me an hundred thousand crowns a year; my vow of obedience has raised me to the rank of a sovereign prince.' I forget the consequences of his vow of chastity."

Yet Gibbon, of all people, should have known better. The footnotes in his *Decline and Fall* show again and again his indebtedness to monastic scholarship—to men such as the Benedictine Mabillon, who pioneered the scientific study of historical documents long before Ranke, or another Black Monk, Dom Bernard de Montfaucon, upon whose excellent editions of the Greek Fathers Gibbon depended. He actually refers to the Premonstratensian Vertot, the great eighteenth-century chronicler of the Knights of Malta, as "that pleasing historian". He quotes the Jesuit Mariana, the Oratorian La Bletterie—a personal acquaintance— and countless other savants who had taken vows of religion. It is ironical, moreover, that Gibbon enjoyed his bottle of Benedictine champagne as much as anybody.

Unfortunately even Catholic rulers subscribed to the ideas of the Enlightenment; bringing such pressure to bear on the Pope that he abolished Jesuits. In *ancien régime* France, opposition to monasticism culminated in 1765 with the *Commission des Réguliers* (Commission on Religious Orders), which, though Louis XV refused to dissolve all monasteries, succeeded in suppressing any community with less than nine members. In the Habsburg domains Emperor Joseph II dissolved as many as 700 monasteries, including every Carthusian priory (one casualty was the exiled English charterhouse of Sheen Anglorum which had survived in Flanders since the sixteenth century). An Imperial decree ordered the closing of all houses of the contemplative life, whose monks "contributed nothing to the good of their neighbour or society". Some allowance was made for scholarship but none for viticulture. The Habsburg lands lost a third of their abbeys, while the orders were weakened still further by the insistence on state education for every novice and on the provision of a pension for any monk who wanted to leave his monastery.

Much worse ensued at the French Revolution. It dealt Western monasticism the most terrible blow in its entire history at a time when the monks were already demoralized by the hostility of the intellectual climate. In 1790 all French monasteries were prescribed. Over 400 Benedictine and 250 Cistercian abbeys went down, together with nearly 600 friaries, 1,500 nunneries and several hundred other houses. The "moderate" Girondine, Mme Roland, declaimed: "Make certain that the Church lands are sold, for we can never be freed from these wild beasts until their lairs are destroyed and they have all been smoked out." During the terror the "wild beasts" were persecuted as enemies of the

Revolution. Far from displaying the cowardice which readers of *Monchologia* no doubt expected, the religious orders produced many examples of heroism. Poulenc's opera *Les Carmelites* tells the story as recounted by Georges Bernanos—based on an actual incident—of an entire community of nuns who went to the guillotine for their ideals. In *Waters of Silence* the Cistercian Thomas Merton has movingly recounted how the White Monks of La Trappe, determined to continue in their austere way of life, wandered through Europe to Russia and then crossed the ocean to North America before returning to France in 1816.

Napoleon shared the same "enlightened" view of monks as Mme Roland—it was one of the few Revolutionary principles which he did not abandon—and outlawed monasticism in every country he conquered. His soldiers waged a cruel war on monks and nuns throughout Europe. In Spain they turned Montserrat into a barracks, hunting the wretched Benedictines up the nearby mountains "like chamois". Even now an excellent sherry, Jerez del Convento, commemorates the ravages of Napoleonic soldiery. In 1812 some nuns of the convent of Espirito Santo at Jerez, fleeing from French troops, buried several casks of their *amontillado* beneath the cloister; it was not discovered for over a century but was quite sufficient to reconstruct the *solera*.

However, it was the spread of the Enlightenment rather than the soldiers' atrocities which caused most damage. By 1810 almost every German and Italian monastery had suffered the fate of those in France—Braunfels describes the government's attack on the abbeys in Germany as being organized like a military operation. By 1814 it seemed as though Western monasticism might die out altogether. The Carthusians, who had mustered 250 houses in 1520 and about 135 in 1789, now possessed only five in the entire world and only one which was functioning properly.

Culturally the loss was appalling. Cluny was blown up with gunpowder and turned into a quarry, a fate suffered by many other monasteries. Some were converted into prisons or lunatic asylums, as at Champmol and Prémontre. Others became farm buildings or warehouses. A large number were demolished for fear the monks might return, as at Romanée Saint-Vivant. In a few rare cases the cellars were used for their original purpose—like those of the Cistercians at Meursault, the Ursulines at Beaune and the Dominicans at Saint-Emilion. Columns and sculptures which were masterpieces of Romanesque and Gothic art served to pave the roads. Wolfgang Braunfels writes: "Precious codices were flung down from the ox-carts taking treasures from Bavarian and Swabian monasteries to the national libraries in Munich and Stuttgart in order to fill the ruts in the muddied roads."

Fortunately, at least some of the monks' treasures survived. Braunfels stresses that every museum of medieval art and every library with medieval manuscripts owes its glories to suppressed monasteries, that this is "the very basis of the existence of such museums as the Musée de

Cluny in Paris, the Germanisches Nationalmuseum in Nuremberg, the Bayerisches Nationalmuseum in München or the Wallraf-Richartz-Museum in Cologne". The very fine municipal library at Troyes contains no less than 50,000 volumes, which were once the property of the Cistercians at the abbey of Clairvaux.

Not a single French or German vineyard remained in monastic hands by 1810. The fabled Benedictine and Cistercian vignobles of Champagne and Burgundy had been put up to public auction very early on. In Germany the Rheingau, owned almost entirely by monks, changed hands practically overnight. Anti-clericals have argued speciously that the expropriation actually benefited viticulture; lay owners were more commercially minded, with more incentive to introduce technical improvements, and were more interested in producing red wines rather than sacramental whites. But, as has been seen, the monks had always been commercially minded and in the vanguard of improved techniques. Far from concentrating exclusively on wine for the altar, monks had made many reds, together with whites for the table. In fact the dispossession's effect on viticulture was disastrous. Frequently vineyards were broken up and parcelled out in tiny plots among scores of small proprietors—Clos de Vougeot is a particularly poignant example—while valuable wine-growing techniques were discarded and forgotten. Some wines have never recovered their pre-Revolutionary excellence—e.g. Saint-Pourçain.

Even the end of the Napoleonic wars failed to halt persecution. In 1835 Portugal suppressed all religious houses. Spain enacted a similar measure the following year; at Jerez the *cartuja* was turned into a cavalry barracks and its cells converted into stables. Latin America copied the example of its former rulers. There was a massive dissolution in Switzerland between 1841 and 1849. In the 1860s the Piedmontese government evicted monks who had returned and while uniting the Peninsula nearly succeeded in eradicating Italian monasticism. In 1874 the Swiss prohibited "the establishment of new, or the restoration of suppressed, monasteries". This unrelenting onslaught was due partly to Protestantism, partly to a desire for "progress" and partly to sheer greed. At Rheinau near Zürich, dissolved in 1862, it was said that the monks' one crime was that their estates were worth two million francs. Their wine always aroused envy—each dissolution provided an excuse for unscrupulous neighbours to get their hands on a coveted vineyard.

The persecution continued until the end of the nineteenth century. In the 1870s the monks who had returned to Germany were threatened by Bismarck's *Kulturkampf,* which caused the expelled monks of Beuron to settle briefly in England. Nor did persecution cease with the new century. In France Emile Combes forced through the "Laws of Association" in 1901 which suppressed all unauthorized religious houses. Here, although the motivation was partly due to the association of monks with royalism, the principal incentive was greed for the "million franc resources" of the abbeys. The Cistercians survived, but as has been seen the Carthusians had to go, while the Benedictines were driven even from Solesmes.

Another wave of senseless destruction began with the Spanish Civil War. At Sigena the Canonesses of Malta were raped and murdered by Republicans, while their superb convent with its thirteenth-century frescoes (possibly by an English artist) was burnt to the ground. Montserrat was sacked once more and its monks hunted down—22 were martyred. At Samos in Calicia—which has excellent vineyards—the entire community died. It was said that the Anarchists preferred destroying the Baroque as it burnt better than any other style.

The New World has shown itself to be no more tolerant than the Old. During this century the religious orders have suffered cruelly in Mexico. Even when the monks were allowed to return they were forbidden to wear their habits.

Needless to say, the Nazis had little time for monasticism. Most abbeys were dissolved and the brethren called up for military service. Some orders like the Teutonic Order were suppressed altogether, even though it had become a clerical instead of a knightly order; it was particularly hated by Hitler because of its Habsburg associations. Besides direct supression, countless monastic communities throughout Europe were dispersed by the ravages of war and many beautiful abbeys were destroyed beyond repair. Monte Cassino is one example, but because it is so sacred to every Benedictine it has been magnificently rebuilt.

After World War II there was persecution in Poland, Hungary, Yugoslavia, Czechoslovakia and China and once again abbeys were forcibly suppressed (though it has to be admitted that their art treasures were treated with more respect than in previous dissolutions). One would have thought that one aspect of monasticism might have appealed to Communists; the abbeys frequently constitute natural collective farms, as appears to have been recognized, if only to a very small extent, in Romania.

No doubt there will be persecutions and dissolutions as long as there are monks. Yet the distaste they have aroused seems a strange aversion in our own day when collectivism, communes and ecology are so much in fashion. It is doubly misguided for wine-lovers to dislike monks, who of all men are best suited to making wine.

Chapter 15
Monks and Wine Today

Monks and oaks are immortal.

LACORDAIRE

They that dwell under his shadow shall return;
they shall revive as the corn and grow as the vine;
the scent thereof shall be as the wine of Lebanon.

HOSEA

Many English historians write as though Western monasticism came to an end at the Reformation. Certainly one may be surprised that it did not do so at the French Revolution or during the recurrent persecutions of the nineteenth century. Yet, with a few exceptions, almost every medieval order of monks, friars or canons still exists today. It comes as something of a shock to learn that there are probably as many men and women under religious vows in modern England as there were just before the Reformation. Other countries have seen a similar monastic revival. Part of this astonishing recovery may be attributed to the Romantic movement of the last century—undoubtedly there was an element of romanticism in the inspiration of such restorers as the Benedictine Guéranger and the Dominican Lacordaire—yet beyond question it owed most to the undying appeal of the true monastic life. This appeal seems likely to survive the upheavals within Catholicism resulting from the Second Vatican Council.

Alas, although a number of monasteries continue to manufacture their traditional liqueurs, few have retained or regained their old vineyards. However, there are perhaps a score of religious houses who have planted new vines. It is surprising that there are not more. The association with viticulture is far from dead.

In 1977 there are approximately 12,000 Benedictine monks and about 3,000 Benedictine nuns. (These very rough figures include a handful of Anglicans.) One of the best known is Cardinal Basil Hume, Archbishop of Westminster and a former abbot of Ampleforth. Most of the monks continue to wear the traditional black habit, belted and with an apron or scapular, and a hood; in cold weather many communities put on the cowl—not a hood but a quilted medieval overcoat. Some still sing the poignantly beautiful Gregorian chant. A monk is styled Dom (short for *Dominus,* "Sir") instead of the medieval English Dan, though Benedictine nuns are called Dame in the old way. There are a number of modern Benedictine vineyards.

Sadly enough, one of these latter-day Black Monk vineyards had to be abandoned as recently as 1969. It was at one of the oldest and most distinguished religious houses in France, the abbey of Saint Martin at Ligugé just outside Poitiers. Founded in 363 by St Martin, this adopted the Benedictine Rule during the Dark Ages and remained a famous house until the Revolution. The Black Monks returned in 1838, Benedictines of the Solesmes Congregation, noted for their historians and liturgiologists; the abbey is now the home of the *Revue Mabillon,* the greatest of all journals of monastic history. Despite such vexations as the deliberate routing of the Paris-Madrid railway through their garden and being expelled for a further period, the community have flourished, providing a haven for Catholic intellectuals—the ex-Satanist J. K. Huysman once found sanctuary there.

For many years the monks of Ligugé produced a dark red wine, undistinguished but pleasant, with a slight taste of gooseberries. Most of this was consumed in their refectory, each monk being served his statutary half-pint a day, though guests could have more if they wished (as the author remembers with pleasure). The monks did a great deal to improve the quality of the local wines and even the most anti-clerical of the neighbourhood's farmers are still grateful to them for this—just as their pagan ancestors would have been in the Dark Ages. The reason for the abandonment of Ligugé's excellent little vineyard in 1969 was exactly the same as that which ruined monastic viticulture in medieval England— a dwindling work force. The abbey had practically ceased to recruit lay brothers, while the supply of novices had temporarily come to a halt. However, novices are returning and as manual labour is an essential part of a Benedictine novitiate one may hope for the vineyard's revival.

In Austria the Black Monks still tend vines. The huge Baroque abbey of Gottweig, which is on the bank of the Danube opposite Krems and marks the end of the Wachau wine district, produces a curious white vintage. But its excellent Benedictines do not necessarily have to drink only their own wine.

Benedictines are once more active in the Rheingau. The abbey of St Hildegard, near Eiblingen just above Rüdesheim, was built in 1910 after a fire had destroyed the old monastery at Bingen over the river (see p. 55). St Hildegard now contains a large community of Benedictine nuns who are completely self-sufficient with their own farm, cattle and generator, and who own vines in some of the choicest areas of the Rheingau. The vineyards closest to the abbey are the Klosterberg, the

Klosterlay, and one on the slopes of the Drachenstein hill. From here high quality wines are produced, ranging from a *"trockendiabetiker"*, suitable for diabetics, to *trockenbeerenauslese,* and on 6 December 1978, the feast of St Nicholas, the nuns picked grapes for what should be a delectable *eiswein.*

An abbey which was also Austrian until 1918 but is now part of the Italian Tyrol is the monastery at Muri-Gries outside Bolzano. It makes an interesting red wine from the Lagrein grape, a Santa Maddalena (or Magdalener) of the Alto Adige, which is perhaps the most individual of modern European monastic wines. The abbey was formerly a castle of the Counts of the Tyrol, who gave it to the Augustinian Canons in 1406; the latter converted its great Romanesque tower into a campanile and eventually built a fine late Baroque church. After the Augustinians' expulsion their place was taken by the Benedictines of Muri in Switzerland, who had also been expelled. (See p. 34). As so often during the later Middle Ages, the abbey vineyard is worked by laymen under the direction of a monk.

In Spain the monastery of Samos in Galicia has revived, and the tragic events of the Civil War have long been forgotten. The monks, who belong to the Subiaco congregation, produce reasonable red and white wine. They also continue to make their liqueur.

In Italy it is peculiarly fitting that the modern Monte Cassino should have its own vineyard. During the Second World War the great monastery was blown to rubble, but since then it has been completely restored with every detail of Baroque ornament carefully replaced. It contains some 30 monks who run a distinguished school. They produce a white wine for the altar, though not for the table, from vines grown in a small vineyard just below the abbey.

So far, modern England's only monastic wine is the tonic wine of Buckfast. This of course is not English at all but good-quality French or Italian red wine to which the monks add ingredients including phosphates, vanilla and green tea. The abbey of Buckfast, in Devonshire, has a romantic history. Founded in 1018, it was dissolved in 1539 and allowed to fall into decay. In 1882 French Benedictines, expelled from La Pierre-Qui-Vire in Burgundy, bought the ruins and, settling in huts on the site, began to rebuild the monastery which they completed in the 1930s. The formula of tonic wine almost certainly came from France—its earliest known name was *vin dynamique.* Originally it was made as a patent medicine with only a local sale, but since 1926 it has been marketed commercially as a medicated, health-giving wine. It is no doubt a worthy successor to the thirteenth-century iron-flavoured wine of Ogbourne St George.

Even in Israel the Black Monks continue to cultivate the grape, growing white wine at Tabgha. In Chile, not far from Santiago, there is a magnificent modern Benedictine abbey of the Subiaco congregation which makes a strong red wine from the Cabernet grape. In Western Australia the monastery of New Norcia was founded in the 1830s by Spanish Benedictines fleeing from persecution in their homeland. For many years they produced some of the best wine in the state, and have only recently ceased to do so.

At present there are about 4,000 Cistercians in the world, of both the Common and the Reformed or Trappist Observances. After the war the Reformed Observance experienced a phenomenal period of growth in the United States, largely due to the romantic spiritual writings of the Cistercian mystic Thomas Merton—his autobiography *The Seven Storey Mountain* caused hundreds of young American ex-soldiers to follow him. This growth came to a marked halt in the 1960s, while in recent years the rule of the White Monks of the Reformed Observance has been considerably relaxed.

In Austria the Cistercian abbey of Heiligenkreuz recovered long ago from its dissolution in the eighteenth century and is now occupied by White Monks of the Common Observance. It is a popular tourist resort in the Vienna Woods and even has a restaurant where one may choose one's trout from a tank. The White Monks not only staff 18 parishes but run a school for mentally retarded children. All these activities are subsidized by the income from the abbey's vineyards whose agreeable white wine is on sale in Vienna.

As wine-growers the Cistercians are once more active in Spain. At La Oliva near Carcastillo (not far from Tudela) in Navarre, they have come back to an old abbey with a twelfth-century church and fifteenth-century cloister; the monastery is surrounded by vineyards which supply an impressive number of parishes with a sweet white altar wine. The White Monk abbey of Poblet in Catalonia, once the mausoleum of the Kings of Aragon, is still one of the glories of Spain. A wonderful amalgam of architectural styles from the Gothic to the Baroque, it has inside its walls the fourteenth-century palace of King Martin with traceried windows and a beautiful external staircase. Poblet was producing notably large quantities of wine as long ago as 1316, according to a French traveller. Dissolved and sacked in 1835, it was reoccupied by Cistercians in 1940. According to reports there is now a flourishing vineyard outside the abbey walls, which is capable of providing the community with its own white wine.

In North Africa Alexis Lichine listed in the 1950s—in *Wines of France*—the wine of the Domaine de la Trappe de Staouëli as one of the best in Algeria. However this Cistercian vineyard may not have survived decolonization.

The Carthusians returned to the Grande Chartreuse in 1940—the only happy event in that grim year. Founded during the reign of William the Conqueror, they are the most unchanged and most unchanging of all monks, but have nevertheless adapted without difficulty to the present innovation in the Catholic Church. Today, including brethren and nuns, there are about 650 Carthusians and 21 charterhouses; among the latter is a monastery of white granite founded in Vermont in the 1960s. Mougères was reoccupied by Carthusians from 1935 to 1977, but its vineyards are now under lay management. Here the procurators and brothers revived the traditional Carthusian skill as vignerons. The wines of the department of Hérault are, it must be admitted, among the least considered in France—"*Les vins de Languedoc, on ne les déguste pas, on les avale.*" However, just as in the Middle Ages, the monks at Mougères demonstrated the value of monastic care and patience and also introduced new techniques of wine production. The vineyards surrounding the chartreuse's pleasant white walls and red-tiled roof cover approximately 75 acres (30 hectares) and produce a surprising number of wines including a rosé, a white and a "*vermeil*"; the cépages are the Carignan, Cinsaut and Terret grapes. Sweet wines are also made—a Grenache, a Maccabeu and a Muscat. They are among the few quality wines of Hérault and have won several prizes. Until recently these wines were served in other charterhouses on a few rare and special occasions but, alas, this is no longer the case. First the commercial demand rose to such an extent that there was none to spare, and then in 1977, owing to lack of numbers, Mougères had to be closed and its community moved to other charterhouses. But its wines remain as a memorial.

After the Order of Malta's expulsion from its island by Napoleon it moved its headquarters to Italy and during the nineteenth century began to place an increased emphasis on its Hospitaller tradition. The Knights, who number several thousand, adhere to the social canons of pre-1789 Europe, their higher ranks being open only to brethren with sufficient quarterings of nobility, while the Prince and Grand Master and about 50 others take full monastic vows and are styled "Fra". At their services all Knights still wear an unmistakably monastic black habit. The Order performs a wide range of Hospitaller activities in the Catholic areas of

western Europe and in African and American countries, with several hundred hospitals and a large fleet of hospital aircraft and trains. Its British association supports and administers the Hospital of St John and St Elizabeth in St John's Wood, together with a home for the aged and other charitable works. Such is the modern Order's international prestige that it has diplomatic recognition from 40 countries and on occasion issues passports; it maintains claims to sovereign status and HMEH the Prince and Grand Master's palace in Rome is held by some to be the world's smallest state. (Since the seventeenth century the Prince and Grand Master has been addressed as "His Most Eminent Highness" and in the Catholic Church ranks immediately after the Cardinals.)

The Order of Malta owns vineyards even today. In Austria the commandery of Mailberg in the Weinvertel has belonged to the Knights since 1128; it is a large and beautiful building, part Gothic, part Baroque. Mailberg produces a Malteser Grüner Veltliner, which Hugh Johnson considers one of the best of all Austrian wines (the Grüner Veltliner is the classic native grape of Austria). The commandery also produces quite a rarity—a good Austrian red wine. The Blaue Zweigelt Rebe is a bit like a German red hock but far stronger (nearly 11½ per cent alcohol), with much more body and bone dry. It is virtually unknown outside Austria, though the firm of Lenz Moser—which since 1969 has managed the commandery's vineyards—is now beginning to export some to Britain, along with some Grüner Veltliner (but not, so far as I know, to the United States). The third wine produced by the commandery is Schloss Mailberg, a *Sekt* or Austrian champagne. This is not to be compared with its two elegant neighbours, being dull and rather sweet, though it seems to taste much better in Austria.

In Italy, in the hills near Lake Trasimene, the Order has a commandery at the ancient Castello Magione, which long ago was a Templar preceptory. Here the Knights own vineyards which make a red wine, which is not dissimilar to chianti, and also a white. They are both called Colli del Trasimeno ("Trasimene Hills"), and should not be confused with neighbouring wines which bear the same name. The cépage of the red is about 60 to 80 per cent Sangiovese, the rest being a mixture of Ciliegiolo, Gamay, Malvasia del Chianti and Tuscan Trebbiano, producing a wine with an alcoholic content of slightly over 11 per cent; the cépage of the white is 60 to 80 per cent Tuscan Trebbiano, blended with Malvasia del Chianti, Verdicchio, Verdello and Grechetto, with an alcoholic content of 11 per cent. Large quantities are produced and it is likely that they will soon receive a DOC certificate. They are most agreeable—the white makes an excellent aperitif—and are served in the Prince and Grand Master's palace at Rome. The labels of a red and a white Capri, both grown on the island by the Marchese Ettore Patrizi, indicate some association with the Order of Malta. (They show the Patrizi arms displayed on an eight pointed Maltese cross, the heraldic achievement of a professed Knight who has taken full vows.) Unfortunately the only bottle I have been able to obtain was a red past its prime, but the two wines have an excellent name. On Malta, near Mdina, a vineyard which had belonged to the Order when it ruled the island produced until very recently a red wine for Lord Monckton, the Bailiff Grand Cross who is President of the Knights' British association.

In 1923 Archduke Eugen (a general who had contributed to the victory of the Imperial and Royal army over the Italians at Caporetto in 1917) abdicated as *Hoch-und-Deutschmeister* of the Teutonic Knights. In 1929 the Teutonic Order was re-constituted as a brotherhood of "mendicant" priests, together with sisters, who serve parishes and hospitals in Austria, Bavaria, Italy and Yugoslavia. Some of the Knights' traditions have been retained. The superior is called the *Hochmeister*, while the priest-brethren wear the great white cloak with its striking black cross (the model for the Iron Cross). The Order also includes a few "Knights of Honour", one of whom was the late Dr Adenauer. Their beautiful church and former treasury in Vienna are well worth a visit. Wine-growing is another tradition which has survived. The *Deutsch-Ordens-Schlosskellerei* is still at the Knights' old castle of Gumpoldskirche on the foothills of the Vienna Woods (see p. 110). Seven white wines and three red are produced—some from Gumpoldskirche itself, some from Lower Austria, and some from the Burgenland in the south-east and south. Among the best are the Grüner Veltliner—fruity, like all its kind—and another white, the original Gumpoldskirchner, from the vineyards near the schloss, full but fresh, and very pleasant. These vintages provide an ironically gentle memorial for the grim crusaders who once ruled Prussia and the Baltic lands.

The Augustinian Canons seem to have owned comparatively few well-known vineyards during the Middle Ages. However, the modern Augustinians of Klosterneuberg are doing their best to make up for this. The canons have been at Klosterneuberg, only a few miles north of Vienna, since the monastery's foundation in 1100 by Margrave Leopold III

—St Leopold. Today their church is, as one would expect, largely Baroque though the Gothic cloisters remain. St Leopold's chapel—where one may see his crowned skull—was originally the chapter-house. Its principal treasure is the "Verdun Altar" (once a pulpit) which portrays 50 scenes from the Bible in blue and gold *champlévé* enamel, and which was made in 1189 by the goldsmith Nicholas of Verdun; during the Russian occupation it was dismantled and hidden down a salt mine. The monastery's other buildings date from the eighteenth century and are in a particularly grandiose Baroque, the roof being ornamented with a huge Imperial crown. The Holy Roman Emperor Charles VI planned to turn the abbey into an Austrian Escorial, but the project was abandoned at his death. Its sumptuously furnished Imperial apartments are a relic of this plan, as indeed is the crown on the roof. Among their other activities the modern canons maintain and staff a theological academy and are also running 26 parishes.

Klosterneuburg produces six white wines, two reds and two sorts of *Sekt,* from a variety of vines grown in vineyards in several different regions. Good examples of the white are the Kahlenberger Jungherrn from Müller-Thurgau grapes, and the Weidlinger Predigtstuhl from Muskat Ottonel; besides winning gold medals at recent Austrian wine fairs, both have the Austrian government's *Weinguetesiegel* (WGS) or seal of official approval, which is awarded only after the wine has undergone chemical analysis and other tests by the Federal Ministry of Agriculture. Of the canons' two white wines from Grüner Veltliner vines, one is the very dry but palatable Hüttenviertel (which has been approved by the British Diabetic Association). The red wines are Klostergarten and St Laurent-Ausstich (from the St Laurent grape); each has the WGS. Of the sparkling wines Klostersekt was awarded the principal gold medal at the 1977 Austrian wine fair.

That most resourceful of all religious orders, the Society of Jesus, has a number of vineyards which are usually worked by their novices. In 1888 the Californian Jesuits moved their novitiate to Los Gatos. Here they built the Novitiate winery, which began to make wine in September 1888. The first wine-maker was Bro Constantine Valducci, who had made wine in his native Italy, while the second was Bro Louis Oliver, who is said to have been the son of a vigneron in Saint Julien in France. Los Gatos is in the south-west corner of the Santa Clara Valley, about 23 miles south of San Francisco Bay. Its original vineyards and those in the Santa Cruz mountains nearby have had to be abandoned because of the high cost of raising grapes on isolated mountain slopes, but the Novitiate winery still grows vines in California—dry wine grapes at Hollister and dessert and sherry grapes at Modesto. The winery is owned by the Jesuit order and is worked by Jesuit brothers and priests who have lay assistants. Its purpose is to produce altar wine for Catholic priests and to sell commercially what is left over, the income being used to pay for the education of Jesuit seminarians. Over the years this has paid for the education of hundreds of Californian Jesuits.

Since 1888 the winery's production has increased from 1,700 gallons to 750,000 gallons. Until 1933 there were only four kinds of wine, a dry and a sweet white, and a dry and a sweet red. The Novitiate winery now produces 12 altar wines and 21 commercial wines; both categories include dry and sweet wines and sherries. The Novitiate's best-known altar wines are L'Admirable (Angelica) and Vin Doré (Sweet Sauterne), while its best-known commercial vintages are Black Muscat (Muscat Hamburg), Muscat Frontignan, Pinot Blanc and Flor Sherry (from Palomino grapes). It is pleasant to discover that L'Admirable is the Angelica of the old Franciscan missionaries; it is made from a blend of Mission and Sauvignon Vert grapes and is 20 per cent alcohol. The Novitiate is particularly proud of the Black Muscat and the Pinot Blanc; it was the first American winery to make a dessert wine from the Muscat Hamburg grape, while the Pinot Blanc has won an impressive number of gold medals—the Jesuits still remember that the Pinot Blanc was the favourite of Graham Greene when he visited the winery in 1960.

The Novitiate also produces that speciality of modern California the Cabernet Sauvignon, which can be one of the world's truly great red wines. Unlike claret, which is a blend of Cabernet and Merlot grapes, Californian Cabernet is an unblended wine being made from the one variety of grape alone. Its drawback is that it needs considerable aging in bottles—far too much of it is drunk too young. The Novitiate Cabernet is perhaps not among the most famous Californian Cabernets but it is nevertheless a very good wine indeed.

There was, until comparatively recent times, another Jesuit winery in the United States. At Florissant in Missouri, near St Louis, the fathers produced an altar wine for many years. However the Florissant winery was discontinued during the 1950s.

In Italy, at their farm near Frascati, the Villa Cavalletti, the Jesuits produce wine, though only enough to supply their houses in Rome. This white Frascati, which averages about 11.5 per cent alcohol, is made from three vines—Trebbiano, Toscano, Malvagia Bianca and Malvagia Rossa. The annual production is about 300 quintals (a quintal equals 220.46 pounds). It has no labels and the Jesuits simply refer to it as the Cavelletti wine. In addition a very limited amount of red Cavalletti wine is made, from For di Passere and Cesane vines. Those who have tasted it say it is excellent.

In South Australia the Jesuit winery at Sevenhill (some 80 miles south of Adelaide, between Clare and Waterville) began in much the same way as that at Los Gatos—first to produce a sacramental wine and then to meet a commercial demand. In 1848 two Austrian Jesuits arrived in the Clare valley, together with a party of Silesian settlers. Three years later these Jesuits built a mud and slab hut in the valley at Sevenhill, with the

intention of erecting a church and a seminary. Sevenhill College has long
been closed but the fine church, consecrated in 1866, still stands amid its
vineyards. As early as 1852 the Jesuits had begun to plant vines in order
to make wine for the mass. Fortunately one of them—Bro John
Schreiner—was an experienced vigneron and seems to have borrowed
vine cuttings from a local brewer at Bungaree. Bro John remained the
Sevenhill wine-maker for 32 years. During this time he introduced the
Crouchen grape, calling it the Clare Riesling, and the Muscadelle,
which became known as the Tokay. At first the grapes were pressed by
feet, but in 1863, with the aid of the new community carpenter, Schreiner
constructed a primitive wine-press capable of pressing four buckets at a
time; a quaint photograph survives of Bro John and the carpenter with
the wonderful machine. A proper underground cellar with slate-lined
tanks was built later. From the beginning the winery's primary purpose,
after supplying the needs of the seminary and the church, was to furnish
Catholic priests throughout South Australia with sacramental wine.
However, red and white wines, and also brandy, were produced for lay
consumption. The most famous vintage was the Tawny port of 1925, for
which remarkable claims have been made; even in the 1970s it is said to
have a long life ahead of it.

Today Sevenhill has expanded so much that the vineyard covers 120
acres with an annual output of almost 200 tons of grapes. It is lavishly
equipped with modern machinery, while many varieties of vine have been
introduced. Sacramental wines of a sherry type, resistant to extreme
climatic conditions, are supplied to Japan, India, Indonesia and the
Pacific countries. As well as these sacramental vintages several other
wines are produced; Sevenhill Shiraz Cabernet (65 per cent Shiraz and
35 per cent Cabernet Sauvignon), matured in oak for two years, is a big,
strong, fruity wine which ages well in a bottle. Another red made from
the same grapes but with the addition of Grenache is softer and drier, not
so distinguished though very pleasant. There are three Sevenhill dry
wines: the traditional Crouchen; a blend of Crouchen and Pedro
Ximénez; and a full-bodied Tokay, said to resemble some white Bur-

gundies, which has recently been introduced. Fortified wines are also made and the *solera* system is emphasized; among them are Frontignac and port. The proceeds are used to train Australian Jesuits and to subsidize their mission in India. The present wine-maker of Sevenhill is Bro John May, only the seventh since 1852. Visitors are welcome at the winery and there are facilities for tasting the wines.

However, even the Jesuits have surpassed themselves in the Lebanon. Until the recent troubles their community at Zahle made not only red and white wine but champagne and brandy as well.

Missionaries are still spreading viticulture. At Hawke's Bay in New Zealand the Marist Fathers are steadily extending their Greenmeadows vineyards and increasing their production of red and white wine. They also make liqueurs. In Tanzania the Holy Ghost Fathers at Dodoma grow some of the best wine in Africa, a strong red which has been compared to Rioja.

The Christian Brothers resemble professed Knights of Malta in that although not priests they take monastic vows of poverty, chastity and obedience. The order was founded in France in 1680 by Jean Baptiste de la Salle as a teaching order. It still flourishes in France—where each brother enjoys the quaint clerical privilege of being addressed as "*très honoré frère*"—but is now active in many other countries as well. In 1868 it came to San Francisco to teach the sons of farmers, miners, trades-people and others. In 1879 it established a training college—or novitiate—at Martinez, where in 1882 it began to make wine for sacramental purposes; for the Brothers' own table and for sale to the general public. The Brothers had the benefit of late-nineteenth-century developments in Californian viticulture and their wine was so excellent that when they started to sell it they found a ready market. Soon the revenue from their vineyard became an important part of their income. In 1930 the Christian Brothers bought a winery with its surrounding vineyards in the Mayacamas mountains above the Napa Valley. Here they built a new novitiate into which they moved in 1932, selling the older property in Martinez. They improved and expanded the vineyards of the new site, which they called Mont La Salle, until today their charming monastery college stands among countless vines which in turn are surrounded by native oaks, maples, firs and redwoods. In the San Joaquin Valley, near the middle of the state, they have a winery noted for excellent brandy.

Like all Californian wines, those of the Christian Brothers are too little known in Europe. Besides clarets, burgundies and Chablis, and of course a Cabernet, they make a delicious white vintage from the Chenin Blanc grape (a cépage from Touraine that is said to owe its origin to no less a vigneron than St Martin himself). The Christian Brothers' Chenin —they call the wine after the grape—is sweetish and full-bodied yet pleasantly light and delicate, rather like a certain type of moselle. They also produce a worthy rival to the old Franciscans' Angelica. This is

Château La Salle, a dessert wine made from the Muscat grape, very pale and very sweet and perfect with strawberries. Hugh Johnson says of their winemaker, "in Bro Timothy they have their own Dom Pérignon".

Many other modern religious communities are making wine. However, the examples already given in this chapter should be enough to show that the tradition of monastic viticulture is still very much alive.

The extraordinary revolution through which the Roman Catholic Church is currently passing has seen a decrease in the number of monks and nuns. (Though there has been something of a boom in hermits.) Recently, however, there have been signs that contemplative orders are once more attracting recruits, and no doubt there will eventually be a monastic renaissance. When it comes it will almost certainly include a return to the contemplative life and to the agrarian culture of pre-industrial Europe. Its communities will require an occupation sympathetic to their ideals and able to provide them with a living. Viticulture seems the obvious answer. Inevitably, in the collectivist and egalitarian society of the perhaps not too distant future, the emphasis in most commercial wine-growing is going to be on quantity. By contrast, using traditional methods the monks could produce wines of quality and find such an enterprise both economically and spiritually rewarding. Morton Shand provides a text with which to encourage them: "Wine is something which, though bought and sold, the Bible and the poets have taught us to revere as the noblest reward of man's immemorial struggle with soil and weather."

Appendix I

The Monks and Wine Tour

The historical relationship between monks and wine can be explored visually, and four famous wine-growing regions are particularly suitable. These are Burgundy, the banks of the Moselle and its tributaries, the Wachau, and the Californian Mission Trail. The following suggestions are made, not as blueprints for guided tours but simply to point out features around which individual tours can be built. Flexibility is essential for such expeditions, and one must bear in mind that the welcome varies just as much in inhabited abbeys as it does in vineyards.

Burgundy

Dijon is the obvious centre from which to begin a tour of Burgundy. Here the fine Gothic church of the old monastery of Saint Benigne stands as a monument to the earliest wine-growing activities of the Benedictines in the region, while in the Logis du Roi—the old palace of the Dukes— one may see some beautiful fragments of Sluter's *Puits de Moïse*, before going to the pathetic shell which was once the chartreuse of Champmol. The town also contains the remains of several other religious houses that once owned vineyards. Before exploring the Côte d'Or one should drive a few miles north-west to the little town of Chablis, undistinguished save for its romantic gateway, and then to its creators 10 miles away—the abbeys of Pontigny and Fontenay. Both are haunting memorials to the Cistercians; the latter much as it was in the twelfth century. Vézelay of the Cluniac Benedictines should also be visted from Dijon, along the N5 then across on to the N6 to Avallon; the wine may not be particularly distinguished but the basilica is superb. (Vézelay is also noted for a delicious goats'-milk cheese.)

The Côte d'Or can be easily explored from the road running south from Dijon to Chalon-sur-Saône, the N74. First comes the Côte de Nuits and to the west are Fixin, once owned by Cluny, and then Gevrey-Chambertin and Clos de Bèze, the two towers of the abbey church of Bèze and Carthusian Brochon. There follow Cistercian Morey-Saint-Denis, Chambolle-Musigny and Clos Vougeot itself, with its great château of a grange. Flagey-Echézeaux, once the property of the vanished Benedictine monastery of Saint-Vivant, is on the opposite side of the road. Still proceeding down the N74 one arrives at Nuits-Saint-

Georges (a wine-shippers' town whose beautiful basilica of St Sympho-rien is well worth a visit), which is near what is left of Cîteaux, the first and greatest of White Monk monasteries. The N74 continues and, after the Côte de Nuits ends south of Nuits-Saint-Georges at Prémeaux, it goes through the Côte de Beaune. Aloxe-Corton is on the west side and the fine Black Monk church of Saulieu, with its twelfth-century barrel vaulting, is not far away. At Beaune itself there is of course the fifteenth-century Hospice, the dazzling Hôtel Dieu, together with the remains of several monastic houses. Still carrying on down the N74 Pommard and Volnay are on the west and also Meursault, which is a pretty little town with a picturesque town hall that dates from Ducal days. The Cister-cians' cellars are in a château on the edge of the town. Driving through Chalon-sur-Saône one leaves the N74 for the N6 (the road to Lyons) to go down the Côte Chalonnaise. This ends at Chagny, but one should go on to the delightful old abbey town of Tournus on the banks of the Saône which is still dominated by the towers of the mighty church of Saint Philibert. Finally, at Mâcon one turns west on the N79 to see the remains at Cluny.

Saint-Pourçain

It is not necessary to spend an entire week exploring a region. A day can be fitted very pleasantly into a holiday for a visit to a single wine and its monastery. A good example is Saint-Pourçain, which can be easily reached from the spa towns of Vichy or Bourbon. After inspecting the magnificent abbey church and cloister (see Ch. 3) one should explore the vineyards which stretch along the rivers Sioule, Allier and Bouble. The co-operative is next to an agreeable little restaurant where one can eat splendidly at a reasonable price, and also taste the red, rosé, white and *gris* wines of Saint-Pourçain.

The Moselle

The Moselle may be explained better in terms of rivers rather than roads. Although full of fascinating little towns and splendid hilltop castles, the region is richer in what were once monastic vineyards than in monasteries. Trier, the ancient city of Trèves, has the remains of some fine abbeys, besides its famous Roman gateway and basilica, while the monastery of St Matthias is still inhabited by Benedictines, though they gave up their vineyards long ago. A few miles down the Moselle from Trier, just up the Ruwer tributary on the right bank, is Eitelsbach Karthäuserhofberg. Alas, it has no monastic remains nor is anything left of the once renowned *Karthaus* of St Alban at Trier. However, on the opposite bank the Benedictine grange of Maximin Grünhaus still stands amid its vineyards. Also on the Ruwer are the Jesuitengarten vineyards at Waldrach and the Dominikanerberg. Eitelsbach Karthäuserhofberg and Maximin Grünhaus may both be visited from Trier.

The Saar flows into the Moselle some miles south of Trier. Its vineyards, which lie well up the river, include those of the Scharzhofberg near Wiltingen which in the eighteenth century belonged briefly to the nuns of St Maria's convent at Trier; the Scharzhof, a seventeenth-century manor house, still stands. The famous vines of Ockfen, which mostly grow on the steep slopes of a small valley, belonged to the monks of St Martin at Trier until 1803. Then there is the vineyard at Wawern still known as the Jesuitenberg. On the middle Moselle lie many vineyards that were once in monastic hands—notably at Graach, Josephshof, Bernkastel, Wehlen, Trittenheim, and, on the Lieser, at Wittlich.

The Wachau

By contrast, in Austria the Wachau is almost overcrowded with abbeys. This stretch of the Danube begins at a great gorge which is crowned by the stupendous Baroque pile of Melk. There are vineyards all along the steep hillsides which overlook the great river.

Benedictine Gottweig and its monks are a miraculously preserved example of a thriving abbey with flourishing monks; visitors can drink their wines at the "Stiftskeller" on the slope above. Undhof has lost its monks though it retains their vines. At Krems there is a wine museum which forms part of the town museum in what was once the Romanesque church of a priory of Dominican friars; the wine section is in the cloisters, which are filled with old presses, vats, inn signs and even corkscrews. However, the centre of the Wachau—both for wine and as an excellent base for any sort of exploration—is the altogether delightful little town of Dürnstein. Alas, the Augustinian Canons were evicted from their beautiful old abbey by the unsympathetic Emperor Joseph II. Nevertheless, the monastery cellars still fulfil their original purpose, having been completely modernized by the Wachau wine-growers' co-operative. And even though the fathers have gone, their Baroque church (with a particularly elegant tower) has at least become the parish church, whose rectory is in the former priory. The co-operative produces several wines, the most popular being, apparently, the Dürnsteiner Katzensprung, which is a Grüner Veltliner, and the Dürnsteiner Hollerin, which is a Riesling. If only the canons could return they would appreciate the achievements of those who have inherited their vineyards.

California

It is possible to follow the Mission Trail in California, though the original track is impracticable. While the missions had to be abandoned and fell into ruin—some vanishing completely—most survived to a greater or lesser degree and have been sympathetically restored. All are worth a visit, but the following are possibly the most rewarding.

From the south northwards, the first is Mission San Diego (1769). Next is San Luis Rey (1797) near Oceanside, an excellent example. The ruins of San Juan Capistrano (1776) in the town of that name are especially beautiful. For the wine-lover Mission San Gabriel (1771), on the outskirts of Los Angeles, should be an object of pilgrimage—it still has the friars' winery, the oldest in North America. Also an essential place to visit is the Mission San Fernando Rey de España (1797), again in a town named after it, which still has its original patio and fountain. Architecturally the church of Santa Barbara (1786) is probably the most important and interesting of the churches built by the Franciscans in California; despite several rebuildings, it remains much as it must have been in mission times. Continuing north, San Miguel (1797) near Paso Robles is another example worth seeing.

However, to obtain a real idea of what a mission was like in its prime one must visit San Antonio (1771), even though it has been heavily restored, in its isolated valley to the west of King City. San Carlos Borromeo de Carmelo (1770), Serra's old headquarters at Carmel-by-the-Sea, is perhaps the most interesting church after Santa Barbara. Probably the most moving relic of the friars is the little church of San Francisco de Assis, all that is left of Mission Dolores (1776), which still stands in the busy centre of modern San Francisco.

Also in San Francisco is the Wine Museum, near Fisherman's Wharf. This contains the Christian Brothers' collection, *Five Hundred Years of Wine in the Arts*. The Christian Brothers' own viticultural achievements are themselves worthy of a visit. Their monastery and Mont La Salle winery near Napa are about an hour and a half's drive from San Francisco, and their wine and champagne cellars are at St Helena nearby.

Appendix II
Wines with Monastic Associations

The following is a list of wines with monastic associations, which range from the probable ownership of a single vineyard for a short period to the creation of an entire wine. The list is not comprehensive, as many wines, although known to have monastic associations, can no longer be attributed to a particular order. The list does, however, give a good indication of the monks' contribution to viticulture.

Burgundy

Aloxe-Corton	Benedictines, Cistercians
Avallon	Benedictines
Beaune	many orders
Bonnes Mares	Cistercians
Brochon	Carthusians, Cistercians
Chablis	Cistercians
Chassagne-Montrachet	Knights of Malta
Clos de Bèze	Benedictines
Clos de Tart	Cistercians
Clos Vougeot	Cistercians
Corton	Benedictines
Côte de Dijon	Benedictines
Couchey	Benedictines
Fixin	Benedictines, Cistercians
Flagey-Echézeaux	Benedictines
Gevrey	Benedictines
Givry	Benedictines
Juliénas	
Mâcon	Benedictines
Meursault	Cistercians
Morey-Saint-Denis	Cistercians
Musigny	Cistercians
Nuits-Saint-Georges	
Prémaux	
Pommard	Benedictines, Knights of Malta
Romanée-Conti	Benedictines
Romanée-Saint-Vivant	Benedictines
Santenay	Benedictines
Savigny	Benedictines, Knights of Malta
Volnay	Knights of Malta
Vosne-Romanée	Benedictines

Loire

Bourgueil	Benedictines
Champigny	Templars
Coteaux de la Loire	Benedictines
Orléans	Cistercians
Muscadet	Benedictines
Pouilly-Fumé	Benedictines
Quincy	Cistercians
Saint-Pourçain	Benedictines
Sancerre	Cistercians
Saumur	Fontevrault, Carmelites

Rhône

Châteauneuf-du-Pape	Carthusians
Chusclan	Benedictines
Cornas	Benedictines
Gigondas	Benedictines, Cistercians
Hermitage	
Saint-Péray	Benedictines
Vacqueyras	Cistercians

South-West France

Cahors	Carthusians
Côte d'Agly	
Côte Roannais	
Côte de Roussillon	
Gaillac	Benedictines
Masdeu	Templars, Knights of Malta
Monbazillac	Benedictines

South-East France

Bandol	Benedictines
Château Chalon	Benedictines
Mougères	Carthusians

Bordeaux

Médoc

Château de l'Abbaye-Skinner	
Château l'Abbé Gorsse de Gorsse	
Château d'Arnauld	
Château la Commanderie	
Château Pouget	Benedictines
Château Prieuré-Lichine	Benedictines
Clos les Moines	

Graves

Château Carbonnieux	Benedictines
Château la Louvière	Carthusians

Château la Mission-Haut-Brion	Vincentians
Clos de l'Abbaye de la Rame	
Cru de l'Hermitage	

Sauternes
Château de la Chartreuse

St-Emilion

Château l'Angelus de Mazérat	
Château la Barbe-Blanche	Cistercians
Château Couvent-des-Jacobins	Dominicans
Château le Couvent	Ursulines
Château les Demoiselles	
Château la Grace-Dieu-des-Prieurs	
Château l'Hermitage	
Château l'Hermitage Mazérat	
Château Montdespic	Templars
Château le Prieuré	Franciscans
Château des Religieuses	
Château Tauzinat l'Hermitage	
Château les Templiers	Templars
Château la Tour-Ségur	Cistercians
Clos des Cordeliers	Franciscans
Clos des Jacobins	Dominicans
Clos des Moines	
Clos des Religieuses	
Le Prieuré St-Emilion	Benedictines

Pomerol

Château la Commanderie	Knights of Malta
Château de l'Eglise	Templars
Château Gazin	Templars
Château des Moines	Benedictines
Château Prieurs de la Commanderie	
Château Templiers	Templars
Clos du Commandeur	Knights of Malta
Clos des Templiers	Templars
Domaine de Grand Moine	
Sabloire du Grand Moine	

Entre-Deux-Mers

Clos des Capucines	Franciscans
Les Carmes-Haut-Brion	Carmelites

Premières Côtes de Bordeaux

Clos de la Monastère de Broussey	Carmelites

Germany

[Some of these names have changed since the Federal Wine Laws of 1971]

Ahr

Marienthaler Klostergarten	Augustinians

194

Rheingau

Assmannshausen	Cistercians
Dom Dechaney	
Eltviller Mönchhannach	
Geisenheimer Klauserweg	
Hattenheimer Hinterhaus	Cistercians
Hattenheimer Engelmannsberg	Cistercians
Hattenheimer Heiligenberg	Cistercians
Johannisberg	Benedictines
Johannisberger Klaus	
Oestricher Klostergarten	
Rauenthaler Nonnenberg	
Rudesheimer	Benedictines
Rudesheimer Dachenstein	Benedictines
Rudesheimer Klosterberg	Benedictines
Rudesheimer Klosterkeisel	
Rudesheimer Klosterlay	Benedictines
Winkler Jesuitengarten	Jesuits

Moselle

Bernkasteler	
Eitelsbacher Karthäuserhofberger	Carthusians
Graacher Abtsberg	
Graacher Josephshoefer	Benedictines
Graacher Mönch	Benedictines
Kasel Dominikanerberg	Dominicans
Maximin Grünhaus	Benedictines
Ockfener Bockstein	
Scharzhofberger	
Trittenheimer	
Wehlener Klosterberg	

Rheinhesse

Bodenheimer Sankt Alban	Benedictines
Niersteiner Brudersberg	
Oppenheimer	Benedictines

Palatinate

Förster Jesuitengarten	Jesuits
Liebfrauenstift	

Baden

Affentaler Klosterrebberg	Cistercians
Zeller Abtsberg	

Württemberg

Gundelsheimer Himmelreich	Teutonic Knights
Eilfingerberg	Cistercians
Stuttgarter Mönchsalde	
Stuttgarter Mönchberg	

Franconia

Escherndorfer Lump	Carmelites

195

Hochheimer	Carmelites
Hörsteiner Abtsberg	
Würzburger Jesuitengarten	Jesuits

Austria

Blaue Zweigelt Rebe	Knights of Malta
Dürnsteiner Himmelstiege	Augustinians
Dürnsteiner Hollerin	Augustinians
Dürnsteiner Katzensprung	Augustinians
Gottweig	Benedictines
Grüner Veltliner	Teutonic Knights
Gumpoldskirchner	Teutonic Knights
Gumpoldskirchner Spiegel	Benedictines
Heiligenkreuz	Cistercians
Hüttenviertel	Augustinians
Kahlenberger Jungherrn	Augustinians
Kahlenberger Weisser Burgunder Auslese	Augustinians
Kloster Ausstich	Augustinians
Klosterdawn	Augustinians
Klostergarten	Augustinians
Kommende Mailberg Grüner Veltliner	Knights of Malta
Kremser (Steiner) Pfaffenberg	
Melk	Benedictines
Rheinriesling	Teutonic Knights
Rittersporn	Teutonic Knights
Ruländer Riesling	Teutonic Knights
St Laurent	Teutonic Knights
St Laurent-Ausstich	Augustinians
Schloss-Kellerbraut	Teutonic Knights
Schlossrosé	Teutonic Knights
Schloss Mailberg	Knights of Malta
Undhof	Franciscans

Hungary

Egri Bikavér	Benedictines
Somló	Benedictines

Switzerland

Cortaillod	Carthusians
Dézaley	Cistercians
Dôle de Sion	Benedictines
Fendant de Sion	Benedictines
Halbrot	Benedictines
Karthäuser	Carthusians
Klevner	Knights of Malta
Neuchâtel	Benedictines
Osterfinger	Benedictines
Siblinger	Benedictines
Soleil de Sierre	Carthusians
Ticino	Benedictines

196

Spain

La Oliva	Cistercians
Poblet	Cistercians
Priorato	Carthusians
Rioja	Benedictines, Cistercians
Samos	Benedictines
Sherry	Carthusians, Dominicans

Portugal

"Alcobaça"	Cistercians
Daõ	Benedictines, Cistercians
Madeira	Knights of Christ
Mateus	Dominicans
Palmela	Knights of Santiago
Port	Knights of Malta
Setubal	Cistercians, Dominicans, Carmelites
Vinho Verde	Knights of Malta

Italy

Capri	Carthusians, Knights of Malta
Cirò	Benedictines
Colli Euganei	Benedictines, Camaldolese
Colli del Trasimeno	Knights of Malta
Frascati	Camaldolese, Grottaferratans, Jesuits
Freisa	Benedictines
Gattinara Spanna	Cistercians
Gragnano	Benedictines
Greco di Gerace	Benedictines
Greco di Tufo	Benedictines
Lacrima Christi	Jesuits
Locorotondo	Templars
Mantonico	Benedictines
Santa Maddalena	Benedictines

Greece

Chalkis	Knights of Malta
Lindos	Knights of Malta
Nemea	Knights of Malta
Patras	Knights of Malta
Rion	Knights of Malta

United States

Angelica	Franciscans
Cabernet	Christian Brothers
Château la Salle	Christian Brothers
Chenin Blanc	Christian Brothers
Los Gatos	Jesuits
Sauterne (sic)	Benedictines

England

Beaulieu	Cistercians
Buckfast	Benedictines
Pilton	Benedictines
St Etheldreda (Wilmerton)	Benedictines

Israel

Latrun	Cistercians
Tabgha	Benedictines

Lebanon

Zahle	Jesuits

Algeria

La Trappe de Staouëli	Cistercians

East Africa

Dodoma	Holy Ghost Fathers

Australia

New Norcia	Benedictines
Sevenhill	Jesuits

New Zealand

Hawke's Bay	Marists

Bibliography

General Reading

H. Ambrosi, *Wo Grosse Weine Wachsen*, Munich, 1975.

P. Anson, *The Call of the Desert*, London, 1964.

M. Aubert and S. Goubert, *Romanesque Cathedrals and Abbeys of France*, London, 1966.

F. D'Ayala Valva, *Maruggio*, Rome, 1974.

A. Boorde, *The Fyrst Boke of the Introduction of Knowledge*, London, 1870.

W. Braunfels, *Monasteries of the Western World*, London, 1972.

C. Brooke, *The Monastic World, 1000–1300*, London, 1974.

A Carthusian, *La Grande Chartreuse par un Chartreux*, Lyon, 1896.

The Catholic Encyclopedia, New York, 1913–22.

Y. Christ, *Abbayes de France*, Paris, 1955.

K. Christoffel, *Wein-leserbuch*, Munich, 1964.

C. Cocks and E. Féret, *Bordeaux et ses Vins*, 12th ed., Bordeaux, 1969.

P. Dallas, *Italian Wines*, London, 1974.

R. Dion, *Histoire du Vin et de la Vigne en France*, Paris, 1959.

T. Edwards, *Worlds Apart: A Tour of European Monasteries*, London, 1968.

J. A. Froude, *History of England from the Fall of Wolsey to the Defeat of the Spanish Armada*, vol. 2, London, 1893.

M. Gattini, *I Priorati, i Baliaggi e le Commende del Sovrano Militare Ordine di S. Giovanni di Gerusalemme nelle Province Meridionali d'Italia*, Naples, 1928.

Gregory the Great, *The life of our most holy father St Benedict, being the second book of the dialogues of Gregory the Great . . .* , Rome, 1895.

Gutkind and Wolfskehl, *Das Buch von Wein*, Munich, 1927.

P. Helyot, *Histoire des Ordres Religieux, Monastiques et Militaires*, Paris, 1714–21.

J. Jeffs, *The Wines of Europe*, London, 1971.

H. Johnson, *Wine*, London and New York, 1974.

—————, *The World Atlas of Wine*, London and New York, 1969.

Dom D. Knowles, *Christian Monasticism*, London, 1969.

—————————, *The Religious Orders in Medieval England*, Cambridge, 1948–49.

A. Langenbach, *German Wines and Vines*, London, 1962.

A. Lefebvre, *St Bruno et l'Ordre des Chartreux*, Paris, 1883.

A. Lichine, *Encyclopedia of Wines and Spirits*, London, 1967.

—————, *Wines of France*, 6th ed., London, 1964.

J. Livingstone-Learmonth and M. Master, *The Wines of the Rhône*, London, 1978.

O. Loeb and T. Prittie, *Moselle*, London, 1972.

F. van der Meer, *Atlas de l'Ordre Cistercien*, Paris and Brussels, 1967.

H. Meinhard, *The Wines of Germany*, London, 1976.

T. Merton, *The Silent Life*, London, 1957.

—————, *The Waters of Silence*, London, 1950.

Comte de Montalembert, *Les Moines de l'Occident*, Paris, 1860–77.

E. Penning-Rowsell, *The Wines of Bordeaux*, New York, 1970.

G. Pillement, *Cloîtres et Abbayes de France*, Paris, 1950.

R. Postgate, *Portuguese Wine*, London, 1969.

J. Read, *The Wines of Spain and Portugal*, London, 1971.

C. Rodier, *Le Vin de Bourgogne*, Dijon, 1921.

V. Rowe, *French Wines Ordinary and Extraordinary*, London, 1972.

G. Saintsbury, *Notes on a Cellar Book*, London, 1967.

F. Schoonmaker, *German Wines*, London, 1957.

P. Morton Shand, *A Book of French Wines*, London, 1960.

A. Simon, *An Encyclopedia of Wine*, New York, 1972.

————, *A Wine Primer*, London, 1970.

S. Sitwell, *Monks, Nuns and Monasteries*, London, 1965.

H. Waddell, *The Wandering Scholars*, London, 1954.

W. Younger, *Gods, Men and Wine*, London, 1966.

H. W. Yoxall, *The Wines of Burgundy*, London, 1974.

References

1 THE COMING OF THE MONKS

St Benedict, *The Rule of St Benedict*, ed. Abbot J. McCann, London, 1952.

Gregory of Tours, *Historia Francorum*, trans. O. M. Dalton, Oxford, 1927

Sulpicius Severus, "Vita St Martini" in *A Select Library of Nicene and Post-Nicene Fathers*, trans. A. Roberts, 2nd series, vol. XI, London, 1894.

H. Waddell, *The Desert Fathers*, London, 1936.

2 THE DARK AGES

R. H. Bautier, *The Economic Development of Medieval Europe*, trans. H. Karolyi, London, 1971.

Cambridge Economic History, vol. 1, Cambridge, 1966.

J. H. Newman, *Historical Sketches*, London, 1872.

E. I. Robson, *A Wayfarer in French Vineyards*, London, 1928.

3 THE BENEDICTINE WINES OF FRANCE

P. Bréjoux, *Les Vins de Loire*, Paris, 1956.

W. W. Crotch, *The Complete Year Book of French Quality Wines, Spirits and Liqueurs*, Paris, n.d.

J. Girard, *La Vigne et le Vin en Franche Comte*, Besançon, 1939.

L. Jacquelin, *Les Vignes et les Vins de France*, Paris, 1960.

J. Mommessin, *Les Origines du Vignobles Français*, Mâcon, n.d.

H. Waddell, *Mediaeval Latin Lyrics*, London, 1966.

4 BENEDICTINE WINES OF GERMANY AND OTHER LANDS

R. E. H. Gunyon, *The Wines of Central and South-eastern Europe*, London, 1971.

Z. Halász, *Hungarian Wines through the Ages*, Budapest, 1962.

P. Lugano, *L'Italia Benedettina*, Rome, 1929.

C. L. de Pollnitz, *The Memoirs of Charles-Louis, Baron de Pollnitz*, London, 1745.

C. Ray, *The Wines of Italy*, London, 1966.

5 CISTERCIAN WINES

S. Beuton, "Nicolas de Clairvaux à la recherche du vin d'Auxerre d'après une lettre inédite du XIIe siecle" in *Annales de Bourgogne*, XXXIV, 1962.

L. Bouyer, *The Cistercian Heritage*, London, 1958.

A. Archdale King, *Cîteaux and her Elder Daughters*, London, 1954.

T. Merton, *The Last of the Fathers*, London, 1954.

6 CARTHUSIAN WINES

J. Evans, *Monastic Architecture in France from the Renaissance to the Revolution*, Cambridge, 1964.

M. Gonzalez Gordon, *Sherry*, London, 1972.

J. Jeffs, *Sherry*, London, 1972.

Dom D. Knowles, *The Religious Orders in Medieval England*, vol. 3, Cambridge, 1959.

T. Merton, *Disputed Questions*, London, 1961.

7 THE MONKS OF WAR AND THEIR WINES

Sir G. Hill, *A History of Cyprus*, Cambridge, 1940–52.

E. Hornickel, *The Great Wines of Europe*, London, 1965.

Sir H. Luke, *Cyprus—a Portrait and an Appreciation*, London, 1957.

J. Riley-Smith, *The Knights of St John in Jerusalem and Cyprus 1050–1310*, London, 1967.

D. Seward, *The Monks of War*, London, 1972.

8 THE WINES OF OTHER ORDERS

G. G. Coulton, *From St Francis to Dante . . . the Chronicle of the Franciscan Salimbene*, London, 1908.

C. Esser, *Origins of the Franciscan Order*, London, 1970.

9 ENGLISH MONKS AND ENGLISH WINE

Anglo-Saxon Chronicle, ed. G. N. Garmonsway, London, 1954.

St Bede, *History of the English Church and People*, London, 1955.

C. Brontë, *Shirley*, London, 1849.

Cartulary of Worcester Cathedral Priory, ed. R. R. Darlington, London, 1968.

S. Hockey, *Quarr Abbey and its lands 1132–1631*, Leicester, 1970.

E. Hyams, *Dyonisius: A Social History of the Wine Vine*, London, 1965.

————, *Vineyards in England*, London, 1953.

M. K. James, *The Mediaeval English Wine Trade*, Oxford, 1971.

Dom D. Knowles, *The Monastic Order in England*, Cambridge, 1949.

G. Ordish, *Wine-growing in England*, London, 1953.

G. Pearkes, *Growing Grapes in Britain*, London, 1961.

R. W. Saunders, *An Introduction to the Obedientary and Manor Rolls of Norwich Cathedral Priory*, Norwich, 1930.

Victoria History of the Counties of England (vols. on Berkshire, Gloucestershire, Herefordshire, Hertfordshire, Somerset, Worcestershire), London, 1904–27.

William of Malmesbury, *Gesta Regum Anglorum et Historia Novella*, London, 1887–89.

H. and B. Winkles, *Cathedral Churches of Great Britain*, London, 1835.

10 DOM PÉRIGNON AND CHAMPAGNE

P. Forbes, *Champagne*, London, 1967.

A. Simon, *The History of Champagne*, London, 1962.

11 CALIFORNIAN MISSION WINES

K. Baer, *Architecture of the Californian Missions*, Berkley, 1958.

H. H. Bancroft, *History of the Pacific States of North America*, vol. 13, San Francisco, 1890.

J. T. Ellis, *Documents of American Catholic History*, Milwaukee, 1962.

T. Maynard, *The Long Road of Father Serra*, California, 1956.

J. Melville, *Guide to California Wines*, California, 1968.

12 "WATERS OF LIFE"

R. G. Dettori, *Italian Wines and Liqueurs*, Rome, 1953.

M. I. Fisher, *Liqueurs*, London, 1950.

The New Catholic Encyclopedia, New York, 1967.

13 BIBULOUS MONKS

W. Beckford, *The Journals of William Beckford in Portugal and Spain, 1787–8*, London, 1954.

I. von Born, *Monchologia*, Vienna, 1783.

G. Borrow, *Wild Wales*, London, 1955.

J. A. Brillat-Savarin, *La Physiologie du Goût*, Paris, 1834.

A. Daudet, *Lettres de mon Moulin*, Paris, 1920.

Erasmus, *In Praise of Folly*, trans. B. Radice, London, 1971.

Walter Map, *The Latin Poems usually attributed to Walter Mapes*, London, 1841.

Marguerite of Navarre, *The Heptameron*, London, 1923.

C. Marot, *Oeuvres Poetiques*, Paris, 1973.

T. L. Peacock, *Maid Marian*, London, 1822.

L. Plattard, *Vie de François Rabelais*, Paris, 1928.

F. Rabelais, *Gargantua and Pantagruel*, trans. T. Urquhart and P. Motteux, London, 1928.

Sir W. Scott, *Ivanhoe*, London, 1819.

Lord Tennyson, *The Works of Alfred Tennyson*, London, 1879.

F. A. de Voltaire, *Candide*, Paris, 1759.

15 MONKS AND WINE TODAY

T. Merton, *The Seven Storey Mountain*, London, 1977.

G. Pimentel, *Unknown Spain*, Paris, 1964.

A. Simon, *The Wines, Vineyards and Vignerons of Australia*, London, 1967

A. Waugh, *Wines and Spirits of the World*, New York, 1968.

Index

Muri-Gries 34, 178
Muscadelle grape (Muscatel) 46–7, 110
Muscat 88, 97, 180, 184
Muscat Frontignan 184
Musigny 69, 70, 173
Muskat Ottonel grape 183

N

Naples 60, 110, 118–9
Neuchâtel 56, 88
New Norcia 179
New Zealand 186
Norbertines *see* Premonstratensians
Normandy 151–2
Nôtre-Dame-de-Cahors 85
Novitiate winery 183–4
Nuestra Señora de los Dolores 145
Nuits-St-Georges 70, 188–9
Nuns 24, 48–9, 55, 62, 69–70, 169–78 *passim*

O

Ockfen 190
Oporto 98, 100, 117
Oppenheim 55, 170
Orval 170
Orvieto 23

P

Palatinate 51, 170
Palmela 110
Paraguay 119, 145
Pedro Ximénez grape 88
Pérignon, Dom Pierre 16, 38, 139–43, 187
Perrières 82, 169
Pershore 128
Pescara 154
Phylloxera 44, 47, 86
Pilton, Somerset 132–3
Pineau de la Loire grape *see* Chenin Blanc
Pinot Blanc 184
Pinot Maltais (Morgeot) 98
Pinot Meunier 130, 138
Pinot Noir 44, 57, 72, 98, 141
    see also Blauburgunder
Poitiers 20, 177
Poland 28, 67, 132, 175
Pomerol 46, 96, 98
Pommard 41, 69, 98, 121, 189
Pont-aux-Moines 72
Pontigny 62, 66, 169, 188
Port 100, 117
Portugal 55, 57–8, 76, 90, 98–9, 110, 113,
    117–18, 145, 165–6, 174
Pouilly Fumé 43
Pourçain, St 43
Pourriture noble 46, 54
Premières Côtes de Bordeaux 118
Premonstratensians 113, 126, 160, 167, 172
Prémontre 113, 173
Priorato 88, 92
Provence 47–8
Prugna 158
Prüm 30
Prussia 94, 109, 132, 182

Q

Quincy 72

R

Reformed Observance *see* Trappists
Reichenau 30
Reims 94, 140
Rheinau 174
Rheingau 51–5, 73–4, 118, 170
Rheinhessen 30, 51, 55
Rhineland 51, 109, 169
Rhodes 93, 96–7, 100, 122
Rhône viticultural area 48, 72
Riesling 53, 76, 110, 113, 171, 185, 190
Rievaulx Abbey 61–2, 134
Rioja 88, 110, 186
Roch, St 34
Rochester 129–30
Romanée 70
Romanée-Conti 70
Romanée-Saint-Vivant 41, 173
Rome 22, 152, 154, 171, 181
Roussan grape 48
Roussillon 98
Ruwer 72, 86, 189

S

St Albans 128, 132, 134
St-Emilion 70, 96, 98, 110, 117, 120, 173
St Gall 30
St Germain des Prés 28, 32
St Hildegard at Rupertsberg 55, 177
St Laurent-Ausstich 183
St Lazarus, Knights Hospitallers of 94, 110
St Martin at Ligugé 20, 177
St Martin at Tours 21, 33, 66, 123
St Martin at Trier 52, 190
St Matthias at Trier 52
St Maur 152
St Maurice 56
St Maximin at Trier 51–2
St Mesmin-de-Micy 72
St Nazarius of Lauresham *see* Lorsch
St-Péray 48
St Pierre Doré grape 44
St-Pourçain 43–4, 174, 189
St Riquier 33
St Romuald 154
St Thomas of Acre, Knights Hospitallers of
    94
St Trinité at Champmol 82–3
St Vanne 139
St Vivant, Vosne 41, 188
St Wandrille 28
Sambucca 158
Samos 152, 175, 178
San Antonio 146, 191
San Carlos Borromeo de Carmelo 146, 191
San Cugat del Vallés 57
San Diego 146, 191
San Francisco 186
San Francisco de Solano 146, 150
San Francisco Xavier 145
San Gabriel 146, 148, 191
San Luis Obispo 146